HARD BARNED!

Gabe, Your sis and I finally got this thing done. Just thought you might be interested in checking it out. Love you bro,

CJD

Babe!
You sis and I finally got this thing done. Just thought you might be interested in checking it out. Love you bro,
CTD

HARDBARNED!

*One Man's Quest for Meaningful Work
in the American South*

A memoir by Christopher J. Driver

With illustrations by Tarri N. Driver

Mill City Press | Minneapolis, MN

HARDJARGON!

HARDBARNED! One Man's Quest for Meaningful Work in the American South
Copyright © 2016 by Christopher J. Driver. All rights reserved.

Mill City Press, Inc.
322 First Avenue N, 5th floor
Minneapolis, MN 55401
(612) 455-2293

www.millcitypublishing.com
www.hardbarned.com

Dear Readers,
I won't actually bore you with extensive legalese or "HARDJARGON" here, but if you want to reference or quote small excerpts from this book elsewhere for your own reasons, I'm all for it (unless you're somehow using it to spread hate). All that I ask is that you please use proper and visible attribution wherever you do, just as I have taken great care to give credit where it is due herein. Thanks a lot for being cool about this stuff, and my sincere thanks again for your interest!
–CJD

Published and printed by Mill City Press: Minneapolis, Minnesota, USA.

First Edition, 2016.
ISBN-13: 978-1-63505-034-9
LCCN: 2016909132

Cover Design by Jaime Willems and Christopher J. Driver
Typeset by Jaime Willems
Illustrations by Tarri N. Driver
Photos by the author, Russ Driver and others unknown

Printed in the United States of America

HARDEDICATE!

For my friend "Mitch" and for my Granddad, Russell Broyles Driver (1918-2010): two of the most honorable men I have ever known and from whom I learned a lot about working.

This book is also dedicated to the worldwide legion of workers who trudge through unsatisfying jobs, never abandoning their quests for meaningful work, whatever color their collars might be.

Too many Americans remain unemployed or underemployed.[1]
—Janet Yellen, Federal Reserve Chair

---

1 Yellen, Janet. United States Senate Hearing: February 24, 2015.

Look at me! I'm a grad student! I'm 30 years old, and I made $600 last year!
—Bart

Bart, don't make fun of grad students. They've just made a terrible life choice. [2]
—Marge

---
2 "Home Away From Homer." *The Simpsons*. Season 16, episode 20: Fox, 2005.

Absurdity is good for comedy, but bad as a way of life.[3]

—**Matthew B. Crawford**

---

3 Crawford, Matthew B. *Shop Class as Soulcraft: An Inquiry Into the Value of Work*. New York: The Penguin Press, 2009.

HARDBARNED!

Prologue..xix

Misty's Barn and The White Whale of Meaningful Work.....................1

Granddad Instills Work Ethic; Boy Dreams of Unrealistic Jobs..........11

Barns: The Healthy Hate Receptacle...24

The Business of Computer Sales..29

How I Became HARDBARNED..38

House Painter/Heart Breaker/Film Renter/Intoxicant Experimenter.......51

In Barn Land, a Way With Words..66

Tennis Player/Music Maker/Restaurant Worker/Shark Researcher?.........70

Barn Equipment, Delivery, Methodology (and Plastic Jesus)..................83

Punks and Hippies Unite to Serve Tourists Fried Seafood....................101

Barn History: The Legend of Samuel and Jim.......................................109

College Begins, Film Rentals Resume…and…Goldschlager!................113

Little Brother Barn, Speedo Guy, Trailer Fire and Torpedo Tire..........117

Back to the Beach: Bikinis and Hurricanes, Karaoke and Dishes........128

Barn Repos, Battle Axes, Meemaw and Muumuus.................................138

"Life's A Bitch An' Then Ya Die"/SUVs and VIPs..................................149

Sweet Old Piss Town and Muddy Bitter Barn Blues..............................164

Magazines, More Movies, Meatball and MAXIMUM ROCKNROLL...173

The Barn-Land DOT…and Deer Semen...185

An Alaskan Ogremonger..194

No Asphalt, No Fiction and "Naw, I Ain't Got No Message."......................210

Lawnmowing, Luggage Toting, Love Connections and Job Rejection....221

Barn Mud, Blue Blood, Detours and Dinars..230

All Hail The Retail King (and Customer Queen)..239

Barn Dogs and Lousy Humans..259

Temp Agency Trials, Insurance Office Bile and the International Lunatics of Logistics..265

Passengers, Hot Tips and The Barn As Art..278

Liberal Arts and Other Effective Ways To Waste Your Life......................292

Hanging Up The Barn Boots for Reflections and Ramifications.............303

Epilogue...309

In 2013 the self-storage industry raked in $24 billion in revenue, more than twice as much as the NFL. The 48,500 storage facilities nationwide—compared with only 10,000 outside the U.S.—could fill three Manhattans, and they outnumber all the McDonald's, Wendy's, Burger Kings and Starbucks in the U.S. put together.[4]

—*TIME* magazine

These vast numbers, while staggering, fail to include yet another incredibly popular self-storage option for Americans in need of even more room for their extra stuff: portable storage barns.

—The author

---

4 Sanburn, Josh. "The Joy of Less: Americans Have More Possessions Than Any Society In History. Can We Finally Take Control of Them?" *TIME* Magazine, March 23, 2015.

HARDBARNED!

One Man's Quest for Meaningful Work in the American South

Prologue

I have straddled the line between blue collar and white and have jumped boldly with two feet into both worlds. I have survived icy cubicles and sweaty truck stops, boring boardrooms and backwoods junk shops, corporate-Kool-Aid swilling loons and barn-salesman buffoons. From keyboards to lug wrenches, at computers or workbenches, between staplers and chainsaws, coffeemakers or rickshaws, inside sterile fluorescent environs or outdoors wielding rusty tire irons, I have battled rogue copy machines and torn my greasy blue jeans. I have shaken my head in dismay at the mad trajectory of my non-career, from business casual in carpeted halls to steel-toed boots and Carhartt coveralls. Whether catered lunches were enjoyed in urban climate-controlled meetings or homemade sandwiches savored between rural bouts with miserable-weather beatings, I have survived—even thrived—in both worlds, doing time and feeling lost, restless, lonely and out of place.

Misty's Barn and The White Whale of Meaningful Work

Everybody has a hard job. All real work is hard.[1]
—Philip Roth

One sweltering Friday, I pulled into the massive gravel lot where the portable storage buildings (AKA barns) were built and had a look around, avoiding the ditch beside the scripture-inscribed mailbox, hopping out into the swirling dirt and sawdust to browse the day's selection of newly completed storage barns of various designs, in sizes ranging from tiny backyard tool shed to massive Greyhound touring bus. I backed my big red diesel pickup and its 30-foot trailer in front of the garage-sized building I intended to deliver. I had already spotted this lofted barn the week before and was dreading the process but eager to banish the behemoth from the lot, which would allow me to clear space for two or three smaller, more manageable barns.

    I called the customer's number on the work order and waited for an answer. I was pleasantly surprised to hear the traditional, dull buzz of a ringing phone instead of distorted and blaring digitized trumpets blasting a fight song from some college football team or the tinny, slurred boastings of a Dirty South gangsta-rapper, all-too common ringback tones in Barn Land. The woman on the other end of the line—Misty—told me that she had known I was delivering the barn today and that she would meet me at the factory in 30 minutes, so I could follow her home. I loaded the barn she had ordered onto the trailer quickly, and after sitting in the truck for

---

1 "My Life as a Writer." Daniel Sandstrom's interview with Philip Roth for *Svenska Dagbladet*. Also appearing in *The New York Times Sunday Book Review*, March 2, 2014.

an hour waiting for Misty and trying unsuccessfully to summon an interest in the first disc of a *Harry Potter* audiobook, I called her again. She made some excuse about tardy children and said that she would be there to meet me in 10 minutes. This time she was punctual, waving from her rusty SUV and launching a sheet of airborne gravel that pinged off the hood of my truck as she peeled out from the barn lot, spinning her tires into a tight 180-degree turn.

I followed Misty's Mitsubishi five miles deeper into the rural countryside from the barn-builder's lot to her mobile home, and from the front it appeared to be a tidy, singlewide, corrugated-sheet-metal structure painted caramel brown. I was grateful for the escort, as there were no street signs to be seen along the unfamiliar tangle of back roads that snaked around the steep hills. Dragging her 12-foot-wide and 30-foot-long barn (known to barn-haulers as a 12X30, pronounced *twelve-by-thirty*) through 10 feet of clearance between the overgrown trees on either side of her narrow gravel driveway, I hoped that the canvas tarp I had nailed to the roof would keep the branches she had failed to trim from tearing off the shingles from her new rent-to-own storage barn.

I arrived alongside Misty's mobile home and promptly began breathing exercises to calm myself, forcing my anger and frustration back into a dark corner of my mind as I drove into the chaos. Misty had done nothing to prepare the site for delivery of the gigantic building she had ordered, one easily the size of her residence itself. No apparent resting place had been assigned, and there was no room to maneuver amid the churning activity in the cluttered backyard.

From the truck I could see an elaborate collection of domesticated, wandering animals, several broken-down vehicles in various states of disrepair, a fantastic assortment of widely distributed feces and several small children in dirty PJs shrieking with unbridled glee as they scurried around the backyard, chasing dogs, chickens, goats and a llama or two. Animal cages, stacked tightly on the back porch and overflowing into the yard, contained at least 10 breeds of dog, from Chihuahua to Shepherd.

Each canine had a loud, urgent comment to share. Many birds called this place home too, although most were invisible, their cages obscured by colorful beach towels. One gigantic, bright red parrot stood un-caged yet tethered by an ankle to his perch, seemingly aware of his privileged status. The exotic bird's intermittent squawk punctuated the otherwise unyielding cacophony of screaming animals, in all its high-decibel glory. Were there monkeys too? It sounded likely. Of course there wasn't room between the piles of discarded junk, broken mailboxes, four-wheeled recreational vehicles, "yard art" and other detritus for me to maneuver my truck, trailer and the barn I was trying to deliver to Misty.

During a barn purchase, the paperwork upon which customers affix their signatures indicates clearly that it is their responsibility to clear the path and prepare the site for the large buildings that they expect to have delivered on their property. Logic (and the rental/purchase agreement) dictates that preparatory behaviors should include cutting tree limbs that block the path of a barn delivery, clearing piles of garbage and abandoned vehicles and generally making room for a building, which can often reach or even exceed the size of a customer's home.

One might assume that civility would enter the equation and demand the decency of putting out leftover trash fires, trimming the grass and removing excess animal excrement and smashed liquor bottles from around the anticipated delivery area, but Civility Demanding Decency sounds like a self-help book from 1952, and it was just as foreign a concept to Misty. She just didn't seem to understand that I was no Jedi and could not use my mind to pick up the barn from the trailer like Yoda lifting Luke's X-wing from the Dagobah swamp, dropping it precisely between piles of her random rubbish. Alas, the barn-hauling helicopter wasn't available. It was too late in the day to rent an industrial-size construction crane, and I would indeed require considerable space to pull my trailer out from underneath the barn in order to escape and move on after placing the huge building somewhere in the vicinity of her preferred resting place. I told her I needed more room.

Misty squinted at me with what was now a familiar, bleary-eyed stare of incomprehension, her mouth agape as her head rotated, slowly noting the truck, the trailer, the backyard, the barn and then me. She started to get it. She realized that our most immediate problem was going to be a pathetically crippled, visibly disintegrating wooden animal cart, a chariot of some pre-historic period that appeared to have been frozen in time as it emerged from the dusty ground in Misty's back yard, or perhaps from the newly excavated set of *Ben-Hur*...precisely where she wanted the barn to be placed. I flashed back to her initial comment on how she was *expecting me to deliver the building today*. I took a couple deep breaths and decided that she had some work to do before I could do mine, so I returned to the cab of my truck and tried to busy myself with my cell phone or paperwork, indulging in a dangerous opportunity for self-reflection, as was often my habit at the time.

How had my life come to this? Was it all the culmination of a series of poor choices? Desperate for a simple but knowing nod, an acknowledgement of camaraderie, I sent an old buddy and former barn hauler a furious text message as the chaos unfolded before me:

"nonstop idiocy. infuckingescapable and almost indescribable. daily. GD barns. unbelievable."

For a while I was distracted, and the people and some of the animals had disappeared. I tried to force myself to stay in the truck, at least for a little while longer, not wanting to give the impression that rearranging the scattered debris on Misty's lawn was part of my job description. What happened next appeared cinematic, witnessed through a dingy windshield in slow motion, a grainy, Zapruder-esque, Super 8-style image, shaky and skipping yet impossible to forget.

The enormous Misty, in her tiny white shorts and gigantic pastel pink blouse, her short and styled gray hair immobilized by Aqua Net, her dangling earrings waggling, emerged from behind her mobile home like a Shriner on a tiny green riding mower, its WEED EATER logo visible under her jiggling waves of girth. This time the shit was quite literally hitting

Misty's Barn and The White Whale of Meaningful Work

the fan. For some unfathomable reason she had engaged the blade and consequently was launching rocks and sticks and dried-up bits of animal poo in every direction. The cloud of excremental dust was massive, and even from inside my truck and 50 feet away, the mower's howl was so loud it drowned out the animals' perpetual shrieking. I watched, captivated as Misty struggled with the mower's transmission and lurched into a pile of broken ceramic flowerpots, sending the children screaming as they fled in their footie PJs from the resulting shrapnel fire. Misty's progress was impeded, but as the motor and animals raged on, she hollered above the din, gesticulating wildly at the kids to help her clear the area of rubble, ultimately managing to free the embattled machine by the sheer force of repeatedly hurling herself against it in the general direction she intended to move. Despite the mower seat's tilt-a-whirl swaying, it held fast beneath Misty and failed to collapse underneath her. Once she cleared the pile of destroyed flowerpots, she backed up to the old wooden rickshaw in her preferred barn spot, and a little kid with a jump rope appeared.

This is gonna be *great*, I thought warily, as Misty's plan unfolded. The above-ground, visible portion of the wooden cart that Misty hoped to yank from its final resting place was falling apart, a shell of crumbing grey pieces of ancient two-by-fours with two flat, dry-rotted tires and a rusty metal cage attached on top. She tied the jump rope to the mower, securing the other end to the disintegrating cart and promptly dragged the rotten old antique over, toppling it into the ground where it lodged, an immobile and unintentional plow, which left the overtaxed mower's tires spinning again in futility. Shouting at the scattering children for help from atop the ailing riding mower didn't seem to work well for Misty, and as much as I wanted to stay out of it, I reluctantly decided to get out of the truck and offer assistance. The little girl in purple animal-print PJs and I grabbed onto the back of the splintered old cart to help dislodge it from the ground. Misty pulled against it with all her might from atop the stuck mower, grinding through various gear and blade settings, lurching forward and back, spewing the wee lass and me with dirt, gravel, dried shit and flower-pot shrapnel, managing merely to wedge herself and her inadequate machine more deeply into the ground.

This *can't* end well, I thought. In the low-visibility midst of the swirling chaos and noise, I squinted through the eye-watering maelstrom and struggled to free the cart. A sizable chunk of crumbling wood broke off and fell into my hands. I grabbed at it again, this time onto what was left of the metal frame, somehow loosening what was left of the cart with minimal injuries. I did manage to accidentally elbow the little girl in the head in the process, but she seemed to be okay. Little girls Down South in Barn Land are pretty tough. Eventually I got the barn in place and prepared to do my leveling work.

Leveling a barn involves the use of a heavy, steel, manually operated railroad jack to lift its sides on the lower end of a sloping yard to a level height, then crawling underneath it to prop up the corners, sides and internal support beams with concrete and wooden blocks, until the structure's floor and sides are no longer sloping in any direction. Fortunately, perhaps sensing my fatigue, Misty had chosen to give me a moment's respite from the craziness and had disappeared into her home with the children, unlike another recent barn customer who had lurked menacingly on her porch in a pastel muumuu, pacing and watching my every move with a disapproving suspicion, shouting at someone who wasn't there:

"It ain't no level! Johnny! Tell that boy that barn *ain't no level!*" just as I was obviously on my back and underneath her barn, in the process of leveling it.

I circled Misty's new barn, using the jacks to lift and shim various sections around its perimeter. Relieved to be left alone to finish the job, I muttered comments toward a curious llama that followed me along a fence line, a couple feet away. He met my gaze inquisitively at eye level over the fence, and I asked what he thought about the crazy people and screaming animals that lived next door to him at this amateur zoo. He seemed rather dignified and concerned with my activity and yet remained unresponsive, showing clear signs of frustration and pacing nervously, snorting and chewing in his exaggerated way. Then it started to rain...

* * *

I don't want to be an employee. I want to be a writer. So I have to write this. To retain my sanity. Yes, I know that was a fragment. I left out a comma somewhere too. A hell of a lot of good a Master of Arts degree in English does when your job is to deliver portable storage barns from a truck in the middle of nowhere. I loved my boss and hated my job. Let's get that straight from the beginning. I made a living as a barn-hauler because I needed to pay off my student loans and earn a living. I didn't want to be a teacher after finishing graduate school, and nobody would hire me to write anything, despite my best efforts to convince anyone and everyone.

A job as a barn-hauling truck driver fell into my lap, and there I festered for the next three years, delivering, repossessing and repairing portable storage barns in a rural, multi-state Southeastern region henceforth referred to as Down South, in what I like to call Barn Land. I was grateful for the work but unsatisfied, able to pay my bills but furious, bewildered and defeated by my inability to make my education work for me. With no anticipation or preparation, never having imagined in my most bizarre daydreams that I might ever even attempt a job anything like it, much less spend three post-graduate years stuck in it, I worked in rural nowhere behind the wheel of a one-ton diesel pickup-truck, dragging a 30-foot custom-built hydraulic lift trailer with a steadily building berserker rage, delivering and repossessing portable storage barns in the backyards of hundreds of unique characters, way out in the sticks of countrified Americana. After three years, I walked away from this job without having another one to go to but before the madness of it all overwhelmed me. What follows are bits and pieces of a working life, job-related stories, lessons and misadventures of an aspiring writer and ex-punk rocker unwittingly trapped in the life of a barn-hauling truck driver who was never able to abandon his search for meaningful work.

My three years of the barn were years of great extremes. I worked for the best boss I'd ever had and made far more money than I had ever seen, most of which, after living expenses, was funneled back into a decade-plus effort to pay off debts incurred while completing my seemingly useless education. Only in the last two months of those three years on the job, late in 2008, did I begin writing about these experiences, as an effort to self-medicate, on a blog that I called—what else? HARDBARNED.

This book is the natural progression of that desire to record the madness before my head exploded, as well as an effort to make use of an eclectic resume that had seemingly rendered me unhireable. Being a truck-driving barn-hauler and repossessing portable storage buildings didn't figure into my career plan, but neither did working construction in an Alaskan fishing village or managing magazine distribution from a cubicle Down South. I didn't aspire to be a dishwasher in an east-coast tourist trap any more than I had planned to be a landscaper, house painter or warehouse worker, a computer salesman, nightclub valet, hotel bellman, grocery cashier, lobster executioner or bikini store clerk at a strip mall on the beach.

My barn experience was so significant that it shook me to the core. It lasted longer than any job I'd ever had before. It made me angrier than anything I'd ever experienced. It became the employment-based measuring stick against which I compared anything I'd ever done for money. I felt trapped and was truly challenged to examine what was important to me in regards to both work and life itself. Barns got me thinking—and eventually, writing—about my many jobs over the last quarter-century, the good and the bad, the funny and the crazy, the frustrations and existential dilemmas threaded throughout and created because of an eclectic blend of experiences that make up my personal version of a working life.

Of course I'm not the only one out there struggling to make use of an education that I can barely even pay for, refusing to give up the hope of one day finding creative satisfaction in The Right Job that has to be out there somewhere at the end of one's search for meaningful work. The best definition of the concept of meaningful work that I know of is my father's. According to Dad, meaningful work is a balanced trifecta that engages one's "interests, values and skillset" simultaneously, a confluence of factors one needs to derive a healthy satisfaction from work. Finding a job that engages one or two of those is a pretty solid victory, if you ask me, but nailing all three is what I'm after. Meaningful work is my white whale, and surely I'm not the only one. I hope it works out better for me than it did for Ahab, but abandoning the search is not an option, and I cannot let these stories of what has happened along the trail of the whale fall into the forgotten chasms of one man's fading memory.

This is the condensed story of my working life over the past quarter century, more or less. Well, at least part of it. I'm still chasing that whale, but here you'll find excerpts from years spent on an assortment of jobs and observations that seemed relevant to my ongoing quest for meaningful work. Names have been changed to protect both innocents and ignoramuses. Timelines have been shuffled occasionally to preserve the narrative. Most locations are intentionally made vague, but all of this happened. Trust me. I was there. I shit you not.

Granddad Instills Work Ethic; Boy Dreams of Unrealistic Jobs

Men labor under a mistake. The better part of a man is soon plowed into the soil for compost.[1]
—Henry David Thoreau

In the 1980s, when I was a little kid growing up Down South, I got paid for a few jobs here and there and learned about the relationship between labor and capital. My parents had divorced, but each still drove me three hours to visit my Grandmother and Granddad—a gentle, thoughtful man of impeccable character with piercing blue eyes, an easy smile and a full head of neatly combed silver-white hair. A retired accountant, university instructor and Naval officer whose supply ship, the George F. Elliott, was sunk by a kamikaze at Guadalcanal, Granddad gave me my first paying job. He offered me a nickel for every tiny white moth I could kill with a badminton racket in defense of his broccoli plants. I chased and swatted at the dive-bombing pests all over the massive vegetable garden that dominated his fenced-in backyard. I was so bad at this that Granddad took pity on me and gave me a 500-percent raise. Even making 25 cents per kill didn't seem to secure my future in wild game hunting, but I fought those moths until I could barely swing the racket and learned along the way that earning money required hard work.

Granddad was always kind and helpful, but he didn't believe that I should be given money without having earned it. He showed me what it felt like to be satisfied by a job well done, whether he was teaching me how to clean his sailboat, organize the garage or weed the garden. I learned the

---

1 Thoreau, Henry David. *Walden; or, Life in the Woods.* Boston: Ticknor and Fields, 1854.

value of a strong work ethic because Granddad led by example and made me want to be more like him.

Gradually I was promoted to a sort of groundskeeper, and I filled Granddad's extensive collection of bird feeders, pulled the weeds and finally got to use the riding mower, which was very exciting. I had free rein of the entire backyard; there were no grownups around, and I was *driving*! Even when I crashed into the fence, ripping an entire section down from the steel posts and hopelessly wrapping the chain links around the front axle of the mower, Granddad wasn't angry. He encouraged me to try again, teaching me to be persistent. He also taught me to fly his two-handled stunt kite and a Batman glider he kept in the garage. Granddad took me out on his sailboat, where he taught me navigation basics and always brought cold cans of soda with little packets of orange peanut butter crackers. I learned that there was quite a bit of work involved in keeping the sailboat clean and running smoothly. I crashed it too—his boat, this time, into the dock—bending the mounted steel hoop on the bow. A little older this time, I felt like a real idiot, but Granddad imparted helpful lessons without losing his temper.

* * *

Not long after the episode with the mower, I drew a real paycheck for the first time, as a neighborhood paperboy. I was obsessed with movies and comic books and needed my own source of income. The paper delivery job kept me flush with multiplex tickets and *Batman* comics, but the deal came with a parentally imposed caveat: I would be required to save half of my money for my college education. It worked for me. I'd finally have some real money coming in—much more than the small allowance I had received for doing chores and homework. I told my Dad I was 12-*teen* because he wouldn't let me see PG-13 movies until I was officially 13. This strategy didn't work. Dad wouldn't budge. Luckily, Tim Burton's *Batman* was to be released the summer I turned 13 in 1989, and after years

Granddad Instills Work Ethic; Boy Dreams of Unrealistic Jobs

of following the caped crusader in comic-books, I was at least as excited as I had been three years before, when I had seen *Top Gun* at the age of 10 in the theatre (somehow it was PG). My resulting fascination with naval aviation for a time eclipsed even my *Star Wars* obsession, as far as the movies were concerned.

After seeing *Top Gun*, like every other 10-year-old boy in America, I wanted to be a fighter pilot. I knew it was the right career path for me and remember being thoroughly convinced of this upon leaving the theatre. This lasted until a guy my mom dated for a while named Dick—who liked to refer to me as "Piss-Ant"—explained to me that Naval Aviators had to be good at math, and that I was probably already too tall, like Goose had been. Buzz kill. My neck would surely snap upon ejection after engaging multiple MIG fighters, or after being caught in a jet wash…and Dick was right. I sucked at math. First career dreams officially crushed.

I lived in a seemingly endless neighborhood of drab, three-story concrete block World War II-era apartment buildings. My parents remained mostly friendly after their divorce and for years lived not far from each other, enabling me to run between Mom's apartment and Dad's within about five minutes, if I sprinted through the small outdoor pool area that was centrally located in a wooded clearing between their perpendicular streets. I rode Dad's 1960s-era French 10-speed bike between apartment buildings, throwing the tightly rolled and rubber-banded newspapers hard, aiming for one mean old lady's third-floor glass storm door, and hoping for the loud BOOM that came with a perfect connect. She'd stumble out the door in her muumuu with rollers in her hair and yell:

"Mah ah-ZAY-lee-uhs! Mah ah-ZAY-lee-uhs! You hit mah ah-ZAY-lee-uhs!"

I rode away laughing, freezing my little ink-stained fingers on cold Sunday mornings. I didn't set out to harass old ladies, of course, but this particular one had a mean little dog that always ran down the stairs and tried to bite me, no matter how hard I tried to make friends with it, much

Granddad Instills Work Ethic; Boy Dreams of Unrealistic Jobs

like the old lady herself. And despite her claims, I never actually hit her azalea plants.

I didn't live very close to any beaches, but I had some bitchin' surfer jam-shorts with Hawaiian floral patterns that my Mom had sewn. I wore these homemade jams with my San Francisco 49ers jersey, *Star Trek* hat and mirrored sunglasses. I favored big, white high-top basketball sneakers, much like my favorite TV action hero, *MacGyver*. I wondered how I could get paid to do *MacGyver*-type stuff. That would be a cool career, I thought. Engineering, maybe? Nope. Too much math. I bought grocery baskets for the newspapers and mounted them on the sides of my rusty old bike. I had yet to discover punk rock, heavy metal, grunge, or indie rock. When I wasn't listening to my Bruce Springsteen, Michael Jackson, DJ Jazzy Jeff & The Fresh Prince or Billy Joel tapes on my Walkman, I was listening to the Top Five At Five on my local commercial rock radio station.

After delivering the papers in the afternoons, I liked to hang out in the basement with a couple neighborhood buddies who had helped me convert a laundry room storage locker into a clubhouse for ninjas because, well, ninjas are awesome.[2] While other residents dropped off and picked up their laundry at the coin-operated machines outside our basement clubhouse, we blacked out the chicken-wire walls with garbage bags, posted pictures of Chuck Norris, ninja weapons and tactics on the inside walls and made our plans after school. We met up again after dark—when I'd finished with the paper route, homework and dinner—with homemade ninja suits and makeshift weapons, fighting battles in the streets and yards and wooded areas behind the apartment buildings. Once we decided to build a clubhouse in the woods and managed to cut down several trees before my Mom found out and crushed our dreams of a homemade ninja log cabin in the woods. Why wouldn't ninjas live in a homemade log cabin in the woods? I had no delusions about my career potential as an elite and shadowy assassin, but it was fun to pretend. I still didn't know what I

---

[2] Of course they are. If you don't believe me, read Robert Hamburger's totally sweet book *Real Ultimate Power: The Official Ninja Book*. New York: Citadel Press, 2004.

wanted to be when I grew up.

During these paperboy years, other than ninjas and all things *Batman*, I got really into BMX bikes. If I couldn't pilot F-14 Tomcats with my hair on fire, why couldn't I become a famous bicycle motocross racer? That sounded like a pretty good career path. I spent a lot of time working on bicycles on the screened-in patio off the living room of the second-floor apartment I lived in with my Mom. I still took my Dad's old 10-speed to work, though. The newspaper baskets would've looked totally lame on my chromoly BMX bike, and when I tried to sling the enormous newspaper-stuffed shoulder bag across my back, I had a pretty hard time keeping the BMX from toppling over. So I stuck with the 10-speed for my job, but on any other occasion that presented an opportunity for a bicycle, I was all about the BMX.

I loved to mix and match parts, trading a set of Redline forks here for a pair of mag wheels there, or maybe a set of GT three-piece cranks for some new Haro bars and a seat post. I was decent with a wrench and had something like my own business, fixing up my bikes and my friends' bikes, buying, selling and trading in the perpetual pursuit of BMX perfection. I parlayed these self-taught bicycle repair skills and my sustained interest in riding and racing into a successful campaign directed at my parents to be sent to the legendary Woodward BMX, Freestyle and Skateboard Camp in Pennsylvania. I wanted to start racing my BMX bikes competitively, and Woodward was the place to go for kids who were into what would eventually become known as "extreme" sports, though this was well before the advent of the X-Games, when skateboarding was still a crime. Little did I know that the most extreme thing that would happen to me at Woodward would involve a plaster cast and some particularly strong anesthetic.

While at Woodward I met some famous professional BMX riders I had admired like Terry Tenette, who got massive air when jumping my bike, making the whole process look way cooler and easier than I could ever hope to, despite the custom BMX that I had built myself from a variety of parts including an MCS Hurricane frame and forks, GT handlebars,

HARDBARNED!
One Man's Quest for Meaningful Work in the American South

and the "007" number plate I had mounted across the front. I stuck black mailbox stickers on the back of my yellow secondhand motorcycle helmet, spelling out RAD, but I didn't feel very rad. I was 12 years old and thought I had style, but I knew that Terry had what mattered: talent. On the second or third day of my week at BMX camp, I had spent long hours riding, racing and receiving instruction from the team leaders. It was announced that we were done for the day, but we were welcome to keep racing the track as much as we liked. I had done okay but knew I needed practice and joined three or four other riders for several more runs around the curvy, high-banked dirt racetrack, pedaling furiously, getting a bit of air here and there over some of the bigger jumps and generally having a real blast, building my confidence little by little. I made the conscious decision to try one last run before heading back to my cabin for a shower and dinner.

The gate at the top of the steep hill dropped, and the remaining riders pedaled hard down the hill and into the first jump, when everything went wrong for me. My front tire hit a divot in the track, and the wheel was instantly flipped sideways. I launched into the air as the momentum lifted my body from the dirt, leaving my bicycle far below me as I soared over the handlebars and the first jump, crashing down the slope on the other side, forgetting all of my tuck-and-roll training and groping out in every direction as I tried to break my awkward fall. I came rolling and crashing down the slope for what felt like an eternity after making initial contact with the dirt. My helmet smashed against the ground repeatedly as time slowed, and I watched a beautiful crimson sunset above our cabins in the distance, waiting to slide to a stop as my limp body rag-dolled its way down the other side of the hill. My bicycle kept bouncing and spinning on, careening haphazardly, high above my head, crashing into the track well beyond where I lay. Someone asked if I was okay. It was nice to just relax there in the dirt, catching my breath and staring at the reddening sky. I felt pretty good until I reached back to prop myself up to stand, when I realized something wasn't right.

"Your arm's broken," Terry Tenette said.

"Lie back down and relax."

I learned that the local doctor was an hour away and unavailable until the next day, so I spent a painful night on my back with a few Tylenol caplets, cradling my broken arm across my chest in a simple splint, waiting for the morning when I could have the bone set and put into a cast. Unable to sleep, my mind wandered to how I'd manage my paper route left-handed.

Rich "The Butcher" Bartlett, another pro rider of whom I was a fan, drove me to the hospital the next morning and was the first to sign my cast, which extended from my hand to my armpit, with a static right angle at the elbow. After we left the hospital, Rich signed one of his BMX jerseys for me and bought me a strawberry milkshake at Hardee's, which I promptly vomited from the window of his car. My stomach was upset from the strong anesthetic the doctor had shot into me before hanging my fingers in traction. On my back on a cold metal table, I felt my arm SNAP and CRUNCH back into place as the doc set the bones. It hurt a lot, but so did the realization that I was not destined for a career as a professional BMX dude, either. Somehow it was clear to me that another potential career dream had been crushed decisively.

Before I'd left for BMX camp, my three-ring notebook for school had contained an eloquent phrase that I had written on the inside cover: "Bikers cruise, skaters lose." I was so enamored with BMX racing, so fond of tinkering with bikes and riding, that I just didn't understand why anyone would want to roll around on a dinky little stick with tiny wheels. But now, stuck at Woodward with nearly a week of camp left, my arm immobilized at a 90-degree angle in a solid cast, unable to even ride the dirt track for fun between the other campers' races, skateboards started to look a little more interesting. From every direction, plenty of talented dudes were pulling off amazing stuff on skateboards on the vert ramps and street courses at Woodward, as The Violent Femmes and Fugazi blasted from boomboxes. I had nothing but time to wander around, watch and listen. I discovered punk rock and decided that my miniscule music collection of popular chart-toppers was hopelessly uncool. I made the life-changing realization

Granddad Instills Work Ethic; Boy Dreams of Unrealistic Jobs

that all kinds of interesting music was happening that wasn't even played on the radio and that infinitely more creative, exciting, artistic and even defiant ideas were happening far outside of mainstream culture, even critiquing it boldly. Woodward opened my eyes to a lot of things.

I got home, lost most of my interest in racing BMX bikes and bought a skateboard. I could barely imagine skateboarding for a living, but I wanted to see what it was all about. As luck would have it, I learned upon my return to the South that my Grandmother had ordered me a subscription to *Thrasher* magazine.

"How did you *know*?!" I asked her over the phone, amazed, first issue in hand.

Apparently, a young man who reminded her of me had knocked on her door, selling magazine subscriptions. We probably had the same stupid haircut. She had asked him what he would like to subscribe to if he had his choice, and he had said *Thrasher*. She had no idea what it was, but she signed me up for two years of it. The timing couldn't have been better. *Thrasher* expanded my knowledge of skateboarding, clued me into punk rock culture and appealed to me like nothing had before. Soon I had posters of Steve Caballero and Tony Hawk soaring over half pipes on the walls of my bedroom instead of Tom Cruise mugging with Kelly McGillis. My Walkman now played Fugazi and Operation Ivy tapes instead of Billy Joel or Michael Jackson.

When I got home from Woodward, the last thing I wanted to do was to deliver newspapers, and I quit soon after taking over from the substitute who had covered for me while I was gone. I couldn't even bend my right arm for several weeks. I could no longer launch the rolled papers up to the third floor. I had to walk every one all the way up all three flights of stairs in each building, and riding my bike was proving to be difficult enough with one arm. I didn't really have to get another job immediately, so after school and homework I read books and played Nintendo instead. I became transfixed by Anne Rice's *Vampire Chronicles* and Dean R. Koontz's and Stephen King's horror novels.

Granddad Instills Work Ethic; Boy Dreams of Unrealistic Jobs

A few years later, when I was in high school in the early 90s, Granddad gave me my first car, a four-door 1971 Chevrolet Impala that I nicknamed The Beast, a seemingly indestructible tank that I used to drive myself to school and to my next job at the grocery store. I also roamed around town with my best buds, Ernie and Joe, smoking cigarettes, searching for skate spots with our skateboards in the back, always on the run from rent-a-cops (whose chief mission seemed to be evicting skaters from office parks and parking lots—there was no skate park back then) and listening to Rancid and Fugazi on the tape deck I had installed in the Impala with the help of another friend. The Beast got nine miles to the gallon. I'm sure it was all part of Granddad's plan to teach me sound money management skills because I didn't get the Honda Accord I had hoped for. Perhaps Granddad had also thought about my tendency to crash into stationary objects (like his fence or the boat dock), and had concluded that the massive Impala would be safer for me to use when crashing into things. He thought of everything.

A few years after I had sold The Beast, somehow managing not to crash it, I needed to replace the old manual transmission in my Volvo station wagon, and Granddad loaned me part of the money to pay for it. After I had paid him back half of the loan, he offered to take me with him on a sailing trip in the Bahamas with my uncle, but he gave me a choice: I could go on the trip or I could consider the debt erased. I went on the trip and paid him back the rest of the loan later. He was never obvious with his lessons on personal responsibility, but I learned them. Granddad helped me discover a strong work ethic and get a jump-start on the road to manhood.

Barns: The Healthy Hate Receptacle

No matter how upbeat they are—no matter how ingenious and flexible—the unemployed and underemployed understand that the clock is always ticking in the background. The longer you are unemployed, the less likely you are to find an appropriate job, and entries like 'sales associate,' 'limo driver' or 'server' do not make an attractive filling for the growing gap in one's resume...when skilled and experienced people routinely find their skills unwanted and their experience discounted, then something has happened that cuts deep into the very social contract that holds us together.[1]

—Barbara Ehrenreich

Though barn delivery was a completely foreign concept to me at first, and I didn't expect to hate the job as much as I grew to, I had to blame someone or something for my inability to land a writing job. Barns turned out to be that healthy hate receptacle. Well, maybe not so healthy, but convenient. I could either hate barns or hate myself, so I chose to hate barns. After some months, I began to perceive barns, irrationally of course, as precisely what stood between me and a writing career. I knew that barns had nothing to do with my own inability to find the job I really wanted, but as the years went by in the truck, my resume *must* have started to look less attractive to employers looking for a writer and hearing from a barn-hauling truck driver.

I progressed through the difficult process of learning the barn-hauling job by day while sending out resumes by night and on the weekends, and I got better with the barns but viewed the job as temporary, always hoping, and (at least early on) assuming that the doorway to my writing career was right around the corner. As this assumption proved incorrect, my anger developed, and because it had to be aimed at something, I directed it toward barns and everything related to their delivery, repair and repossession—even their very existence seemed to be holding me hostage from the life I wanted to live. On the most difficult days (there

---

[1] Ehrenreich, Barbara. *Bait and Switch: The (Futile) Pursuit of the American Dream.* New York: Owl Books, 2005.

were many) of my barn-hauling years, my rage—some of it justified, some of it misdirected—was laser-focused.

Before long, the barn personified itself, transforming from an inanimate object into an outsized personality, an overbearing and ever-present character in my life. As I perceived the situation, it was this character's functional objective to try at every opportunity to unleash havoc upon my days. My job was to get everything moved, delivered, repaired and repossessed without allowing anything to go wrong or ruin my day, while simultaneously striving to secure meaningful, educationally relevant employment elsewhere. The odds were stacked against me.

Still, I enjoyed the solitary freedom of the truck and the open road. I relished the beautiful weather when I worked in it. I wanted to work hard, take pride in my job and represent my employer as a professional to the best of my abilities. I had been raised to understand the value of personal integrity and the satisfaction of hard work. As miserable as I allowed myself to become as a barn hauler, I still strived to maintain a level of professionalism that my employer deserved and of which Granddad would have been proud. I refused to let the quality of my work be dragged down with my deteriorating attitude, but I still screwed things up. A lot.

I blamed anything that ever went wrong on barns, whether whatever had happened was actually the fault of a crazy customer, a distracted or dishonest salesperson, a broken-down truck, a piece of faulty equipment or my own stupid mistakes. I was trapped in Barn Land because of the barn; therefore, the barn was the source of all problems. The barn existed; therefore, I was miserable. These conclusions may have lacked nuance or even reason, but barns served me well as a necessary target for a growing resentment. The perpetual conflict of me versus barn was something like the Coyote versus the Roadrunner. Barns were the Coyote. I was just trying to do my job, so I could go home and get on with the rest of my life. The Barn was the evil nemesis trying at every turn to drop a big fucking rock on my head.

HARDBARNED!
One Man's Quest for Meaningful Work in the American South

Having manufactured a scapegoat for my own issues, I recognized the irony. Barns were keeping food on the table through the early years of my marriage while my lovely wife, herself fresh out of graduate school, was also struggling to find a foot-in-the-door to a meaningful career. Barns also helped me chip away at my considerable student loan debt. In this way, The Barn was a sort of loan shark, offering a nice paycheck but continually taking painful bites out of my ass, and whatever financial aid barns offered was counterbalanced by their detrimental effect on my emotional state, as I was surely a more difficult spouse to live with in those years. It helped to be married to a mental health professional.

Of course I was only visiting Barn Land, or at least I thought of myself as a mere transient there, but barns latched onto me like a field spore with Velcro paws, stowing away on my boots and jeans to hitch a ride home and intrude uninvited on my personal space, manipulating my moods, rearranging my evening plans and invading my dreams. Barns overstepped private boundaries like an unwelcome and forcibly intimate stranger on a crowded subway, impacting far too many aspects of my life and evolving from a mere job into a harbinger of sorrow that threatened to devour me from the inside out. A monstrous, soul-crushing force at the center of my existence, barns gradually spawned a swirling, pulsing, superheated mass of raw emotion and sweaty energy comprised of equal parts frustration, denial, rage, desperation, depression, and ultimately, humor. What had once provoked rage eventually made me laugh.

Most people don't know what the hell I'm talking about when I tell them I drove a truck and hauled barns; they either think I drove 18-wheeler tractor-trailer long-haul trucks, or say,

"Haul barns? How do you *haul* a barn? Do you mean those *PODS*?"

I'd have reacted the same way before I took the job, but no. I'm not referring to Portable On-Demand Storage units, the large shipping containers one can fill and have delivered to transport stuff, though the POD concept is similar to that of the portable storage barns I delivered and repossessed. As it turns out, as opposed to many other places in the world—like Japan, where some hotel rooms are known as mere "capsules" the size of coffins, and average living spaces hover around 400 square feet[2]—plenty of suburban and rural Americans like to have their space. We like big houses and vast, green lawns. We need a lot of room for extra junk, whether it's in a POD, a barn or a walk-in closet, a rented storage unit or just spread across the yard.

The barns I hauled look something like traditional barns on a farm, like the ones you see on a hill when you're driving through a rural area in the middle of nowhere Down South,[3] but different. Usually, they're not gray and falling over and decrepit. They look fairly new,[4] for the most part, except when they're converted into meth labs and accidentally explode,[5] or when they're cut to pieces and modified into dog kennels, horse barns, chicken coops, dance clubs, game rooms, garbage dumpsters, hunting lodges or temporary living quarters for incontinent adults, each a situation I witnessed on the job. They're pressure treated to resist water damage, consist of various designs and sizes and are customizable. They're built to be portable for delivery and aren't particularly unique: many different companies, some Amish, some Mennonite, some neither, build comparable versions and sell them across the country.

Upon hauling these buildings in and out of strangers' backyards, chaos often ensued. In Barn Land, my cohorts and I wore many hats. Though our job title was "driver," we did a hell of a lot more than drive. Drivers were also truckers, mechanics, lumberjacks, construction workers, day laborers, customer service representatives, repairmen, inventory suppliers, roofers, repo men and sometimes detectives. We did whatever it took to get the job done, trying all day, and often well into the night, to avoid being HARDBARNED.

---

[2] Jeremy Hobson, *Marketplace Morning Report*. American Public Media. NPR, February 7, 2011.
[3] See interior title page.
[4] See title page again. This time, look in the rearview mirror.
[5] Barns have indeed been used as meth labs. Several states in Barn Land lead the nation in meth lab busts, injuries and deaths.

The Business of Computer Sales

Is the life of a corporate underling—even acknowledging that corporate underlings are well paid—an acceptable end to our quest for human dignity and worth?[1]

—Wendell Berry

I knew I'd hate working in computer sales the minute my buddy Johnny suggested it we try it temporarily. A talented artist with a recently minted Bachelor of Fine Arts degree, he'd had a tough time landing a job in his field, too. He's since earned a Master of Fine Arts degree but still sells computers for a living. Back then he was eager to take this sales gig at the computer corporation because he was in dire financial straits, selling me on it by accentuating the fact that I was too. Our liberal arts degrees were utterly failing to help us land decent jobs. He emphasized how we wouldn't make sales calls. Customers would call *us*. We assumed that all we'd have to do was to sell them whatever they requested. We were quite wrong, but we didn't know that yet. How hard could it be? Johnny had a point, but I knew it would suck. I didn't want to sell anyone anything, but the writing and editing career I still actively pursued seemed just as elusive with another degree under my belt, and rent was due.

Business and *sales* had long seemed like dirty words to me, necessary evils, but those I didn't necessarily have to participate in directly, other than in my own default status as an American consumer who must capitalize on a skillset of some sort in order to purchase food, shelter, goods and services. I didn't want to manipulate or take advantage of anyone. I

---

1 Berry, Wendell. "Feminism, the Body, and the Machine." *The Art of the Commonplace: The Agrarian Essays of Wendell Berry*. Ed. Norman Wirzba. Berkeley: Counterpoint Press, 2003.

somehow imagined I could heft my idealism over my head while trudging through the mire and the muck of corporate technology sales, at least long enough to save up some much-needed cash.

I knew then as I know now that the empathetic, communal, socially conscious punk rock ethos that resonated deeply within me as an conscientious adolescent is diametrically opposed to the shareholder-appeasing, profit-driven methodology of a global tech giant like the one I was going to work for, but I didn't sign up for a personal paradigm shift. They couldn't change me. I knew who I was. I could go undercover and hold my breath for a few months. I could make some quick cash and get out when someone finally hired me to write something, but I had to pay the bills and pay them now. I could do my best to temporarily appease the soul-crushed overlords who had given their lives to the corporation until it was inevitably, unequivocally time to leave.

Outsourcing the interviewing, hiring and placement for multi-division distribution of new hires, the computer corporation remained safely at arm's-length from the uncomfortable, liability-laden practices of human relations. My group of newly hired staff was funneled into one of two sales divisions based on mysterious algorithms in new-hire testing software. Our test results, for whatever reason, suggested Johnny and I be placed in the business division, so we were groomed to sell to businesses instead of to individual consumers. We submitted to idiotic, context-free personality inventories and told them what we assumed they wanted to hear. We sat through weeks of asinine seminars led by "professional consultants" that the computer corporation flew in from around the country to teach us how to be effective salespeople. One consultant (we assumed she was a former kindergarten teacher) brought a set of brightly colored children's chimes that made annoying metallic ding-dong noises when she hit them with her little matching mallets because she wanted our attention after juice and cookie snack breaks. Yep. She passed out colored markers and had us draw pictures and play games and instructed us on how to perfect our "sales voices." She told us to always *smile* when we were on the phone with customers, tested us on it with fake sales calls, and had us record ourselves pretending to sell something to imaginary callers. We played the tapes back for the whole class until they were good enough for her. Special torture.

Johnny and I barely contained our vitriol for the system or our constantly overwhelming urges to laugh out loud at the moronic corporate culture that was being shoveled at us daily by our trainer, a hipster guy with spiked, gelled hair and a colorful collection of rubber cause bracelets[2], barely older than us, who had clearly blood-inked his unflagging allegiance to the corporation. Divided into teams, we filled out charts on the latest products with magic markers and collaborated on original illustrations and even *poems* about how great some printer or some scanner or some piece-of-shit wireless mouse was. We put our heads together to determine effective language usage and appropriate selling strategies for the abhorrent process of squeezing the most money out of various reluctant customer models, learning how to "slam old ladies" by convincing unsuspecting elderly people that our predatory in-house financing options were actually a good choice for them. We memorized endless acronyms for strategies devised for controlling the conversation with customers over the phone, and we memorized scripts that we were told never to deviate from. We perfected the smoke and mirror techniques designed to mask the actual costs of credit. We played trivia games against other teams based on our rapidly growing product knowledge base. Johnny and I enjoyed making fun of all of it together. It was bad enough, but alone, it would have been much worse.

Then one night after class, Johnny got drunk and fell off a skateboard, breaking his arm. The computer mega-corporation didn't want to pay for his medical bills, so they fired him instead. This was convenient for them, as they had planned all along to have the staffing agency serve

---

2 You know these. Everybody has one. Some people collect many and wear a rainbow on their wrists. Just name your cause: Live Strong. Save The Boobies. Colitis Sucks. Cancer's Bad, Mmmkay?, etc.

as a liability buffer for occasions such as this. Johnny probably could have sued the crap out of them, but for some reason he didn't. Maybe because we were working in a "right to work" state, meaning that red-state labor laws favor the rights of businesses over employees and thus employers are never required to explain why an employee is fired. I finished the training without my friend and became a business sales associate on another "team," this time with a sales manager who was paid according to how effectively his team brought in the bucks.

I just wanted to be cool to people. I wanted to be the guy that I'd like to talk to if I had to call in to buy a computer for my small business, imagining I could ever have one. I wanted to be friendly and helpful, of course, but I wanted to be *real*. *Corporate sales* were about the last two words I could ever identify with, and yet I started to do well. I led myself to believe that somehow I could defy the system, deviate from the scripts and just get people what they wanted. Instead of asking callers the 50 required questions in order to discover how much money they had now and how much long-term earnings potential they might hold for the corporation in the next 10 years, I would treat them like I would like to be treated, talk to them off-script, sell them only what they needed, not pressure them to buy more things and not twist their arm to finance through any of the corporation's myriad schemes.

This approach worked temporarily for me because customers liked me and told my boss. They called back for repeat business and told other business owners about me. I called my customers back when they had problems; I treated them well and tried to help. Because of a few big sales that I closed, particularly one six-figure deal, I was temporarily ahead in the endless rivalry with my peers that was broadcasted throughout the company conspicuously, a policy of public competition that defined the corporate business sales methodology…Constant, relentless competition among peers. Recognition of large sales. Respect for sales performance. Building of expectations through constant pressure and dangled incentives. Public belittlement and shaming of underperforming individuals and teams. Gradually, as the fallout from the sales explosion lifted, my numbers fell off a cliff. I use the explosion metaphor because after closing the six-figure deal, I received an email from my boss's boss's boss, which contained an animated GIF of a nuclear explosion and resultant mushroom cloud, replaying in perpetuity with a huge, flashing, rainbow-colored, division-wide announcement of my sales "detonation" that resulted in congratulatory back slaps and Instant Messages of celebration all day. I wanted to punch my PC.

Once the celebration wore off, I kept getting bad performance reviews for not doing what I was supposed to be doing. I hadn't changed my approach. This method of just being myself had gotten me the sales "detonation," but it couldn't last and was viewed as anomalous. I wasn't doing what I was told. I was veering off-script, selling fewer add-ons and upgrades than my peers, and failing to push the in-house financing plans. My supervisors would sound increasingly ominous in my bi-weekly performance reviews after looking at my numbers and needling through recordings of my incoming sales calls, pinpointing the exact number of words I had failed to read from the script and the number of chances to push the finance plans I had failed to seize upon, as they stressed how essential it was that I get back on track with the program.

What *had* happened last Wednesday at 3:21PM, there on page six of the Financial Documentation Requirement script explaining the details of Payment Plan B to Customer X? Why had I veered off and failed to read the entirety of Paragraph C, line by line? Why had I asked this small business owner only 37 of the required 50 questions that would allow us to quantify and categorize his long-term earnings potential for the corporation *despite* the fact that the poor guy was incredibly frustrated by my endless questioning, only needed a couple of desktop PCs and didn't have patience for my relentless interrogation into the depths of his wallet and the intricacies of his network? Didn't I want to receive another sales detonation email? Wouldn't I like to be recognized on the local and even national sales leader boards as an upper-echelon WINNER? Wouldn't I

HARDBARNED!
One Man's Quest for Meaningful Work in the American South

enjoy earning the free trip with other big sales WINNERS to some tropical paradise for pushing the most shitty house-brand printer cartridges on customers who had called me for help and didn't want, need or ask for anything related to a printer in the first place? Did I really want to be a fucking superstar of sales? Supervisors were unconvinced.

Every Friday afternoon, all of the teams within the business division would gather in a large room for a pep rally. No really, a *pep rally*. I hated them in my junior high and high school gymnasiums, and I hated them at the computer corporation. There wasn't much difference. I didn't have any "school spirit" back then. I didn't wear school colors. I didn't give a crap if my school teams got the most free throws or touchdowns. I didn't even go to a game all season when my high school football team won the state championship. I gleefully competed against my own overly funded, excessively branded, comprehensively outfitted, impeccably coordinated and thoroughly exclusive, high school-affiliated local rowing association, for the next-town-over's ragtag band of misfit contrarian rowers with four leaky old boats. I quit the tennis team to play heavy metal. I definitely wasn't going to stand up, applaud and cheer for someone on a sales "team" who won a golf shirt for harassing the shit out of old ladies to finance preinstalled virus protection software.[3]

The atmosphere was eerily similar to high school, though. Instead of censored versions of Salt N Pepa songs blasting over the PA system with cheerleaders in the background, corporate logos zoomed across a projected PowerPoint display with canned Muzak designed to get us fired up about selling computers. The processed environment and contrived enthusiasm reminded me of the ubiquitous, asinine motivational posters found in fictional conference rooms and office spaces, featuring soaring athletes in

---

[3] Inconsequentially, the virus protection software we peddled for payroll incentives was designed by John McAfee, software developer and former billionaire who was, until recently, living on the run in an RV with his girlfriend, a dog and many guns, convinced that an international gang of hit-men was after him for allegedly murdering his American neighbor when they were both living in Brazil. He's now married, stockpiling supplies while preparing for the end of the world…and running for President.

climactic poses or heroic mountain climbers dangling from steep rocks, high above spectacular vistas with

> **ACHIEVE**

or

> **TEAMWORK**

or

> **DETERMINATION**

stamped across the top, so I wasn't surprised to see these same posters actually lining the walls of the corporation. Instead of regulation basketballs and spirit sticks, here were miniature squeezable stress basketballs and tiny plastic footballs, all stamped with technology vendor logos. Signs with homemade "team" insignias were brandished aloft on broomsticks as banners of pride, just like in the bleachers back in junior high. Instead of trophies presented by flat-topped authority figures in coach shorts at the microphone, polo shirts and sun visors with embroidered corporate logos were awarded by flat-topped authority figures in branded company gear, as grown women squealed with glee like little girls and men pumped their fists in the air, grunting approvingly in monosyllabic unison like cavemen after a successful hunt.

The pressure was building; despite the anomalous sales detonation, my periodic evaluations were sounding more and more terminal, and I knew that my days were limited. I had a clear choice to make. I would have to do all of the things my supervisors were saying I had to do, adopting standard procedure, surrendering to the system, compromising my integrity and treating people in a way that I thought was neither honorable nor fair—but thereby becoming the employee they wanted me to be—because customers were "priority one!" This wasn't going to happen. My old friend Mitch needed a hand with his expanding trucking business and said that I had a job with him if I was interested. He knew I still wanted to write for a living but was happy to train me and offer me a good wage while I looked for writing gigs. It sounded good to me.

After five months in corporate business sales and a steady stream of job applications spewing forth from my computer, I still had zero leads on a writing career, but I had finally earned enough money to buy my girlfriend an engagement ring. I grabbed my magnetic nametag from my half-cubicle and…heard we were getting free pizza for lunch. So I delayed a couple hours, ate my last free meal on the clock, gathered my pens and stapler, and walked out the door for the last time. I drove straight to the mall and bought a new pair of running shoes. I was so tired of sitting on my ass all day at the computer screen that I started running.

I knew nothing of barns or of what was in store for me, or that I'd spend the next three years of my life trapped in Barn Land. I had no idea. I didn't care though. I remained confident that I'd land a writing job soon, and all I knew was that wherever I ended up next wasn't going to be a high-pressure sales environment focused on squeezing people until the change fell out of their pockets. I just wanted to put on those new sneakers and run far the fuck away.

How I Became HARDBARNED

My self-regard as a Master of Arts was hard to sustain through the extended trauma of job-hunting, with its desperate open-mindedness and rising sense of worthlessness.[1]

—Matthew Crawford

HARDBARNED is an adjective, but it can also be a verb, a state of mind or a concise method of summarizing a situation, akin to snafu[2] or fubar.[3] My old friend Bill (a fellow barn-hauler) and I simply turned the object of our disdain into a descriptive way to sum up regularly frustrating, frequently comical[4] and often rage-inducing, barntacular occurrences. Working in Barn Land, the word HARDBARNED became part of our shorthand vernacular. We didn't need complete sentences to understand each other when describing a typical day of barn hauling. HARDBARNED became part of the lexicon we shared, which was well established, as Bill and I had already been friends for years. Together, the two of us had already made it through several undergraduate years of skateboarding, parties and video games, a warehouse job, two years of graduate-school teaching and tutoring, and a super-ridiculous, epic-fantasy heavy metal band.

Somehow we now found ourselves in the craziest job either of us had ever experienced, working as post-graduate truck drivers, delivering barns for a living by day and writing songs for a new punk band, a trio

---

1 Crawford, Matthew B. *Shop Class as Soulcraft: An Inquiry Into The Value of Work*. New York: The Penguin Press, 2009.
2 Situation Normal. All Fucked Up.
3 Fucked Up Beyond All Recognition.
4 Many of these situations only became comical with hindsight. Initially they were blood vessel burstingly frustrating, though eventually I learned to expect the insanity, conquering the rage with humor and laughing at absurd (read: normal) barn incidents before they had even unfolded completely.

we had forged with a drummer buddy of ours, by night. It was a regular occurrence that one of us would be stuck in a barn-induced, time-sucking quagmire that would often result in cancelled band practice. When we would talk on the phone late in the day from our trucks, hours from home and well into the late afternoon, eagerly anticipating our escape from Barn Land to band practice for the evening, our conversations went something like this:

"Hey man, how's it going?"

…silence…

"Ah, barns, eh?"

"Yeah, pretty much barns."

"Sometimes barns and mostly barns and usually barns, but pretty much barns."

"Yeah. Me too. *Barns.*"

Though we'd both been writing instructors, at this point somehow saying less said more. We didn't really have to articulate much after a certain point. We'd both heard all the stories before and knew what to expect. We were both used to crashing onto our respective living room sofas in a defeated fury at night with plenty of cold beer and coiled tension, unable to communicate with friends or wives, stewing and already dreading the next morning's alarm.

This customer or that salesperson. Broken this and broken that. Mud here and blood there. It was all in the tone of the word *barns*. No other words were necessary for those of us who struggled with these infuriating portable buildings, day in and day out. Nothing else held so much sway over our lives. There was no such thing as predictable scheduling. If we made it home in time to do what we wanted to do or even have dinner with our wives or girlfriends, we were lucky. If we made it home earlier than expected, we were even luckier, but barns had a tendency to demand the majority of our attention at the expense of our personal lives.

For an in-depth primer on the etymology of the terms BARNED and

HARDBARNED!
One Man's Quest for Meaningful Work in the American South

HARDBARNED, I offer the following explanation: If your truck is stuck in the mud during a barn delivery, and this ruins at least a significant portion of your day, you have been BARNED. If, due to any number of barn-related problems, your day is extended for four or five more hours than expected, and hence you are unable to do something you had eagerly looked forward to and planned for after work, again, you have been BARNED.

If you start your day with a trailer engine flooded with rainwater or blow out a hydraulic hose or two, break your winch mechanism or snap its cable, crash your barn into other barns on the builder's lot and get stopped by the DOT[5] on your way to the sales lot, then get lost in the country during a delivery because of unintelligible, incoherent or incorrect directions and a lack of street signs, taking out a mailbox or two along the way, tear up the roof of your barn on low-hanging branches, get a flat tire, lose a wheel entirely, set something on fire, run over the customer's septic tank, field lines or water main or tear down her cable, phone or power lines, crash into someone's roof and tear off his gutters or satellite dish, crack the truck's rims so that the tires no longer hold air, bend, break or lose your tools or lift jacks, injure yourself resulting in blood and bruises and curses in any number of ways, flip a barn over from your trailer or onto the ground or get stuck in someone's yard; if the truck breaks down, or parts of it are smashed and broken and you get soaked to the bone and pummeled by golf-ball-sized hail in a thunderstorm and get home at midnight, or any combination of all of the above and more—*each* of which happened to me along the way, *many* of which happened in a single day—you have been HARDBARNED. Well, you get the idea. It happened more than you might think.

My buddy Mitch had been a friend for years before he started asking me if I wanted to work for him, and he was slowly convincing me. A few months out of grad school with the walls of the computer corporation closing in on me, Mitch was in need of a driver to deliver barns for his new trucking company. Short and slim but solid and strong, Mitch is only three

---
5 Department Of Transportation

years older than me, but I had looked up to and admired him for years. We had forged a solid friendship a decade before in the smoky bars where our bands had performed together when we were undergrads. He'd earned a degree in Music Business and owned a record store before diving into the barn business. Gentle and patient like Mister Rogers, with a Zen-like focus and work ethic, Mitch is also a talented musician, skilled mechanic and a fun-loving, occasionally mischievous prankster who shares my love for the genius of Mike Judge. We enjoyed each other's company, and the transition from mere friends to employer and employee was easy.

Mitch had my back, no matter how crazy things got in Barn Land. He understood my predicament and was glad to have me to work for him as long as I wanted, knowing that I was desperately trying to find a way to earn a living as a writer. I was motivated to do the best job I could for Mitch, but I was sure it would only be a few weeks or months before some lucky employer would surely swoop in from a random company and jumpstart my fledgling career, snapping me up to write and edit something fascinating.

Before I ever drove the barn delivery truck, I spent a couple of weeks riding shotgun and simply observing. One of the first days I ever rode with Mitch was memorable. Some crusty old guy in camouflage overalls had purchased (rented-to-own) a repossessed (previously rented-to-own but defaulted upon) barn, which was stuffed to the ceiling with flea-market junk. There were straw hats, mason jars, playing cards, toy cars, broken lamps, dishes, old Coke and Wild Turkey bottles, garbage bags full of old clothes, stacks of bodice-ripper romance novels and dead houseplants in old pots with dirt spilling everywhere. We had to nail the door shut to keep the tidal wave of discarded detritus from erupting into the street. The barn's new steward was actually excited to acquire all the random crap that the previous rent-to-owner had left behind.

The crusty old guy was supposedly building a house, and we had to haul the well-broken-in barn over a mushy dirt bridge that straddled a soft creek bed. When we tried to cross the bridge, the trailer tires sank axle-deep into the mud. I thought we were done for the day, but Mitch sprang into action, climbing and crawling all over the truck and trailer like Spider-Man, tweaking knobs and adjusting levers, making small adjustments to equipment and tools in every direction. He placed large wooden blocks behind the truck's rear wheels, extended the two hydraulically powered rear sections of the trailer, and miraculously—from my green point of view—pushed the truck back up the hill and out of the mud using leverage, ingenuity and the powered trailer, extricating its tires from the creek bed and propelling the truck out of the hole by pushing the far end of the trailer into the ground. I was in awe of Mitch's barn-hauling prowess and wondered what the hell I could possibly have done on my own in a similar or even worse situation. Little did I know that I would have plenty of time to acquire these skills.

Learning to drive the contraption used for hauling barns reminded me of learning my multiplication tables in elementary school. I was never good at math, and I never forgot the torture of memorizing the seemingly endless and inane combinations of numbers while clenching my little-kid fists and punching the walls, the bloody knuckles and the tears. The sheer size of the barn-hauling apparatus is hard to fathom until you actually sit in the truck and begin trying to maneuver the awkward, mechanized beast around so as to back it up and align it perfectly with one, two or sometimes three barns, in order to load them all onto one trailer before hauling them somewhere. The process often made me want to punch something. Sometimes I'd punch a barn.

First of all, backing up the trailer was a challenge akin to blindfolded underwater Sudoku. I couldn't just look over my shoulder and through the rear windshield because the huge gooseneck trailer hitch was right there, standing four feet tall in the middle of the truck bed and blocking my view. Rapidly firing glances across 10 rear-view mirrors (yes, 10, and sometimes 11), I had to constantly shift my view in order to see what was going on behind me, though I often couldn't see what I needed to be seeing through any single mirror at any particular moment because the majority required constant, manual adjustments. Even if they were all remote-controlled, it would still have been a huge pain in the ass to get the things positioned correctly.

With three stock mirrors on each door and a useless one mid-windshield, we relied on three (or four) more mirrors at either end of two square metal poles, which were mounted across the hood of the truck and extended several feet to the right and left of the cab. When preparing to leave the lot with a secured load of barns, drivers could extend or retract and adjust the mirrors by hand to match the width of the barns we were carrying at any given time. A barn might be eight-, 10-, 12- or even 14-feet wide, and drivers were required to place red flags on all four corners of the barns they hauled, along with large, bright, yellow and black

OVERSIZE LOAD

signs stretched across the front of the truck and the rear of the last barn on the trailer, as barns would often extend far wider than the width of the trailer and truck on both sides.

From the driver's seat, we needed to be able to see along each side of the oversize load and from every conceivable angle. As it was, we had to get in and out of the truck 17 times, sitting behind the wheel and looking at the mirrors, then getting out and adjusting each of them by miniscule degrees in order to get the proper angles for each mirror before driving away.

Loading the barns and adjusting the mirrors was hard enough; how the hell to know when to look at which mirror while hauling a monstrous building (or two, or three) and taking up a lane and a half of a narrow, two-lane, two-direction country highway under perpetual construction while dodging mailboxes, cyclists, orange traffic barrels and oncoming big rigs at 55 miles an hour was a specialty skill that required practice and considerable patience. Backing up the truck was made more difficult because when in reverse, the trailer always moved in the opposite direction from the truck, so normally intuitive steering was backwards and confounding. For some people, backing up a car is already an anxiety-ridden experience, but this was an entirely different universe. Sometimes I'd get stuck in the mud,

HARDBARNED!
One Man's Quest for Meaningful Work in the American South

backing too far into the cornfield on the other side of the builder's lot, spinning my useless four-wheel-drive tires in the soft red clay. I'd back the sharp corners of the trailer (or those of the barns already loaded on it) into other barns on the lot, smashing and breaking holes in them. Many times I'd spend half an hour or more driving forward and back and forward and back, like Austin Powers trying to parallel park, scanning mirrors, over- or under-correcting, steering this way and that, the truck going one way, the trailer another, trying over and over to get the damn thing into place so I could merely load the barns and start my workday.

I also learned to drive the big farming tractor that the builders used to move around newly completed barns on their lots, though pulling barns around behind the tractor was often just as tricky, especially when barns were packed tightly together on the lot, as they usually were. I had to back up to the barn, drop the rear end of the tractor, slip the ball hitch underneath the lip of the barn and drag it to wherever it was going. However, because the barn was being dragged by a single ball hitch, it was more than a little difficult to control. The barn would often swing sharply to either the right or the left of the tractor as it was lifted with the ball hitch and crash into the other barns it was sandwiched between. This motion frequently resulted in smashed roofs and corners. I smashed one barn so badly that I had to spend half of the day beating the damaged walls to pieces with a sledgehammer so that the builders could start over. Eventually, I got better with the tractor and learned how to avoid such time-killing exercises, which always lengthened my days and increased my chances of being HARDBARNED. When I was training and Mitch was riding along with me in the truck, I would slam my fist into the steering wheel and hammer my forehead on the horn repeatedly, saying,

"I don't know if I can do this, man."

Mitch would say,

"Sure you can, and you will. It just takes time to learn. Every one of us has smashed up barns and trucks, fingers and shins."

A natural teacher with infinite patience, Mitch would stand on the builder's lot and direct me with hand signals. He'd make circular motions with his fingers, directing me to turn this way or that, like an aircraft marshaller with handheld illuminated beacons directing a plane but without the glowing lava lamps. Sometimes I would get mixed up, and everything was backwards, so I got frustrated, but if Mitch did, he never showed it. Even when I crashed into a telephone pole and demolished the roof along the entire length of one side of a 30-foot barn, or when I smashed out the entire rear windshield of his truck when I jackknifed the trailer in the overstocked builder's lot and exploded the glass into the back of my neck and across the seat, or when I backed into a tree because I had to back the truck into the branches to get in place to load a barn I was moving from one residence to another, not realizing until many miles later that I had dented the rear corner of the truck so severely that the entire taillight assembly had popped out, leaving a huge hole in the truck's tailgate where the light should have been. No matter how badly I screwed up, the worst reprimand I ever got was,

"Try to be more careful."

Mitch's steady, calming presence, regardless of the ridiculousness of the situation or my own ineptitude, motivated me to get it right for him, helped me to stick with it, increased my confidence, improved my skills over time and reminded me—more than a little—of Granddad.

Injuries were a constant concern as well. A few months before I left Barn Land for good, Bill fell on his back from the roof of a barn to the truck's steel trailer, six or eight feet below, slamming his 220-pound frame directly onto the aluminum ladder that fell between the trailer and his body. Nobody was around to hear Bill come crashing down or to help him as he yelled out in pain and tried to stand up, his back cracking and popping as he tried to gulp air. Somehow he managed to get to his feet after several minutes, dragging himself into the truck and driving himself to the hospital. We were all relieved to hear that nothing was broken and that he would recover after many days of rest and several varieties of powerful

How I Became HARDBARNED

painkillers. This was the most serious injury to either of us, and it got me thinking about how Dad had often expressed his concern over how dangerous barn hauling could be, but until someone hired me to write or edit something for a living, what else was I going to do? I wasn't going back to computer sales.

Though Bill and I talked constantly about the potential for serious injury on the job during the years we worked in Barn Land, this was the first time it had happened, other than the usual scrapes, cuts and bruises that we were all accustomed to. Another colleague of ours was once attempting to level a barn he had placed in someone's yard. Somehow the barn shifted and pinned him underneath it, so he had to scream for help until someone noticed and was able to jack up the barn to get him out from underneath the 10,000-pound garage. Luckily he wasn't hurt much. I remember many times when barns fell over from the lift jacks that we used to prop them up, sometimes from three feet off the ground or more, slowly tilting in one direction until the inevitable crash. After jumping out of the way to avoid being pinned by the barn or clobbered by the jack, I'd have to start the leveling process all over again. I was always able to get out of the way, but I never had one come down when I was underneath it. Though we all got knocked around a bit, abusing our thumbs, fingers, shins and foreheads on concrete blocks, hammers and barns, smashing up the trucks is another right of passage for barn haulers. Like Mitch said, it happens to all of us at some point or another.

In one delivery situation, I was trying to drive over a gigantic exposed root system and got stuck beneath several massive old trees in someone's yard. Meanwhile, I managed to hit a water main—a steel pipe sticking out of the ground—and ripped off the running boards along one side of the truck as I attempted to dislodge the Dodge from the huge roots. Once the truck was free, and after picking up the smashed parts that had broken off from it, I had to crawl around in the mud soup of a yard on my stomach and dig through the stinking slime until I found the submerged water main and shut off the steady stream of rotten-egg-smelling sulfur water that was flooding the lawn by closing the valve with a rusty pair of pliers, but I got the barn delivered. In yet another firestorm of personal genius, distractedly alternating looks between mirrors, I backed up with the driver's-side door slightly open and hit a tree with the open door. Until the parts store was able to order the tiny, $250 piece of plastic that would allow the door hinge to latch properly again, I added to my fun by spending a couple of weeks holding the truck's door shut with my left hand and upper arm, all day, while hauling barns.

Bill once smashed the front end of Mitch's other truck into some sharp tree stumps, exploding a headlight into tiny pieces and making a huge dent in this truck's cab behind the hole where the light once was. I was working with Bill that day, and we both should have turned the customer down when he asked us to put his barn in such a difficult-to-reach spot. But we tried anyway. He was a friendly, chatty British fellow in a white Tom Wolfe-style suit. I suppose we thought of ourselves as some sort of Southern ambassadors eager to make a good impression on a recent immigrant, attempting to be both accommodating and mindful of international relations. Another of Mitch's trucks somehow caught fire and burned to a crisp on the job, though that unlucky driver managed to escape unscathed. We all sustained our little injuries, and yet with the exception of Bill's back, we fared far better than our trucks, which were traded every couple of years for a new model with a better transmission or engine or overhaul of some kind.

HARDBARNED!
One Man's Quest for Meaningful Work in the American South

House Painter/Heart Breaker/ Film Renter/Intoxicant Experimenter

The very existence of flame-throwers proves that sometime, somewhere, someone said to himself, you know, I want to set those people over there on fire, but I'm just not close enough to get the job done.[1]

—George Carlin

One summer when I was about 15, having moved on from newspaper delivery and working as a self-employed house painter, I unwittingly created my own flamethrower and almost set myself and my friend on fire, nearly burning down his Mom's house. I opened for business with my old pal Ernie, a kid close to my age I had met on the playground in elementary school. We had bonded over tether-ball and G.I. Joes and were soon close friends. Ernie played the violin and was short with spiky blonde hair and glasses—something like Calvin, from my favorite comic strip *Calvin and Hobbes*. We were inseparable, attending the same daycare center as well, where we also played Transformers and He-Man and got into fistfights with some older kid from the Philippines who always tried to attack us for some inexplicable reason. We lived in the same neighborhood and one memorable year went trick-or-treating as Hans & Franz from *Saturday Night Live*. Eventually, we had the brilliant idea of going into business for ourselves as house painters. As it turned out, our first client was already lined up. Brian, our mutual math tutor, a bachelor who lived alone, built his own sailboat in his garage and gave us sage advice that a 15-year old could never forget:

"When it comes to boobs, more than a mouthful is wasted."

---
1 Carlin, George. *George Carlin: Carlin on Campus*. HBO Movie, 1984.

HARDBARNED!
One Man's Quest for Meaningful Work in the American South

House Painter/Heart Breaker/Film Renter/Intoxicant Experimenter

At some point around this time, I got interested in heavy metal and guitar virtuosos, and I remember hot summer days spent listening to Guns 'n' Roses, Megadeth, Iron Maiden, Slayer, Metallica, Judas Priest, Joe Satriani and Steve Vai. We cranked Ernie's boombox while scraping old, peeling paint from the eves of Brian's house, leaning back and balancing on a ladder, squinting into the sun through watery eyes peppered with tiny paint chips. We proudly displayed our business sign in Brian's yard. It read: ERNIE & CHRIS: HOUSE PAINTERS.

We stuck that ingenious bit of advertising into the ground and got ready for the business to start rolling in. I think we ended up with a grand total of three clients that summer, which was enough work that we could afford our regular trips to the comic book shop. It wasn't the most comfortable job. I found paint chips stuck to my skin in every crevice of my body. One day I sweated so much that I made a puddle on one of the ladder's steps. Paying attention to the eve I was painting over my head instead of my footing, I stepped in the puddle, slipped off the ladder and smashed my shins against several steps on the way down as I splattered paint all over my Airwalks while crashing to the ground and knocking over the paint bucket on my way, my bloody shins tinting the puddle of white paint pooling around me on the grass, like salsa mixing into cheese dip. Pretty smooth.

Later that summer, Ernie and I got an offer from his Mom to seal the back deck on the second story of their house. We'd never tried to seal a deck before, but it sounded about the same as painting. This seemed like the perfect job because we would be at Ernie's house and could take breaks whenever we wanted to play Nintendo, ride our skateboards around the cul-de-sac, practice rock music in the basement or make canned chili and rice with hot sauce (our favorite food). We got started early that morning on the deck and noticed a couple of pesky yellowjackets buzzing around. They multiplied quickly, and soon we were battling an angry airborne battalion, running up and down the deck stairs, clumsily swatting at the swarm with brooms we had used to sweep the deck. Ernie's Mom wasn't home, and we decided the best way to deal with the venomous pests would be to burn them out. We discovered that the aggressive little bastards were headquartered in a couple of old wooden railroad ties under the back stairs to the deck. We found some gas in the garage and without hesitation poured it into every hole we could find in the railroad ties. Together we crept like stealthy assassins under the stairs toward the nest, squatting and reaching as far away from our bodies as possible as we attempted to light the hive. Brilliantly I dangled a burning leaf in the proximity of the seething, gasoline-infused hive.

BOOM!

Ernie and I were literally thrown across the yard with the force of the explosion.

We came to on our backs, smelling the singed hair on our arms and legs, our skin charred like the Coyote after another unlucky encounter with that Roadrunner. I observed with increasing alarm that we were surrounded by puddles of burning gas, patches of burning grass, piles of burning yellowjackets (including airborne ones, also aflame) and assorted, burning bits of exploded railroad ties. Creeping flames were also rapidly climbing the stairs toward the new deck we had just covered with a second clear coat of flammable chemicals.

"I think we used too much gas," I heard Ernie mutter.

"Ya think?" I managed, pulling blackened wood splinters out of my arm and shins.

Ernie started yelling for his little brother, and neighbors appeared outside their houses around the cul-de-sac. Running around to the garage, Ernie grabbed the garden hose while I tried to smother the flames with a broom, which promptly caught on fire too, along with the broom Ernie had brought around from the garage. We stomped and flailed, yelling and swinging our flaming brooms around in an awkward and unintentional imitation of tribal hunters dancing around a ceremonial fire. Eventually we were able to save the day with that garden hose. It seemed a miracle,

House Painter/Heart Breaker/Film Renter/Intoxicant Experimenter

not only that the deck had survived with minimal blackening, but that Ernie and I were neither seriously hurt nor stung by a single yellowjacket. We assured the neighbors that everything was fine and finished the job of sealing the deck.

Ernie decided to finish the rest of the job in the sun without a shirt. Late that afternoon, he had a serious sunburn, and later that evening, after we had eaten dinner and watched a movie, Ernie's entire back was covered with a single, dinner plate-sized blister, and for my second idiotic move of the day, I forgot about it. As we looked out the window together, moonlight reflecting over the shiny new deck coating, I slapped him on the back with congratulations of a job well done and the successful avoidance of potential catastrophe. The blister burst, soaking his shirt, which promptly stuck to the huge wound on his back. Ernie yelled

"FUCK!" and punched me in the arm.

We didn't make much money painting houses or sealing decks, but it was a decent job for a couple summers, anyway, and we always made enough extra cash for a couple new Nintendo games before school started again. Although we both concluded that house painting and deck sealing wasn't an ideal career path for either of us, we enjoyed working together and appreciated a job well done with teamwork.

* * *

Back at school after the self-employed summer, as a junior in high school with a stupid skater hair cut (long on top and shaved on the sides) that I pulled back into an even stupider ponytail, my next job was at the local supermarket, where I bagged groceries but was quickly reassigned to the video department. The promotion was a fantastic move for me, except that the video department backed up to the perfume counter, so I had to sell and offer samples of perfume whenever anyone asked, but I tried to avoid this at all costs. Patrons would arrive in groups and spray sample bottles into noxious clouds that could knock over an elephant while oohing and ahhing and asking for more. But perfume was the least of my concerns. I could take movies home for free. Every day if I wanted! I devoured every VHS tape that looked interesting, and eventually those that didn't, except for most of the children's section. Talking, singing cartoon animals never appealed to me much. I remember being ecstatic to discover several new favorites that blew me away that year, particularly *Blade Runner* and *Army of Darkness*. Another cool thing about this job was that Ernie worked next door to the grocery at the sandwich shop, so we could visit each other on breaks. Working with movies, watching them and talking about them with customers, was the most satisfying job I'd had yet.

The sandwich shop was the venue for a bizarre encounter Ernie had with Casey, a sweet but unpredictable ex-girlfriend of mine. Casey hung out with the same fringe group of high-school artists, musicians, skaters and weirdos that Ernie and I did. I have little recollection of how our casual teenage acquaintance developed into a romantic relationship, but somehow that year I found myself in her bedroom listening to an elaborate description of her undying love for her favorite band. Though Casey's passionate endorsement of all things Fleetwood Mac was no real aphrodisiac, we were young and enthusiastic.

Several awkward, even embarrassing sexual encounters soon followed, as neither of us knew what the hell we were doing. Though I liked Casey, I soon realized that I was not as enthralled as she was. In fact, her enthusiasm was starting to weird me out. I was only 17 and couldn't handle the intensity of whatever it was that Casey seemed to be feeling for me. I never meant to hurt her feelings but just didn't feel whatever she was feeling. I had to end things, but I was clueless about how to do it. I had been the dump*ee* but never the dump*er*, and I couldn't decide whether to make a phone call, write a letter, take her to dinner or send a telegram, but something told me that decency required me to break the news in person. I should not have done this from inside a moving car.

I decided to end my relationship with Casey on the way to my job at the grocery store while riding in her Volvo as she drove through the parking lot. Looking back, it seems like I was a bit apprehensive about her possible reaction—a fear that proved to be well founded—and I had decided that breaking up with her as she was dropping me off at work would give me a way out of the inevitably awkward (at the very least) conversation:

"Let's break up. Oh, sorry. Gotta go. Time for work. Uh, see you at school?"

As I explained to her why I thought we should probably break things off, see other people, etcetera, she began shaking her head slowly, then faster, more erratically, muttering

"No. No. No. No" and so on.

The shaking head and the word "no" doubled and tripled in frequency and volume until she was screaming

"NO! NO! NO! NO! NO!" as her head blurred creepily like in that Ozzy Osbourne video…and then she jumped out of the driver's seat of the moving vehicle.

As I sat bewildered and abandoned in the passenger seat of her still rapidly advancing car, trying to convince her to come back to talk things over or at least hit the brakes, the Volvo rolled across the parking lot, driver's side door open wide, narrowly missing the grocery cart corral as I lunged across the console, grabbing the wheel and trying to climb over to reach the pedals, my newly ex-girlfriend sprinting away across the pavement in tears.

I managed to take control of Casey's Volvo, wrenching the emergency brake upward before it crashed into any other cars or pedestrians, who were staring at me aghast, as if I had attacked the poor girl with a knife. Wearing the official polo shirt and khaki uniform of the grocery store made my position even more awkward. This made the decision of whether or not to chase the screaming and crying young woman across the parking lot rather problematic, so I sort of jogged casually in her general direction, trying to chase her down and talk to her while trying not to *seem* like I was trying to chase her down, smiling, nodding and waving in an assuring "it's all fine, *really*" sort of way at the saucer-eyed shoppers who were pointing and whispering about whether they should intervene. I finally caught up with her, persuaded her to stop and talked it out as we both sat on the pavement together. Crisis averted.

In the parking lot after school the next day, when I arrived at my car—Granddad's old '71 Chevy Impala—a melancholy water-colored note was awaiting me under a windshield wiper. The homemade card read as follows:

"The sky has grown dark. The birds no longer sing. My world is empty without you."

Wondering whether she meant to quote the Supremes or if it was just a coincidence, I started to worry a bit. I felt really bad for causing her pain, and I was truly sorry that she was so sad, but I had recently been privy to gossip about what had happened when her previous relationship had ended. Apparently, Casey had been so distraught over multiple rejections after pleading with her ex-boyfriend to take her back that she had broken into his parents' house and placed a dead bird in the young man's underwear drawer, along with a similarly despondent, water-colored Sad Poem. Whether or not the rumor about Casey's turbulent past was true, I dreaded finding any number of dead things inside Granddad's rarely locked old Chevrolet.

She had plans in store all right, but they didn't involve leaving anything dead in my car or my bedroom. One day shortly after the breakup, Casey appeared in the sandwich shop next door to the grocery and said hello to Ernie. Of course he was surprised and wondered what was going on. She had never come by to visit him at the sandwich shop when we were dating, and he knew that we had just split up. He told me about this later, saying that she had a wild look in her eye and was acting pretty strange. She made some small talk and looked at the menu briefly before leaning over the counter, opening her mouth as if to make an order, then closing it again indecisively, leaning back away from the register, several times in a row, until finally she said she didn't feel hungry and needed to visit the rest room. Ernie was suspicious. She was acting pretty weird. What was she up to? Casey spent a conspicuously long time in the bathroom, according to Ernie, and then she waved mischievously as she sashayed her way out the door. No sandwich. Ernie watched her go with suspicion and inspected the countertop she had leaned over so awkwardly. There she had affixed an enormous gob of freshly chewed bubble gum. He then ran immediately to the lady's room, as there were no other customers at this odd time of the day between lunch and dinner business, and he had just finished cleaning both bathrooms.

The stench knocked him on his heels as he opened the door to the women's room. Casey had decorated the walls, sink, toilet, mirror and floors with her precious bodily fluids, and the mess was awful. Ernie cleaned it up, cursing Casey—and me as well, I'm sure. She knew Ernie was one of my closest friends, and she knew we often worked during the same times, but why attack his clean bathroom to get back at me? Why no dead animal in my house or bio-fluid attack on the grocery store I was working in next door? Why not erase a bunch of the VHS tapes with a magnet or set the perfume samples on fire while I was working? I'll never know, but she didn't do any real harm, and I hope she's doing well.

My job in the video department of the supermarket was memorable for other reasons too. I'll never forget the time my buddy Joe showed up at the perfume counter in drag, his girlfriend in tow. He had on a purple dress, a curly wig with bright makeup and looked like a younger, more butch version of a Golden Girl. I didn't recognize him at first, but then I spotted his giggling girlfriend and did a double take. Joe is quite the manly man, so it's particularly hilarious to think back on this occasion when his high school lady friend had talked him into a public display of his feminine side. I tried this once, a few years later in college, on Halloween with another pal of mine. My girlfriend at the time dressed as a man and made the two of us up in drag with wigs, makeup and miniskirts. The three of us crashed a frat party and nearly got into a fistfight with a swollen, homophobic frat-jock.

Cracking up as Joe leered at me behind some crazy old lady glasses and lipstick, I flashed back six years to when I had first met the future Eagle Scout and talented heavy metal guitarist: Ernie and I were walking up the hill from a trip to the convenience store for candy and sodas, when we ran into Joe. He squinted at us beneath his trucker hat and spat tobacco on the curb, temporarily distracted from his task at hand: super-gluing pennies to a random stranger's car. This was a precursor to the trademark move that Joe and Ernie were to perfect later in junior high, when they'd glue quarters to the sidewalk in front of the school and laugh riotously as students spotted them on the sidewalk and tried to pick them up.

Joe and Ernie and I used to sit on my back porch and drink tea, smoke cigarettes, and wax philosophically about our teenage concerns. On Saturday nights we'd switch between *Saturday Night Live* and *Headbanger's Ball* on MTV, catching all the new videos from Seattle grunge to LA metal. The three of us became pretty much inseparable. We were in a rock band together in high school, we ended up at the same college a few years later, and we worked together on a wide variety of jobs over our teens and twenties. I still worked at the grocery and Ernie was still at the deli when Joe found a job at a nearby pizza place. We spent most of our free time outside of school and work together and would often meet up when our shifts ended at night, either gathering at the local arcade to play video games and shoot pool on weeknights or heading out to our favorite spot in the woods to camp out by a fire and drink beer on weekends, where I once lost part of a tooth in a misguided and foolish attempt to open a bottle of Corona.

Because everyone in our little group of friends was skating in the early 90s, Ernie and I had convinced Joe to get a skateboard too. On the outskirts of our hometown, just at the edge of a massive office park, there was a steep concrete drainage ditch—about 10 feet wide—carved into the side of a hill at a ridiculous angle. Tagged with spray-painted amateur graffiti and littered with the leftover 40-ounce bottles of suburban kids' clandestine parties, The Ditch was an unforgiving training ground for aspiring skaters and the perfect place for Ernie and Joe and I to smoke our first joints. We huddled in the dark and rolled what looked like dry pencil shavings into a thin joint we called a pinner, which we passed around and inhaled. We laughed at each other and wondered what we were supposed to feel like. We stood around for a while and realized that nobody really felt anything. Someone had sold Ernie some bad weed. We were more interested in experimental drinking anyway.

One bitterly cold night I arrived at an elementary school playground without Ernie but with Joe and two other buddies of ours: Mason, a fiddle- and guitar-playing home brewer who often concocted his own potent blends of fruit wine in his bedroom and drove a big green grandma car that looked similar to my big blue grandpa car; and our long-lost friend Tony, a great punk rock guitarist who looked kind of like a slightly overweight, shorter version of Chris Cornell. Once at Long John Silver's, Tony had bet a group of us that he could drink an entire bottle of balsamic vinegar. We dug through our pockets to see what we could come up with, and for eight bucks and some change, Tony had chugged the whole thing. It didn't matter that it had come back to haunt him a few minutes later. He earned those eight bucks.

Tony's mom was out of town, and we were crashing at his place that night. His gay older brother, Ronald, lived with Tony and their mother in a bright red house made of concrete block. Ronald had a crush on Joe that was obvious to everyone, and while Joe did not reciprocate Ronald's affections, he was not above parlaying Ronald's fondness for him to our collective advantage, often convincing Ronald to purchase liquor and beer for our teenage gang in a doomed attempt to win Joe's favor.

On this particular night, we had scored a case of beer and a fifth of whiskey, along with what we hoped was some decent weed. We hiked in the dark though the woods to an elementary school playground and started pounding beers. I'd had beer before but had never really tried liquor. I took a few shots from the bottle as we passed it around between beers but didn't feel anything special. I then turned the bottle upside down and chugged for a minute or so. Painfully ignorant of the ways of the bottle, I drank nearly half of the fifth. It tasted horrible, but as I was still feeling fine, someone suggested that I run around. I did a couple laps around the outdoor basketball court and returned to the wooden fort by the swingset where everyone was stumbling around. I still felt pretty good. Maybe I had a little more energy and a bigger smile, but whatever this "drunk" feeling was supposed to be, I didn't think I was there yet.

Someone handed me a joint. This one wasn't pencil shavings. I inhaled deeply and promptly fell flat on my face in the grass, passing out. When I woke up a short while later, Joe was next to me on the ground. We were both on our backs, staring into the cold night sky, our breath creating clouds of moisture. He had a very big smile on his face and pointed at the trees. I looked up again and noticed that the trees were flying over my head like the Blue Angels in an air show. I never knew that trees could be so agile and graceful, or that they could spin or fly.

"Man! Look at the trees, dude! They're flying!" I yelled at Joe.

"Yeah," he smiled.

"We're *FRIENDS*! We're *FRIENDS*!" Joe repeated, laughing. I laughed too.

This went on for quite some time until we came to our senses and noticed Mason yelling at Tony to wake up. Tony was curled up and passed out in a fetal ball beside the fort. Pretty soon we noticed how cold it was getting, and we were ready to head back through the wooded path to Tony's house, but we couldn't wake him up. Everyone yelled at Tony, pushing him and trying to haul him up to a sitting position, even pulling off his shirt accidentally in the process, but it was futile. Tony slumped back into the frozen mud, half naked, wasted and incoherent. I started to notice my toes freezing inside my Half Cabs. We kicked Tony a few times, yelling

"Wake up Tony! We're gonna fucking *freeze* out here, man!"

It was incredibly cold by now, and all we had were thin sweatshirts with jeans and sneakers.

"Fuck this! I'm getting the car!" Mason yelled and headed up the path through the woods toward Tony's house.

I stumbled after him, arguing that driving a car was probably a very bad idea at this point, but there was no stopping Mason. He peeled out, drove around the block and sped right across the front lawn of the school and into the playground in the back where we were huddled around Tony in the dark. Mason, Joe and I lifted Tony from the ground and shoved him into the back seat of Mason's green grandma machine. We jumped in and made it back around the block to Tony's house, but he was still out cold. We should've carried him all the way from the car to the house, but we could barely budge the guy and figured he'd be fine in the back seat of the car, so the three of us passed out on Tony's bed alongside each other. The next morning we gradually awoke and realized with alarm that Tony was still outside. We found him shivering violently in the back seat, Mason's green hoodie pulled tightly around his face, and he was pretty pissed.

"What THE FUCK, guys?! You leave me in Mason's car in this freezing-ass weather, go sleep on MY BED and lock me out of MY OWN GODDAMN HOUSE! Fuck you guys!"

We laughed, but he survived. We should have carried him inside with us. I was too sick to go to school the next day and told my Mom I had a stomachache and a headache, which was true. I had it better than Joe, who had to show up for a dentist's appointment the next morning.

We all thought Tony had gotten over his anger at us for locking him outside his own house in a catatonic drunk-freeze in the back of Mason's car, but not long after that frigid night, Tony took some acid and was tripping in the grocery store parking lot when he heard the unmistakable voice of God. God, feeling a little kinky I suppose, asked Tony to get naked, even though it was raining. Tony obeyed without question and sat naked in the rain in the parking lot of the supermarket for a while and listened for further instructions. Apparently God wanted Tony to quit the ways of rock and roll, join the Jehovah's Witnesses and find some better friends. Tony quit his band, cut his Chris Cornell hair and beard and joined the church.

Though various members of our original group of friends have tried on multiple occasions to find Tony and catch up, the ties to his previous life were severed forever, and sadly, most of us never saw him again.

Working in the supermarket video store wasn't so bad, especially with my buddies around, and though I knew I had more to offer, I wasn't sure what I wanted to be when I grew up. I knew I could apply myself to whatever job came along, but I had yet to think seriously about meaningful work. I was too busy being a teenager to worry myself with existentialist dread. There would be plenty of time for that.

House Painter/Heart Breaker/Film Renter/Intoxicant Experimenter

In Barn Land, a Way With Words

More than half of Americans at all levels of the workforce are thinking of changing not only their jobs but also their careers. But of those who want to change, roughly 50% have no clue on how to figure out the next chapter. When the times are so intensely and perhaps permanently uncertain, it feels safer to hold on to a job that's only okay or even worse. But is it?[1]
—Anne Kreamer

Though the first few observations recorded here occurred while I was out delivering barns and are fairly self-explanatory, other memorable or noteworthy comments I observed in Barn Land follow these and include a bit of contextual consideration following the quotes.[2]

"You think you kin git it back up in thar between them trees?"

"It looked a whole lot smaller back at the lot."

"I didn't have no time to cut back them bushes."

---

1 Kreamer, Anne. "Why it's risky to be risk-averse" *TIME Magazine*, Monday, June 22, 2015.

2 In the pursuit of absolute truth and despite the inevitable distortion of memory, the decision to re-create dialog here phonetically (and elsewhere throughout this book) is one that I felt would contribute to the readers' understanding of the cadences and distinct pronunciations that certain residents of Barn Land demonstrated. I would also like to note something obvious to many southerners: We don't all sound like this, and nor do all barn customers, but quite a few of the most memorable quotes were uttered with a deep-south twang that adds a modicum of detail to the story and is truly accurate. Although this author is often frustrated by the national or international perpetuation of potentially offensive southern redneck/hayseed/hick stereotypes and recognizes his own contribution to this tendency with significant portions of this book, he is compelled nevertheless to relate his experiences as they occurred, stereotypes be damned. Many more Barn Land quotes are stockpiled in my memory, but these, spoken by real people, forced their way into my book like the voices of so many fictional characters who invade the brains of the novelists who create them, demanding documentation. Writing nonfiction, I had no choice but to oblige their memory and revisit them here, as accurately rendered as possible and with a sincere desire to recreate the experience authentically.

"Sorry bout all 'at chicken shit over thar, but that's wore I need it tuh set."

"I'd 'a moved 'at old car, but it ain't gon' run."

"I need it up in them trees, but I ain't got no saw to cut all them limbs. Does y'all?"

"Beware the THUNDER of God's word."

–Not actually spoken to me, this was inscribed on a plaque and hung on the wall in a barn and used car sales office, but it was memorable.

"You'se supposed'ta KNOW wore I live! I's done TOLT you how ta GIT here. I ain't 'SPLAININ' nothin' more tuh you! Tell you whut. You kin shove 'at barn right up yer GOTdamn ass!"

"All right. FUCK. YOU."

–One customer's comment to me due to anger over my inability to locate his property in backwoods rural nowhere, sans street signs and before smartphones, with his incorrect and incoherent directions, followed by my reply. This was near the end of my barn tenure, and I couldn't take much more. I responded in the only way I could have, hung up on the guy and then called Mitch, telling him that I had just lost it with a customer on the phone.

"Fuck you, you GOTDAMN motherfucker! This here's SPRINGTOWNBURG! Y'all don't know how we do it here in SPRINGTOWNBURG! I'll kick yer GOTdamn fuckin' ass all OVER this lot! This is MY lot!"

"Fuck *you*, liar. Try it."

–A puffy, red-faced, dishonest and drunken redneck—the head salesman in charge of barns and playground equipment at a lot we serviced in Springtownburg—reacting to my physical intervention when he was way out of line, verbally abusing a rookie barn hauler I was training, just before he directed his venom and spittle in my direction, including my response to his tirade before I gladly left his sales lot for the last time in my life. These were the only two times I ever spoke disrespectfully to a customer or to anyone else on the job.

"Oh sure, ma'am. The driver kin fit 'at barn anyplace. It don't matter how tight the spot is. He don't mind cuttin' down trees or doin' whatever it takes. Of course he kin be thare at 8AM next Saturdee mornin' with yer barn, rain 'er shine. Just sign here."

—This same guy in Springtownburg loved to make commitments to customers on my behalf without asking me about it first, as long as he could get the sale. I didn't work weekends unless it was some kind of barnmergency, and (as previously described) site prep work was supposed to be the customer's responsibility, according to the contract they signed initially.

"I DEW NOT KNOW HOO YEW ARE! I DEW NOT KNOW A KREE-US!"

—A voicemail message from a customer, left in response to my own. I had left her a voicemail message identifying myself (as Chris, the barn hauler), noting in detail my reason for calling (an attempt to deliver a barn this customer had ordered and should have expected).

"Would you mind not kicking my seat?"

-I asked this of a child who was sitting behind me and repeatedly kicking the back of my seat while I was in a booth at a Barn Land sandwich shop, on a lunch break from delivering barns.

"YEW KIN TAIL *MAY!*"[3]

-In response to my polite request of her child, the child's mother exploded with rage, yelling this into my face, her features twisted grotesquely, apparently appalled that I would directly address her child, after violently kicking my seat a few more times herself, provoking me to turn around to see who was kicking the hell out of my seat, a lot harder, a second time.

---

3 "You can tell *me.*"

In Barn Land, a Way With Words

"Man, I'm sorry about 'at smell in the barn, dude. My Dad's been living out thar' in it, an' we's been getting' to fightin' an' he knew I's the one payin' fer the barn, it bein' on my property an' all, an' jes' 'cause he's ill at me[4] he done pissed all up in 'at barn, an' now you gotta smell it while you repo it."

–Resident of the mobile-home trailer in the yard from which I was repossessing a disgusting barn that reeked of urine, among other scents.

"Kin y'all call back like, uh, Saturdee 'ar somethin'? He ain't home, an' uh, I don't know whar he's wantin' it ta go. They's still some cars and a trampoline in the way, and them cars ain't run fer a while. I ain't had no chance ta cut back 'em bushes or nothin' neither."

–Typical response from a barn customer after a delivery time has been agreed upon days or weeks in advance, and after I have already loaded and prepped the barn for delivery.

"GIT OHN OUTTA THAR, BOOGER!"

–Yelled by a barn customer from a back porch at a screaming, delighted, rapidly fleeing toddler, naked other than a dirty diaper, who was scrambling around the yard in the mud behind the barn delivery truck, as Bill attempted to back a barn into place upon delivery.

"Some people have a way with words…other people…not have way."[5]

–Steve Martin

---

4 Angry with me.
5 Martin, Steve. "Philosophy/Religion/College/Language." *A Wild and Crazy Guy*. Burbank: Warner Bros. Records, 1978.

Tennis Player/Music Maker/ Restaurant Worker/Shark Researcher?

This world is a place of business...I think that there is nothing, not even crime, more opposed to poetry, to philosophy, ay, to life itself, than this incessant business...Do not hire a man who does your work for money, but him who does it for love of it...There is no more fatal blunderer than he who consumes the greater part of life getting his living.[1]

—Henry David Thoreau

Long before I met Joe or Ernie or any of the other friends I've mentioned here, I was serious about tennis. Even though I wasn't much of a sports fan in general and never could have been called an athlete, the solitary grind of tennis and the mental challenge of being my own greatest opponent appealed to me. For some years I even thought that if I dedicated myself to it and worked hard enough, playing tennis could be my job. At the time it seemed like a pretty great way to earn a living. Though tennis has a well-established international audience and a decent number of players and fans in the USA, it has never been cool in the eyes of mainstream American sports fans. America loves the big three sports: football, baseball and basketball. In the USA, hockey, soccer and even auto racing are more popular than tennis, but I never cared. I loved it. I still do, but I no longer see tennis as a viable career option, as I once did, for a brief shining moment, as an optimistic kid full of unrealistic dreams when anything seemed possible.

Fans of more popular sports have often discounted tennis, thinking of it as something for preppy trust-funders in coordinated outfits with short shorts and matching racquet bags whose parents built a court in the backyard for their precious overachievers to practice with the local pro for a while before teatime en route to their Ivy-League futures amongst

---

[1] Thoreau, Henry David. "Life Without Principle." *The Atlantic Monthly*, Volume 12, Issue 71, 1863.

the global elite. The sport has always had an exclusive air that's still hard to shake, but the image isn't quite accurate.

Plenty of future champions (like Jimmy Connors, Andre Agassi and Venus and Serena Williams) were neither trust-funders nor country clubbers and trained as little kids on hardscrabble, first-come/first-serve, free public-access hard courts, usually with a fiercely dedicated—albeit somewhat maniacal—parent leading the way. A gangly, regular kid like me, with goofy mismatched shorts and T-shirts and stupid hats from my Dad's company BBQ (photographic evidence included here), couldn't wait to hit the courts after school and on weekends. I rode my bike to the free public hard courts not far from the old apartments where I had once delivered newspapers and still lived. In the late 70s and throughout the 80s when I was learning to play, Jimmy Connors brought some middle-American, blue-collar appeal, straight from Ohio to New York City, in a sport that had often been thought of as existing only in the snooty realm of Wimbledon's all-England club. For me, Jimmy's fighting style of heart-on-his-sleeve, baseline hammering, fist-pumping bravado and smart-ass, self-deprecating humor made the game a lot more interesting and inspired me to play harder and push myself to get better.

My dear Dad introduced me to the game and taught me tennis when I was but a wee lad, barely able to hold the racquet and run around without tripping over my own two feet. I played in the competitive city leagues when I was growing up and in junior-high. I was the only sophomore to make the tennis team at my high school, and that was a big deal to me then. I played tennis because I loved it. Dad didn't pressure me to play, even though he sparked my interest, taught me the rules and encouraged me. I tried basketball and soccer, but neither team sport appealed for very long. I liked fighting it out on the court, alone. I relished the mental challenge of knowing what I should be doing and trying to force myself to make it happen, struggling against myself as much or often more than I battled my opponent. When I lost, the only person I was letting down—and the only person I had to blame—was myself.

HARDBARNED!
One Man's Quest for Meaningful Work in the American South

Tennis Player/Music Maker/Restaurant Worker/Shark Researcher?

Something about tennis just felt right. I practiced with Dad regularly, went to a local tennis day camp for a few summers and took lessons, too. I was also a big fan of Bjorn Borg, Ivan Lendl and eventually Agassi, when he arrived on the scene. Dad and I attended a professional tournament in Ohio several times when I was a kid, where I saw many of the top pros play. Though we never made it to a Grand Slam tournament in person, we always watched them on TV together. I was delusional but enthusiastic, and for a while there, I thought I might have a shot at a career as a tennis player, which seemed to me like yet another brilliant idea for the greatest job in the world. I knew I'd never be a champion like Connors or Agassi, but for a short time I thought that maybe with luck and discipline I could somehow break into the bottom end of the pro tour and win a few bucks at some lesser-known tournaments. No big deal—just enough for pizza, comic books, movie tickets and an apartment. Maybe even my own Galaga arcade machine. I was pretty naïve. For some reason, it didn't seem to matter that I'd never even entered a tournament. I had won a trophy for my age group at tennis camp! And I was still the only sophomore on the high school tennis team! I don't know what I was thinking. In fact, pretty soon I wasn't thinking about tennis much at all. As a young person, staying focused on a single interest was never my strongest attribute.

This time, the reason for my lack of focus was heavy metal. I didn't mind that I was the only tennis player on the team with a shaggy haircut, dressed like an idiot with baggy cargo shorts, an Alice In Chains t-shirt, a Queensryche tri-ryche necklace and a hat with Soundgarden and Metallica patches. I was good enough to compete. I didn't want to wear those goofy little tight-white short-shorts or visors or matching polo shirts or cardigans or any of that crap that the squeaky-clean-cut number-one player on our high school team wore. That dude didn't even acknowledge my existence anyway. For me there would be no K-Swiss. If I could compete in my old duct-taped Airwalks or Vans and multicolored thrift-store argyle socks, I would do so, proudly earning the misfit moniker, but after a couple of tennis seasons, a scheduling problem was forcing me to make a decision.

Tennis Player/Music Maker/Restaurant Worker/Shark Researcher?

For the first time in my life, I had formed a rock band. After school, Ernie and I had started playing heavy metal (or our closest slow, simple approximation of it) in our friend Thad's spare storage room, before his Mom came home from work. I played bass and wrote lyrics for silly songs like "Madness Throne" (it sounded awesome at the time). Our growling, semi-intelligible vocalist sounded so awful that we couldn't even stand to be in the same room with him, so we gave him a wireless microphone. He sat in the next bedroom and did his best angry Cookie Monster impression from behind two closed doors. I had my first chance to make rock, and I liked it. It didn't matter that I was too tall for the closet-sized, low-ceiling storage room that we played in, or that every time I lofted my white Yamaha bass to the sky in a triumphant rock pose, the bass crashed into the ceiling fan, taking chunks out of the headstock and nearly knocking me to the floor. I had had a taste of the rock, and it tasted pretty good, but tennis practice was every day, right after school, during the only practice time available for the band, which, unable to unleash our collective storm of creativity on the band-naming process, we had decided to call *Hard To Figure*. Rock beat tennis, and with little indecisiveness, I threw away my unrealistic hopes and dreams of a professional tennis career for an endless series of shitty bands nobody has ever heard of. That's fine though.

No regrets. I had a blast with my bands for half of my life, and I've enjoyed tennis off and on since I could hold a racket. I didn't need formal career or financial success with either to derive years of enjoyment from both. I still love playing in bands, though I haven't for a while, and I still love playing tennis. I may have been better at tennis than I ever was at music, but I was never good enough at either to make a living. Mom told me years later, over Thanksgiving dinner, that I had had a shot at attending a professional tennis camp designed to train kids with potential who might have had a shot at a career, and that I had decided not to do it because it would have required moving alone to another state and would have changed everything in my life to a new, much more intense focus on tennis. I honestly do not remember being given that choice, but I trust my Mom.

Maybe I blocked it out. I do remember picking rock music over tennis. Either way, another career dream bit the dust, and I wasn't looking back.

* * *

After learning how to handle various entry-level intoxicants relatively responsibly yet still managing to finish high school with academic honors, I planned to act on my next career dream. I would become a marine biologist and study sharks! Why the hell not? Daydreaming about an ideal super-hero-style special power, most kids fantasized about being able to fly or having X-ray vision like Superman, running super-fast like The Flash or leaping tall buildings in a single bound and smashing cars like The Hulk. My special power of choice had always been different. I wanted to be able to breathe underwater, like Aquaman or Connor MacLeod. I loved the ocean and wanted to be underneath it as much as possible, even though I was not yet a scuba diver and rarely had the chance to even swim in the ocean. I didn't even live anywhere near it, but I had been to see it a few times, and that was enough to spark a great love. Everyone expected me to go to college, but I had no idea what to do with myself. I knew I loved the sea and wanted to learn more about it, so "shark scientist" became my next great career idea.

I had been fascinated with sharks for years. Getting paid to study the most fearsome, magnificent beasts in the oceanic wild sounded like the ultimate job…other than piloting an F-14 tomcat, playing tennis, racing BMX bikes or being in a rock band. Though I hadn't yet recognized or articulated the concept, somehow I knew that I needed to find meaningful work. I knew inherently that whatever career I chose must be something I had real passion for. Marine biology seemed like the first idea yet that was truly a responsible combination of passionate interest and practical application.

I had been interested in learning about sharks—nature's most precisely evolved predator, perfected by design and hundreds of millions of years of evolution—at least since my Dad had talked me into watching *Jaws* at home on VHS by bribing me with a rare visit to Burger King. Somehow it was okay to watch because it was rated PG, I guess—you'll have to ask Dad, though he claims not to remember the Burger King bribe. Fast food was an unusual treat at the time. I wasn't quite ready for the movie—I had hidden behind the couch when Michael Jackson's *Thriller* came out around that same time—but I ended up loving *Jaws*,[2] even though it was scary, and a genuine, lifelong fascination with sharks was sparked.

Thereafter, as a little kid, I read everything shark-related that I could get my hands on, starting with Peter Benchley's novel, and watched every shark documentary I could find. Whenever I had an opportunity to do a school paper or project about sharks, I jumped at the chance. Though I lived in a land-locked state, somehow it made sense that I'd spend my life studying the most powerful fish in the sea because I couldn't think of any other sort of profession that sounded good, and I knew without a doubt that I loved the ocean and wanted to know it much better. I wasn't all that excited about going to college anyway, but I found a school on the East Coast that had a huge research vessel and a sought-after marine biology program. I applied and was accepted.

I drove to orientation week with my Mom and kept an eye out for good places to skateboard once we arrived in town. The head of the marine biology department opened his "welcome" speech by informing

---

2 Peter Benchley's novel and the resulting blockbuster film by Stephen Spielberg had really done the massive fish a great disservice. *Jaws* instilled a primal fear into generations of readers and film audiences by planting a firm hatred in the minds of millions toward the most magnificent and truly essential apex predator of the sea. Benchley, an avid diver, amateur marine biologist and ultimately a conservationist, would later feel considerable remorse over his own negative contribution to the world's attitude toward sharks in general. *Jaws* played a significant role in the smearing of an entire species' reputation, which in turn contributed to the unregulated, wholesale slaughter of sharks worldwide. Recognizing the folly of his portrayal of the shark as a rogue, murderous monster, in his last three published books, all nonfiction collections of true stories about sharks and conservation advocacy, Benchley found himself at odds with *Jaws*, admitting that he couldn't have written it with the knowledge he had gained since, realizing that humans are an exponentially greater threat to the shark than sharks have ever posed to humans.

my incoming freshman class—in no uncertain terms—that we'd never get to work with sharks, dolphins or whales, and that after spending about 13 more years in school, we'd likely spend the rest of our professional lives in a long white coat with a microscope, staring into Petri dishes under fluorescent lights in a laboratory. Thinking back now, I wonder if the guy was bitter about his own lot in life. Maybe he wanted to work on a shark research vessel too but had been stuck talking to freshman about the degree program and doing boring lab work himself. Whatever his motivations, I had no reason to think he wasn't telling it like it really was, and I thought that his conclusion about my life sucked, so I decided the program wasn't for me and left before orientation week was halfway through.

I sometimes wonder if I was just looking for an excuse not to go to college because I wasn't yet ready to knuckle down and focus, or if that grumpy old professor really got to me. Maybe I didn't want to invest 13 years in a lab to earn my first trip on a shark expedition. Either way, I chose not to begin at university that year. I still love learning about sharks. Eventually, I became a certified scuba diver and plan to one day dive with the mighty Carcharodon Carcharias (Great White Shark) in a cage off California's Baja Peninsula or Australia's Port Lincoln, but I doubt I'll ever become the marine biologist I once hoped to be. I doubt I will summon the drive necessary for another long trek through the halls of higher education as a 40-something freshman in biology, but I could be wrong. My maternal grandmother didn't start her undergraduate study until she was in her late 40s, after working a Rosie-the-Riveter job during WWII, so I guess it's never too late to chase your passion. It's unlikely, but maybe I'll return to that same classroom one day and meet that professor again and tell him I'm there to study sharks. And maybe monkeys will fly out of my butt. Anything could happen, but as I walked away from my first college orientation and dropped out before I got started, I scratched another career aspiration off the books.

* * *

Tennis Player/Music Maker/Restaurant Worker/Shark Researcher?

Back home after deciding to take at least a year off before thinking about college again, it was time to find another job, so I worked as a prep cook at a wine and cheese "bistro" where they played Sade and Seal on the stereo and sold pasta with fancy homemade specialty sauces. I got up super early and learned to make the sauces, including pesto, hummus and homemade breads.

Working in a restaurant is something that everyone should be required to experience at least once in life. There are multiple opportunities to learn about the way the world works within the controlled environment of professional food service. As the menu expanded, so did my cooking skills, and I enjoyed learning more about baking and preparing entrees. I was also taking guitar lessons at the time, and my teacher, Lenny J, would perform jazz guitar live at the restaurant and occasionally hit on my Mom, who would wait tables there, part-time on weekends or after working her technical writing job because she was a friend of the owners and loved the food and atmosphere. On weekends, local actors would walk over from the community playhouse across the parking lot and wine and dine on the patio out front. I'd always been drawn to eccentric characters, and I knew a few of them from school and from a couple local productions I had acted in. I enjoyed visiting with the actors, refilling their baskets with homemade breads and topping off their wine glasses, amused at how they seemed to live and breathe theatre, oozing drama whether on stage or off.

The "bistro" closed, and I moved to a new restaurant across the street, just before it opened. This one labeled itself "fine dining," featuring white tablecloths and white-aproned employees with ties. The Brown Horse had an excellent menu, courtesy of Nico, a skinny and talented chef who sported a black mullet, and his mustachioed older brother Andre, a helpful sidekick in the cramped kitchen. The classy atmosphere, however, was due primarily to the efforts of the spunky and sharp manager, Jay, an attractive, smartly dressed woman in her 30s with short red hair and dangling earrings, who seemed to like me immediately and referred to me with affection by calling out my entire name when she needed something:

"Oh Chris-to-pher *DRI*-ver!"

I started as a busboy, but I was soon doing whatever needed to be done: washing dishes, cleaning bathrooms, sweeping and mopping, taking out trash, splitting logs out back for the hickory grill, bussing tables and taking care of whatever else needed attention. Jay played Sade in her restaurant too, but she also played Everything But The Girl so much that I started to like it, at least their song "Missing," which still reminds me of mopping bathrooms, but in a sort of fun, danceable way. Eventually I waited tables, working under the head server: a sweet, Tom Waits-voiced, Virginia Slims-smoking lady with raccoon eye makeup named Madge, who'd gather the open wine bottles on the server station at the end of each night and finish them off one by one or sometimes all at once.

Madge's Vino Suicide Cocktail reminded me of the time I'd visited the World of Coke museum in Atlanta with my Mom and Ernie. In one room, what appeared to be every type of soft drink the Coca-Cola Company had ever sold—worldwide—was available for guests to sample limitlessly. Ernie and I squirted little shots of each flavor of soda from the immense soda fountain into our single cups, called it a Suicide, and drank it down.

Busing and occasionally waiting tables went pretty well at the Brown Horse for a good while. I worked hard, the food was great, and I had fun hanging out with some of my co-workers, smoking a little weed and drinking beers, but most of that went on outside of the restaurant. Much of the staff would party together after work, and sometimes cocaine and various pills would circulate, but I avoided them. Our after-hours indulgences did not affect our jobs. We were the best restaurant in town, proud of it, and we wanted to stay that way. We served delicious entrees, looked sharp and took care of our guests, and most customers treated us like human beings. However, I hated washing dishes, and I kept getting roped into it again and again. They couldn't keep a regular dishwasher employed, and there was a reason.

What happens to a dishwasher in a "fine dining" restaurant is about the same as what happens to a dishwasher in a sleazy beach bar, diner or tourist trap. I've washed dishes in both places and in several other restaurants in-between. Typically, a dishwasher is faced with either two or three industrial-sized sinks. One sink (sometimes both sinks) is constantly being filled with dirty dishes by bussers and servers who are running in and out. These sinks are also constantly being filled by cooks with steaming-hot, sticky, greasy pots and pans. It usually takes considerable effort to convince the servers that they need to remove the growing towers of clean dishes from the other side of the dish station before they come crashing down on the poor dishwasher.

The only way to make sure that the dishes get clean, and also to ensure that the restaurant follows health codes, is to use scalding hot water that burns your hands. Somehow dishwashing gloves never seem to be within the restaurant's budget, but if they are, they fill with water and your hands get soaked anyway, so with wet hands you pick the dirty dishes out of the rising sink full of muck and rinse them in the scalding hot water, placing them into the automatic dishwasher, if there is one. These hulking, steaming, leaking, sputtering masses of metal are always good for a few burns.

Once the machine is finished and the lid is opened, the steam explodes into your face, and the scalding water drips onto your arms while you remove and stack hot plates. When the machine runs out of liquid, you must slog through the watery mess of used food and hot mud tracked in from outside and collecting at your feet to find a replacement bottle of detergent deep within a floor-level cabinet, or run outside to a storage shed to frantically search for it. With steam burns up to your elbows and red, soft, blistered, raw flesh on your hands, bloody from knife wounds; with bandaged knuckles, sweat soaking your shirt and running into your eyes; with dirty dish water spilling over the counter, down your legs and into your shoes, roaring machines spraying boiling water and spurting little flecks of someone's leftover entree all over the floor and into your face while servers build tottering Jenga stacks of dirty plates and silverware four feet high, the steam obscuring your vision, the grill smoke burning in your lungs, the yelling chefs and expediters arguing, joking, laughing, swearing, slipping on the sloppy mess of food waste overflowing on the thick kitchen mats below the industrial-sized sinks…this is the life of the dishwasher. You get the picture. This is not a great job.

A friend once told me he had loved the dishwashing stints in his past, having reveled in the relative anonymity of perhaps the most anti-social job in a public-serving business. No customers complained to the dishwasher. Nobody cared who he was or what he was on, as my friend attested. While my teenage friend had enjoyed being drunk or high and anonymous on the job, in those years I had hated being burned and soggy, sober and uncomfortable. Some people have risen to great heights from positions as anonymous dishwashers. Examples include my aforementioned friend (now a dedicated teacher) and Sidney Portier (the legendary, groundbreaking actor) both men I admire a lot—but dishwashing, for me, was one of the low points on my thick resume of customer service positions. I swore to myself that I'd never again agree to a job that required it.

Barn Equipment, Delivery, Methodology (and Plastic Jesus)

It is, above all (or beneath all), about daily humiliations. To survive the day is triumph enough for the walking wounded among the great many of us...a man's singular preoccupation with work...may affect his attitude toward all of life.[1]

—Studs Terkel

Often the barn-hauling driver would battle the laws of physics with his truck, trailer, winch, chains, jack and barn. Though the equipment was rather simple, it was creatively designed, elaborately conceived and prone to daily challenges. The truck used for hauling was either a three-quarter or one-ton pickup, diesel of course. Only a diesel truck would have the engine power necessary to move a whale-sized 10,000-pound barn across four states, up a gravel driveway, around nine abandoned vehicles and between 14 trees of various sizes.

Trucks would need to be versatile enough to pick up the barns, haul them on the interstate, across fields, streams and ditches, and deliver them in tight suburban spots as well. Tractor-trailers were too large to maneuver in yards, as were dualies.[2] Preferences shifted annually in the barn business among Ford, Chevy and Dodge, depending almost entirely on the variety of engine and transmission released each year. I didn't have an allegiance to any of these brands, though some drivers swore by one or another. At best, some trucks survived a year or two of hauling barns without major repairs, though most trucks seemed to require them regularly anyway. I often wondered why Toyota or Nissan or Honda never ventured into the market

---

1 Terkel, Studs. *Working: People Talk About What They Do All Day and How They Feel About What They Do*. New York: The New Press, 1970.
2 Pickup trucks with four tires (two on each side) in the rear, AKA *Dual Rear-Wheel* drive (as referenced in the movie *Cooties*).

of full-sized diesel work trucks. Maybe they did the research and decided they didn't want the headache and the battles with barn haulers who would inevitably torture the hell out of the trucks and demand warranty coverage. After beating a Chevy into the ground for about a year, I spent the next two years in a Dodge, a truck that broke down a lot less than the Chevy at first, but often enough. The Dodge had a longer, extended bed that I could pile high with concrete and wooden blocks; it was less often plagued by irritating electrical and fuel system problems than the Chevy was, and it had a better stereo, but I didn't know much about the insides of it—the why or how the engine managed to do what it did.

I always felt like an imposter when some dude in coveralls would approach me at a gas station and quiz me on torque, displacement, powertrain, gear ratio or whatever. These things didn't matter to me, so I didn't know about them. I may have had coveralls on too, but I couldn't say what the gas mileage was. I didn't keep track of it. It wasn't my truck, and I didn't know all its specs, but you can bet your ass I learned how to drive it. I was constantly in fear of crashing some part of the oversize apparatus of truck, barn and trailer into someone's car, particularly at busy intersections, convinced that I would smash someone's windshield to smithereens and squash their little heads like Gallagher with a sledgehammer and a watermelon. Somehow I never did, and the only car I ever smashed in three years of barn hauling was my own, when one day I pulled the truck and trailer out of Mitch's driveway. Failing to steer wide enough into the 90-degree turn to accommodate the long trailer, I dragged its tires against my poor little car, caving in the door on one side. Smooth.

Once the type of truck a driver would use to haul the barns was determined, the portability issue was solved with a barn design featuring thick wooden runners (heavy, parallel four-inch by six-inch rectangular logs that ran the length of each barn under its floor) installed from front to back. The runners lifted barns a few inches off the ground, and each perpendicular floor joist fit into custom-cut notches spaced equidistantly along each runner, creating a gap for the driver to run a chain through in order to drag the building, like a sled, up and onto his trailer.

A powerful winch with a thick steel cable was installed at the front end of the trailer nearest the truck, designed to drag the chained barn onto the rear end of the trailer, its runners centered on the trailer's steel rollers, pulling the barn into place against the opposite end of the trailer, which would gradually be lowered parallel to the ground again for travel. The runners along the length of the bottom of the barns glided perfectly across the tops of the smooth, steel rolling-pin-like rollers on either side of the length of the custom trailer. Barns would then be secured with more chains and straps. If there was room left on the trailer after extending it with the gasoline engine-powered hydraulics, more barns could be loaded behind the first one and held in place with yet more chains and straps.

The unique steel trailer, designed by a talented friend and former barn hauler, was approximately 30 feet long when fully extended, conceived and built specifically for hauling barns and capable of accommodating the smallest 8X8 barn and the largest 14X40 monstrosity. The outboard gasoline engine was situated on its top section above the truck's tailgate, so that the driver would need to stand with his head very close to this very loud engine to operate the controls for the hydraulic lift and extension. This made communicating with customers or other drivers on the premises via anything but improvised hand signals virtually impossible when the noisy little engine was started, with a key or a pull of the rope.

Once activated and roaring at deafening volume a foot or two from the driver's head, the engine would power the lifts, raising the trailer's front end approximately 10 feet into the air, placing the lip on the far opposite end of the trailer onto the ground.

The trailers we used for most of my three years in barns are known as "gooseneck" trailers, meaning that the trailer connects to the truck in the bed, over the tailgate, rather than on a bumper hitch. This allows the trailer to swivel around almost 90 degrees, perpendicular to the truck, on either side of the cab, creating much more maneuverability than a bumper hitch would allow. However, one must be careful not to turn the truck too

HARDBARNED!
One Man's Quest for Meaningful Work in the American South

86

far in either direction, which can result in a "jackknife" wherein the cab of the truck is smashed against either iron edge on the high side of the "gooseneck" or forward-most portion of trailer, as I did to Mitch's Chevy.

A driver also had to be careful not to crush consecutive barns together when loading two or three at a time, as these collisions would smash the shingles on the edges of the roofs and require time-consuming repairs performed from a ladder or while dangling over the roof-edge of the barn. In order to prevent these collisions, drivers would construct bumpers from discarded, imperfect 4X6 wooden blocks originally intended as barn runners, cut them to fit, and nail them to the base of the rear end of the forward-most barn, thereby creating a bumper-like barrier that would keep the next barn in line from squashing right up against it and damaging either barn's overhanging roof. In his truck's cab, bed and toolbox, every driver carried a full set of cordless power tools, manual lift jacks, a chain saw, an adjustable aluminum ladder, multiple sets of wrenches, screwdrivers, hammers and knives, shovels, hatchets, flashlights, crowbars, extra shingles, metal roof trim, and plenty of barn accessories like door handles and knobs, window sealant, metal air vents, barrel bolt latches, D-ring fasteners, duct tape, electrical tape, liquid nails, and various assortments of nails and screws for the inevitable repairs and on-the-fly fixes.

A driver arriving at the builder's lot has three things to accomplish before he can begin to deal with an actual barn delivery: he must make sure he has enough concrete block, wooden block and barn accessories loaded onto his truck; he must locate the particular barns he intends to haul amid a large collection of barns; and he must load and secure them on his trailer before leaving on his way to the sales lot, or in some cases, heading directly to a customer for delivery.

Because they are the principal materials used to level the barns in people's yards, concrete and wooden blocks are essential stock on every barn hauler's truck. Perfectly flat spots, accessible and carefully selected by discerning customers for barn placement, are an extremely rare and welcome surprise for the barn hauler. He is accustomed to setting up barns on the sides of hills; in between garages and broken-down cars; in creek beds and piles of mud and garbage; and amid rotten tree stumps, fire pits, discarded motor oil, broken High Life bottles, animal shit, charcoal and anything else imaginable, including dead bodies.

Though most rotting corpses encountered upon delivery were animals, at least once, one of us unknowingly delivered a barn above the hidden resting place of a murder victim. Whichever of us delivered the barn either didn't notice the smell or didn't differentiate the odor of the corpse from the usual odiferous bouquet on display in many barn customers' backyards. We found out a year or two later that a man had indeed murdered his own wife, thrown her body down a deep backyard well, tossed in a bunch of cinder blocks and gravel to cover her up, and sealed the well. He then ordered one of our barns and had one of us place it above the hidden well. The body was eventually recovered, and the barn customer/murderer was incarcerated.

A barn hauler learns to expect the worst from every situation and becomes unexpectedly surprised and elated at the infrequent occasions that allow him to place barns on even semi-level ground. Prepared concrete pads, level and ready for barn placement, are generally mirages brought on by dehydration and barn-hauling-induced madness, but I can attest that much like the elusive Sumatran tiger, a smattering still exists in the wild.

More often than not, a driver is tasked with finding a way to level a barn on hillsides or in other places completely devoid of flat spots, and wooden and concrete blocks are required. A driver must cut his own wooden blocks from the long, square, telephone pole-sized runners, (irregulars that are cast aside by the builders) and lug them by hand across the lot and into the path of the fixed circular saws. The driver cuts the huge square logs into pieces approximately the size of a large shoebox, stacks them, and loads his truck. Some will be used as bumpers or barriers between loaded barns on the trailer, as described earlier, and will later end up underneath barns for leveling support blocks. The driver must load two or three sizes of concrete blocks onto his truck by hand, or if the builder has none available onsite, the driver must travel to the nearest home supply store in search of them.

After securing a full load of blocks at the beginning of his day, the driver must then locate the barns he needs somewhere on the builder's lot. He could be looking for certain styles of barns that are low in stock on particular sales lots. He could be in search of custom-built orders for particular customers, or he might require a combination of both. Locating a particular barn on a builder's lot is often more difficult than it sounds. One would tend to assume that it's hard to misplace a barn big enough to hold several horses, or at least several people, or a couple of cars. The fact is that barn styles are limited, barn builders' lots are vast, and there are many duplicate styles on every lot. Sometimes the builders will provide identifying tags for the doors of the barn, and these simple additions make finding specific barns much easier for drivers, who often arrive at the same time as several other drivers, creating a traffic jam of trucks and trailers on the lot and resulting in considerable delays for everyone.

At least one of the manufacturing lots I frequented organized different barns by a colored tagging system. Each regional sales lot or hauling company was assigned a corresponding color, so drivers on this particular lot could quickly identify the barns they were looking for. The technological marvel of color-coded yard-sale stickers did not occur until late in my three-year career as a barn hauler, and it had only been implemented on one of the many lots I serviced before leaving the job. I assume that chaos still reigns at many of these lots, and drivers are still forced to wander across acres of barns, opening doors and looking inside every building for paperwork in an attempt to identify particular orders or suitable barns to haul for inventory. Thus, the daily barn search became a great way to use up a lot of time. I did suggest once that we implement an automated inventory tracking and control system, just like a grocery store, with bar codes and scanners and a real-time website—all in the name of efficiency—but alas, my dreams for a technological overhaul of barn manufacturing and transport were not realized by the time I had left the profession for good.

Once the barns were loaded on the trailer, tarps were secured over their roofs to protect the shingles from flying off in the wind on the way to the sales lots. Though metal roofing has since grown in popularity, when I was hauling barns it was relatively rare, and a lot of work went into protecting shingled barn roofs. This was particularly fun in winter, when barn roofs were often covered with sheets of ice. Drivers carried telescoping aluminum ladders to climb onto the sloped roofs, where we unraveled the tarps and arranged them evenly, carefully avoiding a fall. Once the driver climbs back down, he nails the tarp along both sides of the barn to secure it.

The driver then makes his way to the sales lot, which can take any number of hours, depending on whether one of his eight tires goes flat, or if any wheels catch on fire or fly off the trailer, or whether the DMV decides to detain and interrogate him on a hunch that he might be a threat to homeland security, or whether his tarps break loose in the wind and he has to pull over and secure them, or if his transmission gives out on a steep mountain road. If he makes it to the sales lot and doesn't have to deal with any of these or many other potentially schedule-obliterating problems, he unloads his cargo, rain or shine, and enters the Barn Dimension: the unpredictable great unknown of the barn delivery process, a fantastic world that seemed often to be as peculiar and unlikely as one created by Henry Darger, where a series of mind-boggling and hair-tearing events can unfold in as many ways as an origami pterodactyl.[3]

---

[3] Darger was a prolific artist-hermit who lived in obscurity and worked as a Chicago janitor by day, creating his unfinished, unpublished 15,000-word fantasy novel *The Story of the Vivian Girls, in What is Known as the Realms of the Unreal, of the Glandeco-Angelinnian War Storm, Caused by the Child Slave Rebellion*, an original manuscript written on a series of phone books along with hundreds of illustrations and paintings that were not discovered until after his death in 1973. Darger's fascinating story is told in the 2004 documentary *In The Realms of The Unreal*. An origami pterodactyl was featured in an old Little Caesar's pizza ad that I always liked. It's on YouTube.

Barn Equipment, Delivery, Methodology (and Plastic Jesus)

Having finally completed his journey from the builder's lot to the regional sales lot, the driver first must find room for his inventory barns, unload them, remove their tarps and make sure they are relatively level and that their doors are functional. Pausing to ask enormous barn browsers—oblivious in their sweat pants, pastel tank tops, NFL hats and big orange Oakley shades—if they would mind not parking their Chevy Avalanches right behind his work rig, clearly blocking his path and entire sections of the sales lot that require his attention, is not an uncommon occurrence for the barn hauler, as it is somehow only obvious to him that he is in the process of unloading barns and in need of quite a bit of space to maneuver his 40-some feet of truck and trailer.

He has hopefully reached at least one or two customers via telephone on previous days and has a few deliveries scheduled. Otherwise, he must sit in the truck at the sales lot and begin the process of trying to reach barn customers to ask if they are ready for delivery. After stocking more block (if concrete block stock was low at the builder's lot), the determined driver must now identify the particular barns he is to deliver, again looking through a large collection to find the ones he needs.

At times, and much to his dismay, after another ordeal of merely locating a particular barn on the sales lot, the driver will discover that he will still have to load and unload several other barns before he can get to the one he needs to deliver. The barn he needs may have a gigantic garage in front of it. It may take an hour to move five other barns out of the way and play musical barns all over the lot in order to find new places for each of *these* barns and get to *his* barn, only to find out that the customer had cancelled the order and was no longer buying the barn in the first place.

If he is lucky, the driver is working on one of the rare sales locations that marks barns conspicuously with SOLD signs, which he finds immensely helpful, spotting the right barn almost immediately. If he is on one of the majority of sales lots that don't, he wanders around for half an hour or more, climbing in and out of every barn on the lot in an attempt to determine which barn is the one he needs to deliver first, reviewing every work order stapled to the interior of each barn. He could go into the office and ask the salesperson, who could be a substitute or a regular and may or may not know the answer to his question, but either way he'd likely be forced to listen to a long story about the lonely salesperson's cousin who is in jail again or the restraining order on his daughter-in-law who ended a recent argument by beating him with her cell phone, or the barn that sold today and really *must* be delivered today, despite the fact that the driver has overbooked his delivery schedule and is already running late due to the traffic jam at the builder's lot, the extra trip to the concrete block store, the Chevy Avalanche, the waddling browsers in sweatpants, the lack of the SOLD sign, and the family feud filibuster.

One way or another, the driver unloads his inventory barns from the builder's lot, locates the appropriate barn for his first delivery of the day and moves a few other barns out of the way so he can get to it. The driver finally proceeds to load this barn onto the trailer, making sure to face it in the proper direction, according to the customers' specification on the work order, which is incorrect approximately 75 percent of the time. Sometimes a driver is suspicious of the work order and calls the customer to verify which direction he would like the barn to face on the trailer for optimal delivery, but this is not a reliable method of determining the facts either. When the work order or the customer is incorrect regarding which way the barn should be facing on the trailer for optimal delivery (which depends entirely on the lay of the land where the barn is to be delivered), the driver often does twice the prep work, loading and unloading the barn twice, or even more, either on the sales lot or in the middle of the road in front of the customer's house when he arrives on the scene and confirms that the customer did not—in fact—know what he was talking about when he insisted that the barn be loaded with the doors facing away from the truck. Sometimes it is difficult for a customer to mentally envision the barn, both on the truck and in his yard—in the perfect spot—and simply discern which way it should face in his yard and therefore which way the driver should load it, taking into account that the driver must have room to drive out from underneath the barn with his large truck and long trailer without crashing into a tree, a septic tank or an above-ground swimming pool. Often such details are not resolved until the barn arrives onsite and is loaded and unloaded repeatedly.

Once our determined driver confirms that he is on his way via his cellphone, he's off! He must now follow "directions" obtained by the salesperson from the customer and transferred to the work order. Rarely legible, usually incomplete, likely dyslexic and often simply wrong, directions on work orders regularly consist of a chicken-scratched homemade map of local "landmarks" with a few jumbled, misspelled words on the side. From this mess, about as useful as an empty Fritos bag found on the side of the road, the driver must discern the location of the customer's preferred delivery site, usually way the hell out in the middle of rural nowhere, where there are no street signs worth mentioning.

Often times, making calls to the customer isn't much help either. If the driver is somewhat experienced and therefore at least moderately familiar with the delivery region, he is at an advantage, for inexperienced drivers in unfamiliar locations are ticking time bombs of frustration looking for a spark. It's easy for twitchy young fellows such as these to encounter such a colossal snafu of unfortunate and idiotic circumstances throughout a single day of hauling barns that he is indeed reduced to a simmering, shaking, physical manifestation of rage itself. At least that was true of me in the first year or two. After raging against the barn machine for a couple years, I was no longer shaking in fury from behind the wheel of the truck; but, weary, battered and bedraggled by daily Barn Land madness and my fruitless quest for more meaningful work, I'm sure I had a burned-out and defeated look best described as a thousand-barn-stare.

Striving merely to get his work done and get home, knowing well the plethora of problems potentially positioning themselves to slow him down along the way, the driver tends to avoid human contact as much as possible throughout his work day, preferring not to encounter salespeople *or* customers, gradually becoming more misanthropic with every delivery.

HARDBARNED!
One Man's Quest for Meaningful Work in the American South

Barn Land was almost completely a man's world. Though certainly a woman could haul barns, I never met one who did. A few older women worked on sales lots, and young Mennonite women helped build barns occasionally, but it seemed like a rare occurrence. I once saw a teenage girl, barefoot in her long dress and bonnet, on the roof of a barn nailing shingles.

I don't know if there is a typical barn hauler, but the overwhelming majority of the ones that I knew were dedicated, hard-working professionals, quick to smile or laugh and just as eager to lend a hand. A lot of them stuck with the job year after year, though many hated it. Some felt trapped by obligations to debt or family or both. Many realized that there were no other job opportunities that paid as well, especially in the depressing job and economic climate of the late 2000s. These men soldiered on and endured a lot for little thanks other than the money in their pockets or the privilege of working for someone like Mitch. Some couldn't take it and quit quickly. Some were injured and gave it up. Some got sloppy and lost their jobs, but many kept at it and lasted much longer than I did. And yes, a few of them really enjoyed it, didn't feel trapped and weren't desperate to escape, but the only guy I knew who admitted to this was actually a fireman and hauled barns as a part-time side job. I wonder if he'd have felt the same enthusiasm if he were a full-time (overtime) barn hauler. Anyway, here's to the brave and hardy men still out there hauling barns. I feel your pain, and I salute you with the respectful toast of a cold one.

Barn haulers manage to complete a lot of hard work despite frequent adversity. They are natural problem solvers. Despite a catalog of potential difficulties including bad directions, frequent incidents and obstacles that often intercede and conspire against him to cause catastrophic breakdowns (mechanical, mental, emotional) in the course of a day of hauling barns, it is not at all uncommon for a determined driver to find his way to an actual delivery site. Relieved to have made his way to the correct address, he turns into the driveway, trying hard to swing wide enough to avoid the fence posts, mailboxes, tree limbs, bushes, ditches, culverts, bird houses, lawn decorations, potholes, children and various canine (or other species

Barn Equipment, Delivery, Methodology (and Plastic Jesus)

of) pets in hot pursuit. He hopes the customer spots him from the window and emerges from the home to greet him and discuss placement of the barn. Pleasantries are exchanged along with comments on the weather. Unreasonable requests for barn placement (such as steep hillsides with slopes greater than three feet) are denied. Possibilities are discussed. Alternatives are suggested. Negotiation begins. Neighbors weigh in, complicate things and are (hopefully) ignored. Delivery ensues.

As mentioned earlier, steel lift jacks are an essential part of the delivery process. Once a barn has been maneuvered into place and the driver is able to drive out from underneath it, he's going to have to prop or "jack" up whichever side is sitting low (according to the slope of the land) with a powerful, manually operated lift jack. The Hi-Lift jack is the jack of choice for the barn-hauling professional, and apparently for the rock and roll-loving, SUV-driving adventure junkie as well, as I discovered when I unwittingly activated an online promotional video—complete with an upbeat, active-lifestyle-themed instrumental rock soundtrack—when accessing the Hi-Lift website for the first time while writing this book. For some reason, the barn-hauling professional is neither glamorized nor featured whatsoever in the squeaky-clean, action-packed ad on the home page for the Hi-Lift jack, a commercial set in a fun world where spotless Jeeps and newly waxed Range Rovers ascend steep rock formations and are rescued by anonymous men in clean jeans and fresh, white sneakers, bearing brand-new Hi-Lift jacks without a hint of dirt, rust or grime, and they aren't even bent or missing any parts! This particular jack is a hefty, formidable tool that can allow a single delivery driver to lift just about any barn as high as he needs in order to level the building, but my jacks were always dirty, rusted and often bent or broken, requiring regular repair and lubrication. The clean-sneaker guy in the commercial probably didn't use his much; he probably didn't leave it in the rain in the bed of a truck either.

When leveling a barn, the driver first lifts one long side of the building, whichever is on the lower side of a slope, centering the jack in the middle, which sometimes requires digging a hole to get it underneath the edge of the barn. If the barn is large (between 24 and 40 feet long) the driver may use two jacks, walking back and forth between them as he uses his body weight to pull the manually operated jack handle, making sure that each one is lifting evenly. Once the long side is measured with a level, the driver braces the corners by digging out flat spots with a square-tipped shovel, placing either concrete or wooden blocks or a combination of both under the corners until the barn is sufficiently supported.[4] He then removes the jacks and lifts whichever short end of the barn is below the level mark, as is often necessary because Barn Land is hill country, and delivery spots regularly feature slopes heading in more than one direction.

The jack can be a dangerous tool, as its heavy metal handle has a tendency to snap back toward the user if it fails to engage fully upon each pull/push cycle. Mitch told me about smacking himself in the throat on one such occasion, which rendered him temporarily unable to speak or breathe, and I had my own collection of bruises from the thing. On other occasions, if ground conditions were less than ideal, the jack would sink into the soft mud or topple over, causing the heavy barn to crash to the ground, pinning the jack and forcing the driver to dive out of the way to safety and begin his leveling work again.

Assuming he was able to level the lower of the two long sides of the barn, the driver would then install temporary supports on the corners of that side, remove the jack(s) and move on to lift the lowest of the short ends of the barn to a leveled height, whereupon he would be ready to install permanent supports all around with various sizes of concrete and wooden blocks. This setup would inevitably involve crawling around underneath the barn in order to access some of the more difficult-to-reach points of support that ideally are distributed evenly along each of the two (or four) runners that line the bottom of a barn, depending on its width.

Crawling underneath a barn, wondering what the hell I was

---

[4] Pressure-treated wooden blocks used for leveling are included with the barn purchase, but some customers prefer concrete, which was sold separately.

doing with my life, I encountered myriad creatures and hazards ranging from spiders, hornets, wasps, snakes and centipedes to broken glass, animal feces and/or carcasses, motor oil, septic seepage, hot coals from recently extinguished or still-smoldering fires, yard trash, exposed nails spiking into my skull, splinters, and of course mud, rocks, thorns, poison ivy and excessive amounts of existential ennui. Digging out flat spots on the sides of steep hills; lugging concrete blocks from the truck; ignoring a predictable fusillade of misguided instructions spouted from the on-looking customers, family and neighbors; crawling around in the muck underneath a barn, I often floated to another time and place in my mind.

At one of these moments I drifted back to a time when I was a little squirt, a mere five years old, playing with my cousin Grace on the floor of my great-grandmother Nana's house. Content and energetic, our bellies full of Nana's famous Boston Coolers—a tall, frosted, old-fashioned soda-fountain glass filled with Pepsi and topped off with a generous scoop or two of vanilla ice cream—Grace and I finished our *Empire Strikes Back* coloring book and decided to play with Nana's old Fiddle Stix, "an exciting, fascinating, tantalizing game." Fiddle Stix were the thick, wooden, precursor to Pick Up Sticks, a child's game. Dumping the colorful rods from the tin can into the thick living-room carpet, we stretched out on the floor, balancing our chins on our hands, our elbows elevating our heads barely higher than the pointed tips of the bright sticks that poked up vertically from the rug. Somehow I slipped. My five-year-old face fell fast into the deadly child-spikes.

Surely I wasn't their only clumsy victim, but somehow Pick Up Sticks managed to avoid banishment into the pantheon of recalled dangerous toys like Lawn Darts (Jarts), an unwieldy variation on horseshoes that impaled many a hapless child, three-wheeled all-terrain vehicles (ATVs) that flipped far too many outdoor revelers toward their doom, Snack Time Cabbage Patch Kids (WTF? A doll that ate stuff and…well…processed it) and the Easy Bake oven, which easily burned down many an adult-sized home. My eyes escaped puncture, but I fell nose-first onto a green fiddle stick and felt neither fascinated nor tantalized. After a moment's pause, I lifted my head and tugged at the green spear, blasting a steady stream of bright blood onto the crème carpet and unleashing a first-degree ultra-scream reserved for the worst moments of an otherwise pleasant and relatively injury-free childhood. There was an ambulance ride and an X-ray to make sure there were no splinters in my brain, but maybe that injury was what had knocked my life off track, I thought, on my back under the barn, wrestling concrete blocks into place in the dirt. Mom likes to say that Nana's first comments upon seeing me as an infant were something along the lines of

"That boy's going to be very smart. He's got a big brainpan."

Well maybe the fiddle stick had pierced my big brainpan after all. Maybe the inexperienced X-ray technician had missed it so many years ago. Clearly this latent, unrecognized brain injury had manifested itself decades later, dooming me to a useless education and a fate involving an uncomfortable intimacy with cinder blocks and chicken shit. Perhaps I had unwittingly initiated my own progressive mental deterioration with that fiddle stick long ago. Maybe this barn thing was just the next step that would eventually lead me into a heartbreaking, drooling, lobotomized stupor like Jack Nicholson's sad fate in *One Flew Over the Cuckoo's Nest*. I had to stop thinking like this. Hole in my head or not, I was still stuck under the barn.

Frustrated one day by the job in general, my continual inability to find a writing job, and the overstocked barn lot's immediate lack of space available in which to load barns and maneuver trucks and trailers, I screwed up. I spun the rig around and over-corrected, jackknifing too quickly beyond the point of no return. The result of my mistake brought the front side of the trailer (the raised section above the bed) smashing into the corner of the cab of the truck, pounding a couple of sizeable dents into the frame and causing the back windshield of Mitch's Chevy to implode instantly, as if hit by a shotgun blast in a car chase.

I had to just sit there and laugh at myself as I picked out the broken bits of glass from my T-shirt collar and the driver's seat. What else was I going to do but laugh? Get out of the truck and start smashing it with a crowbar in a rage? Sit in the dirt and cry? I was finding little pieces of glass in the cab for months. I was glad that nobody seemed to have witnessed my bout of idiocy in the dusty parking lot; apparently everyone else working that day had been busy with his own work, either loading barns or building them.

I sheepishly called Mitch and told him what I'd done, disconnected my truck from the trailer and drove it to the nearby paint and body shop for an estimate. After explaining my predicament to the owner, an enormous man in a leather chair who responded with a friendly chuckle, I called my wife in a neighboring town for a ride home and retreated to the parking lot to wait for her. Sitting in the broken truck in the late-afternoon sun for an hour or so, I stared at a four-foot plastic Jesus statue that presided over the small cemetery next to the body shop.

Though he lacked any plastic disciples, he seemed calm, extending his plastic hands affectionately over his interred followers, his head tilted slightly in perpetuity. I felt a sort of communion with Plastic Jesus, as that familiar wave of existential ennui crashed over me, a little harder than usual this time. I longed for the peaceful feeling he seemed to have. This was madness. What was I doing with my life? I didn't feel much more useful than the petroleum-based savior presiding over his long dead flock. I tried to forget my own situation, staring into the serene eyes of Plastic Jesus from my broken truck as I listened to Stephen King describe his own near-death experience in his memoir *On Writing*. He spoke of endless rejections and dogged determination to be a writer against all odds, his struggles with alcoholism and of course the van driven by the drunk that almost killed him and took away everything, much later in his career. King had decided to soldier on, and so would I. My wife picked me up. On the way home, I told her about my adventures in truck abuse. Attempting a new approach to exorcising barns for a few hours, for the first time I started to write about them.

Punks and Hippies Unite to Serve Tourists Fried Seafood

In order that people may be happy in their work, these three things are needed: they must be fit for it; they must not do too much of it, and they must have a sense of success in it.[1]

—John Ruskin

I met a fun, friendly girl named Lena who started working with me soon after the Brown Horse restaurant opened. Not long after withdrawing from the marine biology program, having returned home to live and planning to take at least one post-high school year off before considering college again, I had worked at the small lunch and dinner establishment for a few months when Lena walked through the door with a server application. She was a tall, 21-year-old brunette; I was 18 and in awe of her. Lena had a natural ability to derive joy from everyday life, which I found a refreshing break from my teen angst. She drove a Saab and loved the Grateful Dead, a band I hated. I still had The Beast (my old Chevy Impala) when we met and preferred Fugazi, Jawbreaker and Rancid to Jerry Garcia or Trey Anastasio, but somehow we tolerated each other's music and grew close despite our differences.

Lena taught me to appreciate a wider range of spicy foods and bitter beer. She loved marijuana, with which I had experimented but had never acquired much of a taste for. When I smoked pot, I usually felt about as intelligent as a tree stump. Still, I wanted to please her and find the plateau she seemed to float on, and mostly I just tried to keep up. After a few months of dating, Lena asked me to move to the beach with her for the summer. One of our friends from the restaurant, a bubbly blonde

---

1 Ruskin, John. *Pre-Raphaelitism*. New York: John Wiley & Sons, 1884.

named Kayla who drove a pink Ford Probe, came along with us. In May of 1995, we quit our jobs and moved to the Outer Banks of North Carolina. The morning we left, I sold The Beast and bought my Mom's '87 Volvo 240 wagon. I've been hooked on old 240 Volvos ever since Dad and I road tripped around North America in his '82 stick-shift 240 sedan, on which I then learned to drive. That one still ran when he swapped it at 373K miles.

I worked three jobs over the course of my first summer on the Outer Banks. We started with what we knew. At the seafood restaurant on the north end of the beach, Lena worked as a cocktail waitress, and I worked in the huge basement kitchen. I ran the fryers and steamers behind the counter in the misty, boiling hot station next to the sauté chefs. I peeled hundreds of pounds of shrimp by hand and dumped mountains of fries and hush puppies into sputtering hot oil. I breaded and fried oysters, clams, scallops and crab cakes, coating my fingers in sticky batter and splattering the boiling oil as I tossed the seafood bites into the fryer to soak up the fat. The worst part was killing the lobsters. I was required to grab them live from their crates, put rubber bands on any open claws, flip them on their backs and quickly dispatch them with a large butcher knife, bisecting them from head to tail, splitting their brains and scraping out their guts into the sink, rinsing them out, stuffing them with a crab cake, and tossing them into the steamer. Sometimes people don't believe me when I tell them that lobsters unleash a high-pitched scream when they're stabbed to death, but it's true.

I turned 19 that summer and shared a beach house with seven other seasonal restaurant employees who ranged in age from 21 to 24. We partied at night with our college-kid roommates who were on summer vacation and working restaurants jobs too. We spent most of our days on the beach, and we all typically went into work around four in the afternoon. The day we arrived at the house to move in, there was a wild alligator in our yard, and the Fish & Wildlife professionals showed up, cornered, captured it and took it away in a truck. Little did I know I'd soon have a second run-in with the wildlife authorities.

One of my hippie roommates had long hair and lots of necklaces and liked to entertain the housemates by juggling fruit in the kitchen while making mixed drinks. He left the house a couple times for Grateful Dead shows and came back depressed when Jerry Garcia died that summer of '95. I wasn't devastated. Several other roommates were frat dudes who liked jam bands, but they were nice guys for the most part and were easy enough to be around. I became good friends with a couple of these guys but haven't stayed in touch. Our neighbors across the street were truly dedicated hippies who tripped on acid and mushrooms almost every day. They were two of the most friendly, generous people I'd ever met. We'd all gather to hang out on our deck, cook crabs and drink beer from the omnipresent keg. Nobody wore shirts, everyone smoked weed every day, and the mood was always mellow. Other than Lena, Kayla was the only other female roommate and shared a room with Lena and me, but she wasn't around as much due to her lifeguarding job at the other end of the beach, so we usually had the space to ourselves.

Another housemate drove a green 1960-something Mustang convertible. We'd pile in and drive down the beach road listening to Dave Matthews cover "All Along The Watchtower" on our way to the restaurant. I often wore my old Fugazi T-shirt (counterfeit, as Fugazi never sold merchandise), so my hippie roommates nicknamed me Fugazi. As a music minority of one in our eight-person household, I was forced to endure my roommates' endless marathons of The Grateful Dead, Blues Traveler, Widespread Panic, and even worse—Phish, or some abomination known as The String Cheese Incident. This noodle music was in polar opposition to the precision and focused intensity that I preferred from my rock. These bands sounded so sloppy that they could barely hold the song together (or didn't really care to), and their lyrics were silly nursery rhymes. My roommates would bring the speakers out on the deck and blast these selections while we played basketball at the house next door, and I learned to tolerate a couple of the groups more than the others. Of all of my roommates' horrible music, Dave Matthews Band and Ben Harper grew on me a little that summer. At least they both had tight rhythm sections and lyrics that made a little sense. Compared to the endless jam bands I was pelted with daily, these guys sounded fantastic, but I'd have much preferred Rancid or Jawbreaker, Archers of Loaf, Face to Face, or my old favorite, Fugazi.[2]

Even though my teenage friends and I would joke about dirty hippies back home, I got along great with my hippie neighbors too. I got along with most people pretty well anyway. I tried to treat people with respect, and I had my own understanding of the punk rock ethos, one that differed from the one projected by much of the mainstream media for decades. I identified clearly with the music and the communal, DIY, anti-establishment message, but I didn't shoot heroin or cut myself, get Nazi tattoos, rob convenient stores or pick fights with immigrants, like in many Hollywood interpretations of so-called "punk" lifestyles. Actually, in the years since that summer at the beach, having played in bands and toured some within the punk rock underground, I've almost always found

---

[2] I was first intrigued by Fugazi's unique, creative, exciting, energetic and original, precise and intense yet melodic and almost jazz-like punk rock music, but I was drawn to their ethical sense and values, and inspired by their actions. Fiercely independent, always insisting on all-ages venues and adamantly non-violent, Fugazi formed in 1987 and performed until 2002, when they began an indefinite hiatus. They ignored the mainstream music business and supported social-justice causes, managing to sell around 200K copies of each record they self-released, regularly playing sold-out shows around the world despite receiving only college radio airplay, selling their own records on their own terms, without major label support, MTV or commercial radio, on founding singer/guitarist Ian Mackaye's label, Dischord Records, which he and friends ran out of his parents' DC home, without financiers, managers, promoters, producers, booking agents or A&R types. Despite their insistence on low ticket prices, often in the $5-$10 range, Fugazi raised considerable money from their concerts, benefiting a wide range of organizations like Amnesty International, the American Civil Liberties Union, Community for Creative Non-Violence, Emmaus Services For the Aging, Food Not Bombs, Positive Force DC, Helping Individual Prostitutes Survive, Women's Advocates To Terminate Sexism, and countless other organizations for social justice, the homeless, battered women and abused children. Fugazi led by example, and many bands over the years, in towns all over the world, have come together in this DIY community spirit to use their music to effect positive change in the world while raging against its many injustices. Dischord records is still running strong today. Here's hoping that circumstances align, some day, for Fugazi to become an active band once again. Now that would be an exciting time.

the inverse of these stereotypes to be the rule, but there are still jackasses to be found in every culture and subculture—not just in the mainstream—but everywhere you go.

Still, it's not easy to find a universal definition of the punk rock ethos. Ask a hundred people who either identify with the label or don't but think they know what it means, and you'll likely hear nearly as many definitions. The "punk rock" label has often been hijacked by racist fools or elitist assholes who like to beat people up for various reasons, but the fringe make the headlines. My understanding of punk rock was not that of being a misanthrope, though I was used to feeling like an outsider. Punk to me was an international community that welcomed outsiders, weirdos, misfits and non-conformists. It was about a safe expression of creative, artistic identity outside of mainstream expectations, authority and establishment conventions like religion, sports and politics. It challenged the status quo defiantly and raged against conformity.

Punk said it was okay to be different. It wasn't about acting fucked-up or being violent, and though it challenged the mainstream, to me it was ultimately about respect. Yes, punk rejected traditional, exclusionary religious dogma and explicitly questioned all forms of authority and the influence of mainstream popular culture and media, but punk rock to me was *and is* essentially about being creative in your own way—defining your own culture through whatever sort of art you are motivated to create—and all the while simply being tolerant and accepting of all people—treating them as you'd like to be treated—whatever their interests or beliefs, culture or background and however these might differ from your own worldview. The punk community I knew was about respecting individuality, diversity, human rights and everyone's right to be different—*pride* in difference. Maybe punks see the world through a more negative filter than hippies do, but I think a punk is just more of a realist, so maybe a hippie is a bit more of an idealist. Perhaps hippies just have a sunnier outlook. Either way, both labels reflect independent-minded individuals, keen on living their lives their own way without having anyone else impose their ideologies, expectations or choices upon them. When it came down to it, as I realized that summer as the only self-identifying punk amongst hippies, other than the choices of music and clothing and hairstyles that we all made, there wasn't a huge chasm of difference between hippies and punks and our worldviews. And I don't like to box people in with labels, either. They're tired, diluted, subjective and often completely inaccurate, but sometimes I use them. It's human nature to categorize when we communicate, but generalizations are usually a bad idea.

That summer at the beach, one of our older roommates took me under his wing and invited me to the gym to help me try and add some muscle to my skinny teenage frame. Jim was the oldest guy in the house and a psychology major. One day at the multi-tiered, tourist-trap restaurant where we all worked, he decided to create his own special of the day on the kitchen blackboard where all the servers started their shifts. Jim wrote "Grilled Osprey with Lemon Butter Glaze" on the board. In the kitchen we laughed when some of the servers actually added the fictional special to their notepads, one after another, but it wasn't long before customers started reacting. Apparently one astute couple was offended at the idea of being offered an entrée from the endangered species list, so they called the authorities.

It was even funnier when the Fish & Wildlife suits showed up, but they didn't seem to get the joke and interrogated the entire staff until they were certain that we didn't actually have any dead birds and that the whole thing was a farce. There was serious talk of a lawsuit. The entire staff was interrogated in the hopes that one of us would crack and reveal the source of the joke that had become an ordeal, but nobody squealed on Jim. We all quit the tourist trap soon after the osprey fiasco and the following witch-hunt.

In the mood for a change of scene, I took a job as a sandwich maker and prep cook at a quiet, comparatively tiny sandwich shop on the sound side of the barrier island. I worked for a nice lady but got bored fast in the kitchen no bigger than a taco stand, serving very few customers in search of veggie pita sandwiches and shrimp bisque. I moved on to work as a clerk at a souvenir junk shop and miniature golf course, where I spent many an afternoon stocking salt-water taffy, selling mini golf tickets and ringing up piles of plastic souvenir beach crap from behind a cash register. At one point I painted the outside of the shop. Balancing precariously from a high ladder in the sun, scraping old paint from the crumbling eaves into my eyes, I flashed back to my house-painting summers back home with Ernie and smiled, the sweat helping to flush out the paint chips. This time nothing was exploding, and there were no yellow jackets to be found. The salt-water breeze smelled sweet, and I could see waves crashing across the street on the beach from atop the ladder. What I did for a buck didn't matter so much at that point. I was a lucky teenager at the beach with no worries.

Through Lena, I met a local kid my age named Neil who was also into skateboarding. His summer beach job was making tableside Caesar salads at an authentic Italian restaurant. Whenever we'd all get together for dinner, he'd make one for us, and the combination of garlic with raw egg, anchovies, olive oil, lemon juice and Dijon mustard became another new (and now an all-time) favorite flavor. I've never had a better Caesar salad than the ones Neil made, not before or since, and I still use his recipe. Neil and I would skate around the parking garage at his parents' condo, and before long he showed me what his real source of summer income was: making bongs. He would buy lengths of clear and sometimes colored plastic tubing from hardware stores and bring them back to his workshop—a storage locker beneath the condo—and use a welder's torch to carefully heat, bend and mold all kinds of crazy psychedelic shapes for multi-chambered smoking pipes. I decided that summer that smoking pot was definitely best experienced with one of Neil's homemade bongs, even though my marijuana intake paled in comparison to that of my roommates. Weed wasn't the only intoxicant on the beach, of course.

At one party I remember clearly, someone brought a medical tank of nitrous oxide and sold balloons. It just seemed like a normal summer night at the beach. Nobody was trying to hide anything. There was a keg and plenty of weed, and people were wandering all over the street, no cops to be seen. The nitrous tank was set up right in front of the house. I sat down on the driveway in the warm night air with a few people and inhaled a balloon. Everything slowed down so fast that I felt like life was on an LP record spinning at the wrong speed. Voices around me sounded like Will Ferrell's after shooting himself with the tranquilizer gun in *Old School*. The feeling was pleasant but brief, and I liked how I didn't feel foggy for a while afterward like I did with pot or magic mushrooms, another house favorite. I liked beer but wasn't much into getting wasted, and though I tried nitrous and mushrooms a couple times, I never tried any drugs harder than these and mostly stuck to beer and a little weed now and then.

Before the summer came to its inevitable close, Lena and I hopped the ferry and escaped south to a small island, a charming colony of artists, writers and recluses, for a final getaway. We didn't see a single soul on the beach and took long walks, talking about what might be next for us. It was nice to have time to just be together and avoid the parties and tourist-serving jobs for a few days. Lena was planning on moving home and going back to school near the restaurant where we had met, and after a year of working in restaurants and messing around at the beach all summer, I felt the call of the classroom and decided that maybe I should start thinking about college again too. I found a university about three hours from home that looked interesting, but it was also three hours from Lena, which was less than ideal. I'd found the right program to get me into study mode again and wasn't ready to move back home, so we decided to embark on a long-distance relationship. I missed her but figured it could work. I could not have begun to imagine the assortment of craptastic jobs that awaited me in college and beyond.

Barn History: The Legend of Samuel and Jim

A real job is a job you hate.[1]
—Bill Watterson

As legend has it, sometime after the reign of GHW Bush and prior to that of W, in the rural South, before various Mennonite, Amish and secular barn companies had built many a personal fortune and nearly stretched their meteoric sales across the entirety of North America, there was a Mennonite named Samuel. Samuel, like many Mennonites, was pretty good at building portable storage barns—so good in fact that he started to speculate about financial opportunities in the secular world. After all, the Mennonite market was rather limited, and Sam knew as well as anybody else the necessity for junk storage that an individual or family of any religious notion (or lack thereof) was desperately in need of Down South. All one had to do was drive down a few county roads or pass a couple of trailer parks to see the plethora of lawn junk.

A culture of excess is not endemic merely to southerners; it is an all-American tradition, born of capitalism, easy access to affordable products and a natural tendency to spread. Nor does an affection for collection appear contingent upon income. Barns are just as easily filled with rummage-sale clutter as they are stacked with any number of items of great, albeit difficult-to-discern, value. Down South, no true collector is limited by her economic means, and one man's trash is another man's treasure, as the cliché dictates. Different strokes for different folks.

---

1 Watterson, Bill. *Some Thoughts on the Real World By One Who Glimpsed It And Fled.* Kenyon College Commencement Address: May 20, 1990.

Nowhere do these axioms ring truer than in Barn Land, where yard sales remain incredibly popular. Some barn customers augmented their collection of barns with more and more barns—even five or six in one yard—sometimes turning them into guest rooms or workshops but often simply using them to house the abundance of stuff they didn't have room for anywhere else. Sometimes a few of these people intended to buy and resell this excess stuff at yard sales and flea markets. In these cases, business was the goal—never actually ridding oneself of all the excess stuff—but buying and selling it in perpetuity, forever. A constant revolution of things—an ancient mercantile tradition of trading, buying and selling but ultimately maintaining a stable collection of goods with which to do business—made more sense than simple accumulation, but these cases were exceptional. Most barn customers seemed to be junk accumulators, not junk merchants. Exchange or trade seemed the exception rather than the rule.

Most barns were dedicated purely to the acquisition and storage of random stuff. Some folks fill attics, garages and junior's old bedroom to house their stuff. Some live in tiny apartments and pile their stuff to the ceiling. Some rent storage units. Some rent barns. Others annex their homes or construct additional homes to house their extra stuff. Some customers instructed me to install a barn as close as possible to the structure they were living in, so that they could actually attach the barn to their trailer, house or barn. Yes, some folks already lived in a barn I had previously delivered to them and wanted to attach another. To house more stuff.[2]

But let's get back to The Legend. Samuel knew inherently that people in his region of the country would buy barns. It was that simple. There were plenty of Mennonite mouths to feed, and Samuel was the best barn builder he knew, so bigger business seemed inevitable. Sam met with

---

[2] If you have a moment and somehow have never witnessed his masterful, hilarious and spot-on soliloquy on the subject of our national obsession with the acquisition and storage of all our stuff, just whip out that smartypants phone and google "George Carlin Stuff" for the video. I won't quote it here because George deserves your full attention for the whole bit. It's a classic.

a non-Mennonite investor named Jim. Jim checked out Sam's barns and liked what he saw. A partnership was born, and the Mennonite barns, which have always been well designed and solidly built, were unleashed on the masses. Jim arranged for sales lots to be set up in towns across the rural South, and Sam hired extra builders to help crank out several different designs and sizes for inventory to fill up the sales lots, which were created by renting open lots from used car vendors, doughnut restaurants, RV dealers, muffler shops or from whomever had the space and was willing to handle the sales.

At some point early in this rapidly expanding business venture, someone realized that the barns would have to be delivered, not just from the builder to the sales lots, but also from the sales lots to the customers' yards. A major selling point (albeit a massive liability for the outsourced barn delivery company) would be free delivery and setup. Buying a barn wasn't anything like picking up a new doghouse and some two-by-fours at the Tractor Supply and bringing them home in the back of the family pickup truck. Most customers wouldn't be able to pick up a multi-ton barn at a sales lot and deliver it to their own backyards. Of course, some yards were not accessible, so there would be times when only a built-on-site barn would do, but Sam and Jim hoped to avoid those situations as much as possible, as they would tend to be more costly and time consuming and would defer builders from their efficient, productive factories, also requiring all materials to be hauled to the site.

According to The Legend, Samuel and Jim sold so many barns and got so rich so fast that their lifestyles changed noticeably. This wasn't a big problem for Jim, but for Sam, who still lived in a tight-knit religious community, living large was conspicuous and frowned upon. Samuel was instructed by community leaders either to change his ways or face banishment from his community. No one knows what Samuel was doing that was so displeasing to the elders. Did he sport a red Ferrari with all the bells and whistles instead of a brush-painted black pickup truck with the stereo and air conditioning removed (the standard, acceptable transportation in his community)? I don't think so. Did he host raucous hot-tub parties with local harlots and adult beverages or a special Mennonite edition of MTV's *Cribs*? Doubtful. Maybe he bought a cell phone or hosted a kegger for his bearded bros in the back yard. We can only speculate.

All we know for sure (well, it is a *legend*) is that Samuel sold his share of the venture to Jim and preserved his standing in the community. Jim went solo, becoming a barn baron and going on to claim his fortune in the secular world of portable storage barn sales and rentals. And claim his fortune Jim did indeed. So says The Legend of Samuel and Jim.

College Begins, Film Rentals Resume…and…Goldschlager!

The college student interviews for a job as a knowledge worker, and finds that the corporate recruiter never asks about his grades and doesn't care what he majored in. He senses that what is demanded of him is not knowledge but rather that he project a certain kind of personality, an affable complaisance…There seems to be a mismatch between form and content, and a growing sense that the official story we've been telling ourselves about work is somehow false.[1]

—Matthew B. Crawford

A week after turning 19, in August 1995, I entered college, having decided to study the recording industry. A year after the shark study letdown at freshman orientation, I had let go of the marine biology idea. I couldn't face the prospect of 13 years of school followed by a career in a white coat under fluorescent lights in a laboratory. If I couldn't be out on the open sea chasing sharks, I could pursue another passionate interest: music. Here was a chance to get a college degree while learning about music production. If I wasn't skilled or talented enough to play music professionally, at least I'd be close to where it was happening, and I'd surely meet other below-average musicians with whom I could create music along the way.

A few years prior to enrolling, I had printed out (and practically memorized) independent recording engineer, musician and producer Steve Albini's anti-recording industry cover story manifesto from *MAXIMUM ROCKNROLL* entitled "The Problem With Music" which featured a close-up of an anonymous man holding a pistol in his mouth, with a caption below, asserting: "Some of Your Friends Are Already This Fucked." Though he worked with big record companies on occasion and is particularly known for having recorded Nirvana's *In Utero* and The Pixies' *Surfer Rosa*, Albini's thesis vehemently damned major record labels, portraying

---

1 Crawford, Matthew B. *Shop Class as Soulcraft: An Inquiry Into the Value of Work.* New York: The Penguin Press, 2009.

them as pimps and the bands as whores, and the whole transaction between the two as a poison that was killing creative output across the independent, underground DIY music scene that I had grown to love. Despite his fervent analysis of the mainstream music machine, Albini made a lot of money working for the big labels but channeled it into his real passion—his personal studio in Chicago, where he has recorded thousands of independent and never-known bands at affordable rates without any interference from overpaid corporate executives concerned only with the potential of their investments. This strategy made a lot of sense to me and inspired me to study audio engineering. A few years later, my own independent, unknown band was lucky enough to record an album at Albini's Electrical Audio studio in Chicago.

I figured I could learn practical skills from my mainstream-music-industry studies at school, eventually channeling that knowledge into the punk rock underground to work as an audio engineer, recording the outsider music that mattered to me most, regardless of its radio-play or commercial potential. That was the plan, anyway. I'd figure out how to make enough money to live on, somehow. I spent my first semester in the dorms, lying on the bunk with my old Walkman from my paper route days, listening to cassette recordings of Henry Rollins' *Get In The Van: On the Road with Black Flag*, imagining how great it would be to tour the country in a punk rock band, playing songs I had written to people who actually wanted to hear them.

The first day I walked into my freshman dorm room, there was a 10-gallon cowboy hat on the top bunk. As it turned out, my roommate was a frat dude and not a cowboy. I was still suspicious of frat dudes, but this guy wasn't the douchebag stereotype I had perhaps naively expected. Smitty was a nice guy, studying to be a pilot, and though we didn't have much in common, we discovered that we both liked tennis, and we played together once in a while. Even though we didn't hang out that much otherwise, he was a good roommate, and we got along well. While focusing on required freshman core classes and managing (if I was lucky) to land a spot in one or two of the overcrowded introductory audio engineering classes in the recording industry department every semester, I still needed to work.

My first job during college was at a major video store chain. Akin to the supermarket video store where I had worked in high school but several times larger and with the same khaki-pants-and-blue-polo uniform, this house of movies also offered the fringe benefit of free rentals for employees. With an extensive inventory, this place was the perfect enabler to feed my movie fix. I spent endless hours wandering the dusty shelves of VHS tapes, memorizing titles and box covers, bringing home whatever looked interesting and making several friends along the way. There were customers I really liked, including one middle-aged family man who reminded me of Roger Ebert and was always eager to discuss the current batch of new releases, relate his own reviews of whatever movie he was returning and hear my suggestions. Customers were memorable for a variety of reasons. One old lady just couldn't comprehend why

"them black bars was on my screen again" when she rented a letterbox edition of *Forrest Gump*, no matter how many times I explained the difference between widescreen and pan and scan, and we had the same discussion on preserving aspect ratios whenever she was in the store.

One creepy mouth-breathing regular only rented the worst low-budget gore fests we stocked, like *Island of the Cannibals*, *Faces Of Death*, and *I Spit On Your Grave*. He was always hunched over in a grimy jumpsuit, squinting and measured in his speech and mannerisms, yet methodical and insistent. He once asked if I had any "good movies." I asked what he had in mind, though I was familiar with his rental history.

"Somethin' with a lot a' killin' in it," was his reply.

I smiled. He didn't. I knew that he was well acquainted with the horror section, but I walked him over to it anyway. Probably the dude was harmless, but who knows where he ended up? He tended to creep out the clientele and was definitely a low-talking lurker.

I had a good time at the video store for the most part. It was fun to share the work with friends, and it often had the atmosphere of a party. Sometimes it *was* a party. I remember one Halloween when somebody brought in a liter bottle of Goldschlager. We were all angry with management at the time anyway, and each of us ended up quitting in solidarity soon afterward when one of our favorite shift managers was accused of stealing, but before that happened we had a great Halloween, stashing the bottle behind the counter and doing shots throughout the night shift. We ran a tight ship at the video shop but were extra friendly that night.

It was the end of an era, as DVDs were replacing VHS tapes and Netflix was lurking on the outskirts, preparing to decimate the industry entirely and erase rental shops from existence. I'm glad I had a chance to work in two video rental stores before they all disappeared. The human interaction with a stranger over a shared appreciation or disdain for an excellent (or horrible) movie is something to be missed. Even Netflix eventually dismantled their online mechanism for sharing ratings and recommendations with friends.

Little Brother Barn, Speedo Guy, Trailer Fire and Torpedo Tire

Maybe you don't like your job
Maybe you didn't get enough sleep
Well, nobody likes their job
Nobody got enough sleep
Maybe you just had
The worst day of your life
But, you know, there's no escape
And there's no excuse
So just suck up and be nice[1]

—Ani DiFranco

It's amazing how many barn customers live in insanely remote areas with no street signs whatsoever. Apparently, it's great fun in Barn Land to fire shotguns at these signs as you drive by, leaving little more than tiny green nubs at the top of the now useless posts:

"Ha! That there'll teach 'em city slickers to try and deliver nuthin' to us!"

It seems counterproductive. Early one sunny weekday morning, I was delivering a barn to a man who lived in a small house next to a main road that lacked a street sign. When I say "main road," I still mean out in the country, but it was pretty much the only road out there, hence the significance. Anyway, this guy's little house was approximately 50 feet from the road, and he had a short gravel driveway with a gentle slope above the street, alongside a big tree. The other side of the road was a steep drop-off into a field below. I blocked traffic on the narrow road as I pulled my truck perpendicular to the man's house, then parallel to the

---

[1] DiFranco, Ani. "Pixie." *Little Plastic Castle*. New York: Righteous Babe Records, 1998.

road, wheels half on pavement, half on the grassy slope below the other side of the street. Attempting to jackknife the trailer backwards into a 90-degree turn without jackknifing it too far, I needed to back the barn up the perpendicular driveway alongside the tree and place it next to the little house, also facing the road. A short, scruffy, smiling man in his mid-30s wore jeans, a Miller beer cap, work boots and a stained white T-shirt. He emerged from the house sipping a tall, 24-ounce breakfast—*the champagne of beers*—encouraging my efforts to back up the barn with the usual

"Cut 'er this way! Cut 'er that way!" accompanied by furious, unintelligible hand motions, squirting High Life here and there from his can like a drunken grade school crossing guard. If he'd had a whistle, he'd have been letting loose.

"How you doin' man?" he said after I got the barn in place and jumped out of the truck. "You want a beer, man? I got plenty more 'a them cold ones where this come from."

"Wish I could, sir. Thanks though."

"Well suit yerself. Yuhssee, this here barn's fer my re-tard brother. He cain't hardly do shit fer himself—seein' as how he's a re-tard an' all—so I'm the one's takin' care of him. Momma an' Dad said they's tard 'a both of us livin' in the house with them 'an said we better get a barn fer my brother. This way he's close ta home an' I kin help out when he needs it. He's a re-tard. Did I mention 'at? We'll cut him some holes fer a towlet an' all."

I got to work leveling the barn while the man regaled me with stories about his many adventures with his brother and how nice it would be to move him into the barn in the driveway. Suddenly a brown UPS truck pulled to the side of the road in front of the house. At this point the man began to jump up and down with glee, spilling his beer, knocking his hat from his head, slipping on the gravel and almost falling on his face with delight.

"Aw hell yeah! My Nigh-kees! My Nigh-kees is here! You don't need no new *Nigh-kees*, do ya dude?"

"Uh, no thanks. I'm good."

The man scrambled down the steep front yard to accept the package and returned shortly with an enormous cardboard box balanced precariously over one shoulder. I estimated it could probably contain 20 or so boxes of new Nike shoes. As I continued to finish my work around the edges of his barn, I learned of the man's sales scheme:

"You see now, most a' them uther eedjuts around here like's 'em new Nigh-kees whenever they kin' git 'em, and 'at store down there don't sell shit. I get ta thinkin' I could order me some a' them Nigh-kees myself an' jack 'at price up all I want, sell 'em around here to whoever needs 'em. I sell out fast, man. Fast. Shit sells better than weed, an' sometimes I even trade up for a bag or two. You don't need no weed, do you?"

"Nah, thanks. I'm good."

* * *

Aside from the difficulty I regularly encountered because of missing street signs and inadequate directions, even more amazing was the number of customers who couldn't clearly explain where they lived, even after I got them on the phone.

"You sound like you ain't from around here. Izzat rhyte? You know 'at big-ass tree over by 'at old fence up by the old Gooch place? Down past 'at holler where the Burger Barn use tuh set? You know, turn on down by the first trailer 'an then…what? Naw, there ain't no street signs. Oh, left. No, right. I mean left. Yep. Turn left 'at the first trailer after 'at old fence and the big stump. Sorry."

For this reason, I preferred MFS to GPS. Anytime I could arrange for a Meet & Follow Situation, I went for it. Global Positioning Systems were tried by a few drivers but often failed because many unmarked "streets" we delivered to were not recognized by Google Earth or Garmin or Magellan or TomTom, or anyone other than the locals who frequented them. Sometimes they were paved, sometimes not. Often they were an uneven, treacherous hybrid consisting of equal parts asphalt, gravel, dirt, mud, trenches, potholes, partially decomposed fast-food trash, crushed Bud Light or Natural Light Ice cans, roadkill, deer guts and exposed roots. At times there was room for two vehicles to pass each other when going in opposite directions, but frequently there was not. This made it particularly fun to drive a 12- or 14-foot-wide barn through these narrow areas, crashing through overhanging limbs, dragging the tires of my trailer off the sides of the road and into the ruts and potholes, hoping not to encounter anyone coming from the other direction, particularly anyone excessively fast and stupid.

On another occasion, I had plans to move a barn for a guy who already owned the barn. He told me he wanted to move the building 20 miles. We agreed on a place and time and price. I arrived, met the guy and loaded his barn. I was to follow him to the new destination. This is one reason I preferred moves, as opposed to deliveries or repos: when you are following the customer, it's harder to get lost. Following the man in his little blue truck, we pass the 20-mile mark (I'm clocking it on the odometer). I'm trying to pick up the local NPR affiliate so I can catch the Unger Report, which is often pretty damn funny, but the station keeps cutting in and out due to my extreme (and routine) middle-of-nowhere situation. My phone vibrates; I take it from my pocket, and the man I'm following says something I can't make out, except to note that there is some problem with the delivery site and that we are about to lose cell phone reception. The already poor reception is indeed lost entirely. I continue following.

I figure we'll be there soon. I figure maybe his estimate of 20 miles was a little off, and that it would be more like 24 or 25 miles. Wrong. It was 42. Not sure how that happened, but I was pissed. This wasn't the only customer I'd scheduled for the day, and I had already spent a lot longer at it than I had anticipated. We get to the delivery site, and the man stops in the driveway, leaving me behind, blocking most of the road. I turn on my emergency flashers and wait as he walks down the drive. Cars plow through lawns on either side of me, weaving around mailboxes in the grass of front yards around me as I wait, giving everyone the SRW or Southern Road Wave, which consists of lifting an index finger in recognition when gripping the steering wheel as they pass. A barely perceptible nod of the head is a suitable accompaniment to the SRW, albeit optional. Some return the gesture; others shake their heads in frustration or respond with the ESD or Eat Shit and Die look, or even, on occasion, the FUMF (Fuck You Motherfucker) look and gesture combination. The man returns shortly thereafter and walks to my window saying,

"I've got some bad news. The roofers are working on the roof of the house today, and they parked one of their trucks right where that barn you've got needs to sit. Looks like they've all gone to lunch and left their truck right there in the way, and to top it all off, it's got a damn flat tire. I guess all we can do is wait."

I wondered why this guy didn't plan a little better for the day, time and spot that *he* picked.

"I've got some bad news too," I said.

I went on to tell him that I had quoted him a price based on less than half the actual distance I had moved the barn, based on what he had told me in our first conversation. Not only had he shorted me on mileage, but he wasn't the only delivery scheduled for the day. Though he initially disagreed, he was reasonable, soon apologized and promised to "set things straight" with me. I must give this man credit for being an exceptional customer because not only was he a rational and fair man with a firm grasp of the reality of the situation, he immediately decided to put the barn in a different place rather than deal with or wait for the roofers, and I quickly got to work unloading and leveling his barn. He agreed to pay what was actually owed and sent me on my way with a sizable tip and a local restaurant recommendation. These stories don't always end in chaos.

Most barn customers didn't seem to feel out of place on their home turf, like I did when I entered their unpredictable properties for dicey and dubious barn adventures upon delivery. Of course most people are content and relaxed when they are in or around their homes, but some of these customers were excessively relaxed. I once delivered a barn to a man who was as comfortable in his environment as any stranger I had ever encountered on a barn delivery. So comfortable, in fact, that he greeted me in his underwear, drunk.

Just as the sun was slipping behind a mountain on the horizon, I crested the hill in front of his property and could see his steel-gray trailer at the top of a long, steep gravel drive. The tidy mobile home stood out against the green backdrop of the tree-lined slope that framed it. I remember how beautiful the deepening amber sunset looked across the field in front of the property. I turned into the driveway, shifted into four-wheel drive and began the slow creep up the hill, gravel shifting under the tires and shooting out from beneath the truck on both sides. Immediately a man appeared, launching out from behind his mobile home on a four-wheeled all-terrain vehicle. All I could do was stop and watch. The inebriated pilot of the mudslinging machine careened from one side of the driveway to the other, zooming toward me down the steep hill at an amazing rate of speed. Barely able to maintain his grasp on the handlebars, the man bounced wildly up and down on the seat as his ATV catapulted him toward me. He arrived in front of my truck and immediately spun in a circle, spinning tires, launching a sheet of gravel at me as Misty had done, shouting

"YEEEHAAWWW!" as you might have guessed, followed by

"FOLLER MEEEEE—YUH!" (the "yuh" at the end reminding me of James Hetfield).

Before the man had a chance to head back up the hill, I got a good look. He was 40-something, slender, hairy but darkly tanned from head to toe, with a Magnum P.I. mustache, a green NASCAR cap, mirrored sunglasses, a gold necklace and a pair of men's black bikini briefs. Maybe it was a Speedo, but it was all he wore. He stood up, jerking the throttle with one hand and taking a pull from a Bud Light long neck with the other, roaring back up the hill. I followed him with my truck, trailer and his barn, and the man pointed to the area where he wanted the barn to go. He didn't seem to have any intention of talking to me about anything, because as soon as I nodded in agreement, he went right back to tearing back and forth around the property on the ATV, standing up most of the time, kicking up dust and gravel as he spun in circles, screaming nonsense. I decided the best plan was to take advantage of the rapidly diminishing daylight and the man's distraction and get the barn in place, level it and get the hell out of there. I got the truck into position and unloaded the barn, all the while keeping an eye on the man who seemed to be quite oblivious to me or to my work, content and happy to entertain himself. After the barn was on the ground and I had started leveling it, I noticed that the enthusiastic new barn-renter, mumbling to himself and stumbling off the ATV, was headed in my direction, wasted.

"Getcha one'nem beers, why don'cha?" tumbled out of his mouth beneath the 80's 'stache.

"I wish I could, sir, but thanks anyway,"

It was getting dark now, and I could tell he was in the mood to socialize.

"Whaaa? Y'all cain't drank no beers on'a job?"

He smiled a crooked grin and took a pull from a freshly opened bottle. I said something about making it home for dinner, and he talked about how great a cook his wife was and invited me to stay and eat, and I politely declined. Sure, dinner sounded good, but I had a long drive ahead to get home to my own wife, my own dinner, my own beer. He stumbled over to the back porch of his trailer to get another bottle, and when I next looked in his direction, there he was, black bikini briefs pulled down, taking a piss right off the porch and into the yard. He came back over and tried again to get me to drink a beer and stay for dinner, but I said my thanks and was on my way. Reflecting on it later, I was struck by the childlike enthusiasm in this man. Barn delivery day was clearly a celebratory event. The recipient had a healthy supply of his choice of long-neck bottled domestic corporate swill, his cop shades, his four-wheeler, his favorite NASCAR hat and bikini-brief combo, and he was giddy like a kid on Christmas morning. Inexplicably it reminded me of one holiday when I was a little kid; I was so happy to open a gift package containing a Transformers Optimus Prime action figure that I did a backwards somersault.

Speaking of NASCAR, I'm no race fan—I've never been to one—but the idea of watching incredibly loud cars drive around in circles hundreds of times for hours (*Here they go around to the left! They're turning left again!*) just doesn't do it for me. Sitting on bleachers under a burning sun with ear plugs under a shower of hot rubber dust that's collecting in my $10 watery lager as I scream at a friend sitting next to me over the din of 50 racecar engines and an announcer describing the next left turn to me sounds about as fun as being subjected to Count Rugen's torture machine in *The Princess Bride*. Anyway, I'm told that a single racecar can go through 40 tires in one NASCAR race. I couldn't compete with that level of genocidal rubber slaughter, but my tires did tend to take a beating during my tenure as a barn hauler; mine were super thick and steel-belted, as opposed to NASCAR tires, which are merely a quarter of an inch of thin rubber because of the immense heat generated on the track. However, dragging tires sideways on pavement with my trailer when tying the rig in knots to try and complete an impossible delivery and pulling them through all kinds of crazy junk in the woods and trailer parks caused me many puncture wounds and blowouts, some more memorable than others.

I once was heading down the interstate at a steady 70 miles an hour with a full load of barns when a heavyset bald man in a Cadillac drove up beside me and started waving his arms frantically. I checked my mirrors, and all seemed well. Maybe he was drunk, or just pissed off at having to share the road with an oversize-load-bearing truck, as plenty of frustrated drivers had made clear to me with their ESD and FUMF looks and gestures in the past. Probably he was some freak who wanted me to pull over so he could ask inane questions about the barns. This too had happened. I didn't have time for such foolishness, and I was not about to pull over so some guy could shop. Then I remembered the scene from *Planes, Trains and*

Automobiles when a disoriented John Candy and dozing Steve Martin are driving the wrong way down an interstate at night. A couple flags them down from their car across the median and yells,

"You're going the wrong way! You're going to kill someone!"

Candy looks over from the driver's seat at Martin and says:

"Ah, they're drunk. How would *they* know where we're going?"[2]

Martin nods sleepily in agreement, and the two men continue ahead into the path of two speeding 18-wheelers, Martin hallucinating Candy-as-Satan next to him, cackling maniacally as he drives them both to hell…and then their car burns up.

Maybe I should pull over, I reconsidered as Cadillac Man shook his head and sped away. I got to the next-closest rest area, parked and jumped out for a look. One tire on the driver's side of the trailer was almost completely gone. There were blackened marks on the barn above it and scorch marks on the tire behind it, and it was nothing but a shredded, smoldering piece of ruined rubber, melted like chocolate on the axle. I was pretty lucky that the flaming tire of madness didn't set the whole rig on fire. If the barn had caught, I would have been in for a real adventure. Thanks, Cadillac Man, wherever you are.

The rest of my day was spent waiting on a ride and then waiting for repairs at the closest garage, as the steel bearings within the hub of the trailer's axle had liquefied and fused together in the superheated core of the flaming wheel. Serious repairs were in order, along with that new tire.

On another memorable occasion, I had noticed earlier in the afternoon that one of my trailer tires was loose. I tightened it with an impact wrench and went on with my day, though I did notice that some of the threads on the axle bolts had somehow become damaged, but the wrench worked fine, and the wheel seemed secure, so I thought I would be okay to finish the day's work. I made a mental note to take the truck back

---

2 *Planes, Trains and Automobiles.* Dir. John Hughes. Perf. Steve Martin, John Candy. Paramount Pictures, 1987.

HARDBARNED!
One Man's Quest for Meaningful Work in the American South

to Mitch's house that night for repairs. Everything worked fine all day, but on my way home, coming down a steep mountain interstate around 60 miles an hour in the right lane with an empty trailer, I heard a dull thud behind me. I looked back just in time to see the trailer wheel sail high into the air, bounce against the concrete divider in the center of the four-lane freeway ahead and to my left, then launch itself upward again, its trajectory crossing back over and above to my right. My heart seizing in my chest, I pulled over as quickly as I could, losing sight of the flying torpedo of death as it soared back over my lane, the truck, the shoulder of the road and into the dense woods below. My greatest fear—a little car with a huge trailer tire smashed through its windshield—was avoided. I took a few necessary moments to sit and silently process what had just happened and focus on slowing my heart rate. Crisis averted, I tried to relax and drove home, short one wheel.

Realizing that this was yet another close call that this time could have actually killed people, I started thinking more about walking away from the job. The stress of being saddled by student loans for an education I could not manage to make use of to earn a living was one thing, but I didn't need this kind of stress in my life. I couldn't imagine what I would have felt like if that wheel had hurt someone. I wanted a way out of barn hauling more than ever. Still, nobody seemed to have the slightest interest in responding to my continual barrage of applications for writing jobs, and by this time I had started to apply for other kinds of more predictable delivery and service jobs again. Maybe I could deliver pizza or laundry or watermelons. I could handle the pay cut and stress reduction of working at a bookstore. That would be pretty cool. I'd rather be surrounded by books every day than barns. Surely I could find something. Any alternative was starting to sound good; I had passed a tipping point of sorts, and barns were officially on their way out of my life. At least that was what I tried to tell myself.

Back to the Beach: Bikinis and Hurricanes, Karaoke and Dishes

> *There is something even more central than job security that white-collar corporate workers lack—and that is dignity...what sets [them] apart and leaves them so vulnerable is the requirement that they identify, absolutely and unreservedly, with their employers...the CEO may be a fool; the company's behavior may be borderline criminal—and still you are required to serve unstintingly and without the slightest question.*[1]
>
> —Barbara Ehrenreich

After my first year of college, in May of 1996, I returned to the same beach with the same girlfriend to work the same restaurant and retail jobs, more or less, but as I said, the jobs didn't really matter. Lena and I had seen each other periodically over the course of the school year, but now we were together at the beach again, which was all that mattered. Though Kayla elected to return with us, this time the three of us had a different house in another neighborhood with a new set of roommates. The schedule most of us were on again allowed for late nights, late mornings, early afternoons on the beach and more of the same after working a three-to-11PM shift most nights.

Kayla followed our Saab and Volvo caravan to the beach again in her pink Ford Probe, and again she had a radically different schedule than the rest of us, working as a lifeguard at the far end of the beach and getting up early in the morning. She'd usually get home from work in the late afternoon when the rest of us were about ready to head to our restaurant jobs, and as in the previous summer, we didn't see her all that much, but when she was around, she made sure to make an impression. Kayla was a sweet kid, but she was an exhibitionist at heart, eager for attention. With her pink car and provocative pout, she liked to strike sultry poses in beach photos

---

1 Ehrenreich, Barbara. *Bait and Switch: The (Futile) Pursuit of the American Dream.* New York: Owl Books, 2005.

and hung a black leather whip on the wall of the bedroom she shared with another Brown Horse alumnus named Rachel who tagged along with us that summer. We didn't ask Kayla about her whip. We didn't have to. Buffed lifeguard beefcakes from the covers of romance novels would regularly show up at our beach house at random hours, wearing nothing but tiny red shorts, their long brown hair flowing in the wind, unable or uninterested in conversing beyond the requisite two-syllable utterance,

"KAY-LUH?" when we'd answer the door.

A veritable cornucopia of unintelligible yet multisyllabic utterances pulsed from Kayla's upstairs bedroom when such visitors were present, so we usually just left the house when Fabio the lifeguard or one of his heavily muscled friends arrived for a visit.

This time, I applied for work at an Italian restaurant. I had server experience. I was good with people. I knew how to make pesto. Maybe I could even learn Neil's art of the tableside Caesar salad, I thought. I shouldn't have gotten my hopes up. I was hired on as a server but was immediately banished to the dishwasher station.

"Ees jest for leetle while" was what I kept hearing from the mustachioed owner with hairy Popeye forearms who'd agreed to hire me to wait tables and immediately assigned me to the kitchen where I did nothing but wash dishes, scalding my arms and hands, again finding myself miserable and alone in the sloppy, steam-filled kitchen. After two weeks and more of the same after reminding the owner of our original agreement, I walked out and didn't come back.

That summer, I learned another important lesson about working. I learned that you can't please everybody, no matter how hard you work, and that a lot of times a selfless, mindless, opinionless robot can be an ideal employee in the eyes of many employers. After leaving the Italian restaurant, I was hired promptly at Brisco's, a sleazy little karaoke/sports bar/restaurant on the beach. Luckily for me, my roommate Christy was a bartender there, and he recommended me enthusiastically to Erica, the manager.

HARDBARNED!
One Man's Quest for Meaningful Work in the American South

Christy reminded me of the Ram Man action figure and character from the *Masters of The Universe* line of toys and cartoon show. Everybody liked him—the huge, friendly weightlifting dude with the effeminate name—so I was hoping that his vote of confidence would be the clincher. After trying my best to convince Erica that I was worthy of her restaurant during the interview, I had left, unsure of whether or not my impression was even moderately impressive. Sure, I had worked at several restaurants in the past, and I did have good references, and come on, a monkey could bus tables. Yet I knew Erica saw me as just another student looking for a summer job that he probably wouldn't take too seriously. She was right about that, but I meant what I said. I wasn't looking for a career as a busboy, but I always intended to work hard at whatever task I managed to get paid for, at the beach or anywhere else, but don't hire me to wait tables and expect me to be a dishwasher.

Before the tall blonde had a chance to greet me from behind the counter at Brisco's, a rainbow-colored parrot was screeching,

"Hello! Hello!"

Elaborate aquariums lined two sides of the bar, but what immediately drew my attention was the enormous green iguana in a refrigerator-sized box, lounging on a tree trunk behind thick glass, the size of a large dog. I learned later that this was Brisco, the restaurant's namesake, whose likeness appeared on all the T-shirts as well. The familiar coastal aromas of fried seafood, cocoa butter, cigarettes and beer gently reminded me of why I had come. Oh yeah! A job. I barely even noticed the overweight, lobster-colored woman stumbling sloppily through "Margaritaville" with a microphone and a beer. Brisco's refrigerator-sized, clear plastic box with a tree limb and a heat lamp in the front lobby looked like a prison to me. What a horrible fate for such a spectacular creature, I thought.

This time they didn't need any servers, but they needed a busboy, so I went for it, on the explicitly expressed condition that I would not be demoted to dishwasher. By this point I was a restaurant veteran and knew the drill. I was perfectly accustomed to the eccentricities of restaurant managers, and I had been warned about Erica. Most supervisors are driven, and many are difficult; some can be vicious. I remember my new co-worker Steve saying,

"If you can get along with Erica, you'll be fine. Just don't cross her."

The first time I met Erica, I knew that somehow, whether I wanted to or not, I'd be crossing her. She walked up with a definite air of superiority. She looked me up and down with a skeptic's eye for defect, obviously wondering what use I might be. She surprised me with a smile and I then realized she was actually pretty, her middle-aged face framed with long curly blond hair. She meant business though, and I could tell. Her face was pinched with deep lines of concentration or irritability, and she radiated a sense of complete control. I knew that this was her show, and I was definitely an outsider, not yet even considered a rookie. Seriously though—I had applied for a job that essentially consisted of wiping tables down with a rag—what could possibly be so tough for her to decide? I went home and waited to hear back from Erica. To my surprise, Christy came home a couple days later with a message from her. I was to come in to work the next afternoon.

Great, I thought, she liked me. I showed up and was given a Brisco's was told I would have to pay for later, and I was promptly been the point of the trip out there? Was she just was the boss, a not-too-subtle control trip? shift would be. My duties were to bus to get bread for guests, and to run and mop the kitchen at the end her restaurants, but before I

kid, you are simply at the short end of the stick, can't really get shafted into a ated job in the business, and I not a team player or willing to be

131

helpful or flexible. I understand what is involved in running a successful business, especially a restaurant. Teamwork is essential, and if you don't help each other out, everything comes crashing down. I didn't mind filling in for dishwashers from time to time at the other restaurants but had reached the point where I was no longer willing to be demoted into the full-time job of the dishwasher.

When I followed Erica into her office on that first day at Brisco's, I knew just what I would be willing to do and what I would not. I made it crystal clear to her that I was there to bus tables, and that I would perform that job to the best of my abilities; I would do it cheerfully and with great care. I also made it perfectly clear that I did not intend to be her dishwasher. I even related some of my unpleasant past experiences at other restaurants, and I thought that she was listening to me, until I heard,

"Would you be willing to fill in for a dishwasher sometime, if it is necessary? Everyone pitches in around here."

This was not what I wanted to hear, but I considered the money I would make, and I reluctantly said yes, that I would fill in if there was no one else for the job and it was absolutely necessary, but only a couple of times, and only in emergencies. I was very explicit in my intention to be a busser, to do the best possible job bussing tables that I could, and that was not interested in a dishwashing job. Erica agreed and hired me. I some kind of monkey. I did a fantastic job, and I was fast, *really* fa skills had been honed back home at the Brown Horse, and I was sti game. Servers were impressed and the word got back to Erica qui the best busser Brisco's had ever seen, and they let me know i appreciated among the staff, and Erica even told me that she doing a good job. Cool, I thought. I'm finally breaking th managerial persona. Maybe there's a real person in ther

The rest of the staff was easy to work with, that Erica was pretty much the pure personificatio she wasn't around very often, and most of us b there. Each staff member helped out everyone

Back to the Beach: Bikinis and Hurricanes, Karaoke and Dishes

Erica was right, there was a real team spirit at this little tourist trap. We were all aligned against the manager, united in our mutual dislike for her pettiness. We knew we did a great job, but we were all just kids at the beach, looking forward to the keg party almost every night somewhere on the beach after work. Every night around closing time, a tired old drunk would take the stage and perform her rendition of what I already thought of as the worst song of all time: 4 Non-Blondes' "What's Up?" I had never imagined that the song with the "what's going on" chorus could possibly get any worse. Turns out I was wrong. As Colonel Kurtz put it,

"The horror…the horror."[2]

I spent most of the summer at Brisco's, happily bussing tables until I was again railroaded into becoming a dishwasher. After a few weeks of work, it happened. Erica asked if I could do dishes for a single night. Reluctantly, I said that I would. Of course, one night became two, two became three, and before I knew it I was washing dishes almost as much as I was bussing tables. I felt used, abused and more than a little stupid for having agreed to fill in at all in the first place. At this point, weighing my options was the next step. I made good money when I bussed tables, but I hated the dish trap with a passion. I pitched in a few times to help out as I had agreed to, but I was so angry at having been forced into it that I told Erica one night after a shift. Covered in muck, shoes and socks soaking wet from dishwater, hands raw and worn, I knocked on Erica's door in the gloomy darkness beneath Brisco's kitchen. I think she saw it coming. Looking up at me with accusatory eyes from her paperwork, she knew exactly what I was going to say.

"What do you need, Driver?" she snapped.

I told her exactly what I felt. I reminded her of how she hired me to be a busser, not a dishwasher. I pointed out the skill and efficiency with which I performed my bussing duties, and the fact that all of the servers

---

2 *Apocalypse Now*. Dir. Francis Ford Coppola. Perf. Marlon Brando. American Zoetrope, 1979.

thought that I was the best busser that had ever worked at Brisco's. I told her how I didn't mind doing this crummy job if it was absolutely necessary—if the dishwasher was sick or something. I really liked the usual dishwasher; he was a great guy, but I wasn't going to take over his job. This was it. I gave her a choice:

"Let me bus tables, and I will do a great job, or let me go."

"If you are told to wash dishes, around here, you will shut up and wash dishes."

"You hired me to bus tables."

"I just don't think I want to deal with you anymore."

"That's fine," I replied, literally throwing in the towel as I left her office for the last time.

* * *

Unsure of what to do next and in need of some beach income to help me through the rest of the summer, I was offered part-time employment by a friend of Lena's who owned a bikini store at a local shopping center. One of her girls had left the job, and she needed someone to cover the day shift a few days a week. Hey, it was retail—it was bikinis—how bad could it be?

What might sound awesome to the average guy about working in a bikini shop is not exactly correct, and whatever another guy might dread about it isn't quite what he'd expect either. Yes, there were plenty of attractive women at the beach who came into the store to try on bikinis. This of course was impossible to ignore. Many of them were surprised to see a 19-year-old male keeping shop, but most of them didn't mind. Not all of the women who shopped for bikinis were necessarily women who should have seriously considered *wearing* bikinis, however; and fairly often these women would ask my "professional" opinion on the suits that they were trying on. I tried to be kind. Guys would come in with their girlfriends and either eye me suspiciously from the other side of the room or walk right up to me, slap me on the back, and congratulate me on scoring the greatest job known to man. Ultimately, I felt a little silly working in the bikini shop; the girl who had worked there returned, and I decided I wanted to do something a little more physically active. I returned to work again for my friend Joey who owned the souvenir shop on the beach and soon found myself outside in the sun on a ladder again, scraping paint chips into my eyes. I missed Ernie.

Hurricane season was upon us, and our beach store was about 50 yards from the Atlantic Ocean. I didn't have much time to finish painting the building before Hurricane Bertha began tearing her way toward the Outer Banks, and we scrambled to board up the windows and prepare for the worst. A zoomed-in close-up of my hands putting screws into the plywood boards over the shop's front windows made it onto the CBS Evening News with Dan Rather, though no agents contacted me afterwards, and unfortunately for me (and for George Costanza), a lucrative hand-modeling career did not materialize.

Lena and I argued over whether to heed the mandatory evacuation from the barrier island with all the tourons (what the locals called tourists, even though technically we were neither locals nor tourists), but Lena won the argument, and we ended up having a hurricane party with all the other dumb kids who were riding out the hurricane at the beach with kegs of beer, tanks of nitrous oxide and bags of weed. As I remember, it was a pretty great party. It rained hard and was super windy but otherwise no big deal. The next day, my roommates and I spent several hours picking up, accumulating huge trash bags full of cups, cans, bottles, fast food containers, and cigarette packages, cleaning the inside and outside of the house. The shop I worked in survived unscathed as well, except for the huge sign out front that had been twisted and smashed like so many beer cans in the back yard.

My second and final summer on the Outer Banks went out with a bang. For a surprise celebration of my 20th birthday, Lena and two of our friends—the married owners of the beach store and bikini shop—took us on a sunset cruise on a beautiful work of art, a 60-foot wooden sailboat. We drank red wine, nibbled birthday cake and watched the sun drop across the shore, its brilliant red colors reflected on the gentle waves. The end of a season was upon us, and it was time to head back to school for my sophomore year, where I hoped to learn more about how to turn my interest in the recording industry into a satisfying career in audio engineering.

Back to the Beach: Bikinis and Hurricanes, Karaoke and Dishes

Barn Repos, Battle Axes, Meemaw and Muumuus

If I show up at your door, chances are you did something to bring me there.[1]
—Martin Blank

Some say the most dreaded aspect of barn hauling is the repo. It was often amazing to witness the lengths that people would go to prevent repossession of a barn full of useless junk. An entirely different animal from deliveries, unpredictable and occasionally exciting, a repossession can often lead to outrageous frustration, like when a buddy of mine was trying to repo a barn in the rain and was stuck in the mud for hours, or when he went on a repo and was physically threatened by an 80-year-old man in overalls who appeared to be concealing a firearm, or when a man dug huge trenches around a 12X30 barn that he knew was up for repo, creating an actual moat, so that our trucks could not reach it. When I couldn't get a 12X20 barn I was repossessing through the thick tangle of trees on either side of a long road in front of the house I was removing it from, I had to drag the thing on the ground for a couple hundred yards to prevent the trees from tearing off the barn's roof. People will chain vicious dogs to barns up for repo. The moat guy did this too. I guess he couldn't find a dragon.

People will nail makeshift walls to the sides of a barn with whatever materials they have in the hopes of creating the impression that a barn has become part of another structure in the landscape and thereby avoiding

---

1 *Grosse Pointe Blank*. Dir. George Armitage. Perf. John Cusack. Caravan/Hollywood Pictures, 1997.

repossession, but these add-ons just came crashing down into a pile of scattered junk when I dragged their barns away. They will park an armada of cars, boats and recreational vehicles around the barn, attempting to create an impenetrable defensive perimeter to avoid repossession. Sometimes this works.

Repossessions were classified by those of us in Barn Land as either a "turn-in" or a "sneak attack." When people decide they don't need or can't pay for the barn anymore, they call and request a turn-in. No big deal. They expect us to come and get it. However, this doesn't necessarily indicate that they will either A: clean out the barn or B: get all their broken-down vehicles and garbage out of our way so that we can actually load the barn and haul it away. A sneak attack is pretty self-explanatory but warranted only after many attempts to convince a customer to pay long-overdue barn bills have failed.

Once I was attempting a sneak attack and noticed that an old pickup truck was strategically parked so that I couldn't get my trailer near the front of it. I looked closer and spotted the keys in the ignition of the truck, though the doors were locked. I crept into the truck bed and looked around to see if any neighbors were watching as I pried open the sliding window in the pickup's rear windshield and squeezed through, turning on the engine and unleashing a spine-crushing blast of music from the stereo. I managed to turn it down, move the truck, grab the barn and get the hell out of there before anyone noticed or came after me.

Sometimes, as in situations like these, pulling off a challenging repo can bring a sneaky sense of satisfaction. Don't get me wrong here; there are many reasons to dislike the repo process, but it's part of the job. You can't sign up to haul barns and opt out of repos. I was talking to a nice Mennonite fellow on the builder's lot once who was interested in hauling barns for a living. He asked me several questions about the job, and I answered truthfully and in detail, including my frustrations with the job.

"You have an education, yes?"

I said that I did, and he made the following assertion without hesitation:

"I have an eighth-grade education. This job is perfect for me because *I have no ambition.*"

What could I say?

"Maybe you're right," I said with a sad smile.

He went on to ask me if I was required to repossess barns. I said yes, and he replied that he didn't think he'd be able to do that. I couldn't blame him. His reluctance to commit to a job that would require repos got me flipping through a mental catalog of my worst experiences on repo duty.

One crowning achievement in my personal chronicle of barntacular mishaps was definitely the time I became stuck in a concrete culvert in the front yard of the man whose barn I was trying to sneak away with. As I was attempting to repossess his barn, the angry, skinny old man sat on the front porch in his overalls and trucker hat, glaring at me with sunken cheeks, no visible teeth and a smoldering intensity, sipping an Old Milwaukee in the late morning sun.

Folks in Barn Land can get pretty territorial. Repos can be stressful enough when you're already trying to be as discreet as possible and avoid encounters with angry residents or neighbors, though discretion is often impossible when you show up with a huge diesel truck and trailer, fire up your lawnmower-loud winch engine and rip a gigantic building out of its resting place with heavy chains, often forcing furniture and all kinds of junk to come crashing down both inside and outside of the barn. If there are dogs in the vicinity, they are barking relentlessly. Neighbors are taking notice. Heads are turning. You tend to hope for the best and avoid human and animal contact as much as possible.

Sometimes you can sneak onto someone's property and get away clean; however, showing up in a backwoods rural area to see a seething barn customer already on his porch, visibly angry and drinking, tends to ratchet up the tension level. Getting stuck in his front yard while attempting to escape with his barn—which he claims is paid for—as he watches in fury and *then* having to approach him to *ask for his help* is in another category entirely.

I got out of the truck, sheepishly approached the man's porch and didn't say a word. His screaming diatribe began well before I was in range of his scattershot spittle, but I slowed my approach to a halt just out of range and just let him get it all out. Most of his complaints were focused on the barn rental company and his assertion that those running it had

"done got they gotdamn munny!"

As I gently asserted that no, the company had sent several letters and made several phone calls due to the customer's unpaid rental agreement, he shook his head repeatedly and yelled

"Naw! Naw! Naw! Naw! Naw! Naw!" until I realized the futility of my reasoning and stopped talking.

The guy was incensed, and now I was trapped in his yard. Incredibly, he just happened to be a tow truck driver and had a truck on the premises. I didn't even have to ask for help. He knew that in order to get rid of me, he'd have to help me out of the culvert and assist me in my efforts to repossess his barn. He started moving his truck into place without even a suggestion from me, and his screaming diatribe never ceased. The only problem was that his tow truck was a rusty bag of bolts from a bygone era, and the weight of my much newer and much heavier truck snapped his winch cable easily.

And thus he rained more curses down upon me, his toothless jaw yammering at an unnatural distance up and down, his lips loose, spittle exploding from his face, his floppy jowls reminding me of the slobbering dog in *Turner & Hooch*. I shrugged my shoulders. His second winch cable did the trick, and I retreated with a wave and a word of thanks.

If I showed up at someone's home to repo a barn, it should never have been a surprise. Fair warning was given. Notices were mailed. Phone calls were made. The customer knew that he or she had been behind in

HARDBARNED!
One Man's Quest for Meaningful Work in the American South

payments for a number of months, and that someone was coming to take the barn away. This doesn't mean I looked forward to the process or wanted to be involved in any way at all, but I needed my job and did what I had to do to keep it. I felt like I was forced to play the title role written for a character trapped in some alternate universe, and the portal leading back to reality was slowly closing in without me, but I could never reach it.

Sometimes it was like an out-of-body experience, particularly on brutally hot summer afternoons. I would look down at my barn-hauling self from another perspective, floating above in the shimmering heat waves and not recognizing myself because surely…that sweaty guy down there on his knees in the mud and chicken shit, struggling with the barn and the jack and the chains, rushing to sneak away with the building before the neighbors noticed, between the barking pit bulls and snapping tree limbs and screaming rednecks…he couldn't be me…could he? Wait a second, he *was* me. I was the guy who joked around with little kids who liked to watch me delivering barns, telling them to make sure they went to college, so they wouldn't have to do *this* for a living. The problem was that I was the only one who got the joke. College had not provided me with any golden key to anything. It had nothing to do with barn hauling.

As far as I knew, I was trapped in Barn Land, and continuing with the job meant I had to do repos, like it or not, but something about the situation got my adrenaline pumping. Maybe it was because there was an implicit threat of physical violence or action-packed confrontation on every repo, though no one ever attacked me with anything other than curse words and threats to call the cops or the husband or the neighbor Billy Ray, whoever he was. Maybe it was because I had finally accepted that I was trapped in the job, and that if I had to do repos, I was going to try my damnedest to be successful at it. I hated it and yet still, I wanted to do it well. Part of that was borne of my respect for Mitch, my desire to be a good employee, and my work ethic, which dictates that if I'm getting paid to do something, I need to make my best effort to do it well. Though I didn't fully approve of the predatory rent-to-own pricing scheme, it made sense that if you didn't pay for something you'd signed a contract to pay for that it would be repossessed. It wasn't like we were evicting people from their homes. We were simply abbreviating their storage options for a bunch of old crap that they probably didn't need anyway.

One rotund fellow, a shorter version of George The Animal Steele or Frank Black from The Pixies came running out of his house as I ripped his 12X24 storage barn from its foundation, crushing the cinder blocks beneath it and ripping its aftermarket electrical wiring from the ground. Furious Francis stood fuming in his gray sweat pants, bare chest and shaved head. He threatened to call his buddy, a state trooper; Frank claimed this officer would come over right away and arrest me. I called Mitch on the cell phone and was instructed to ignore the threat, continue the repo or accept the amount of money that was overdue on the rental agreement in cash. Frank spewed venom for a while, as if I had anything to do with his circumstances, but he ended up handing me the wad of cash he owed the barn company. I hated being in that position.

The overwhelming majority of barn customers didn't think of purchasing their barn in terms of the total cost. They thought in terms of the monthly payments and whether they could afford them or not. The crushing reality of the 40-percent profit margin was lost on the average rent-to-own barn customer. I know this because I witnessed many of them telling their neighbors how much the barns cost them, solely in terms of monthly or even weekly payments. The neighbor never asked for the true cost, and it was instantly agreed that barns were "reasonable" or that the weekly price "ain't bad at all!" Though 40-percent interest is indeed steep and has definitely allowed a select few people in the barn business to make *very* comfortable livings, the math wasn't that difficult, even for someone who is terrible at it, like me.

Any customer who could afford it was welcome to save considerable money by purchasing a barn from the lot—free and clear and upfront—thus avoiding the interest rates, should they elect to do so. Few customers did so, as most couldn't afford to, and interest rates were high. Yet the terms were flexible. A customer could back out at any time with no late charges and no questions asked. All they had to do was communicate. I felt that someone who signed the contract but ignored the payments, failing to respond to multiple letters and phone calls from the rental company, deserved to have his barn taken away. It was that simple. After all, many opportunities were given for a person to make up late payments, and there were no punitive penalties whatsoever. All customers had to do—if they found themselves unable to afford the barn—was admit that they couldn't make the payments, clean out their barn and let us know it was ready for pickup, but instead they had to push their luck as far as it would go, ignoring the company's sustained attempts to communicate long enough for me to be sent out there, daring us to do what the contract they signed said we would do, defiantly leaving their buildings packed full of junk, and often lying to my face as if they knew nothing about the impending repossession.

I suppose the inherent irresponsibility and the assumption that repossession was an empty threat made my many forays onto private property to repossess barns both dreaded and exciting, somewhat scary yet also satisfying when completed successfully. I did my best to sneak in and out of a yard and disappear without discussion, conflict or confrontation with residents, neighbors, firearms or wildlife. On repo duty, I wasn't getting paid much unless I was hauling the barn away from the property, though Mitch was always good about compensating his drivers for wasted time.

It wasn't as though there were valuables involved. In nine of 10 repos, Bobby Q. Barn Customer's outside storage building was crammed full of useless crap. Maybe Bobby should have thought about getting rid of some of his junk. He could have unloaded it into his home, or under it, if it was mobile. He could even have dumped it in the ditch on the side of the road or over the edge of a cliff, which seemed to be a pretty common way to dispose of old appliances and trash in Barn Land. I've found all kinds of interesting things in repos. Once I found a collection of cheap ornamental swords: a jewel-encrusted katana, a towering broadsword, a flimsy-looking rapier, even a battle-axe! In the same barn, there were throwing stars, nunchucks, and *Magic The Gathering* trading cards. I took this barn from a trailer park while a scary-looking woman in a pastel muumuu stared at me with angry, bloodshot eyes from behind a screen door. It is extremely rare that I have any interest in keeping anything that I find in a barn, but I decided that my boss and co-worker should keep these weapons and display them at Mitch's headquarters as comical barn-hauling trophies. Unfortunately, the scumbag salesman at the barn lot in Springtownburg decided to claim them for himself, for reasons I cannot begin to fathom.

Other random items discovered regularly in barns I had repossessed included multiple collections of VHS movies, CDs and obsolete computer hardware and software; life-size cardboard sales display cutouts; boxes full of 80s hair-metal band cassettes, Barbie and Ken and their extended families, vehicles and accessories; Transformers, Go-Bots, G.I. Joes, He-Men, and their endless generic doppelgangers; Hooters playing cards, fireworks, live dogs, broken kitchen appliances and smelly furniture; nasty old clothes and dirty dishes, seasonal decorative items of monumental hideousness, grubby discarded car parts, filthy dishes, broken tools and refuse of every kind, organic and otherwise.

One repo began with kids of varying ages playing in the back yard, as I backed the long trailer to the edge of the lawn, near a closed gate that stood between the end of my trailer and the front of the barn I planned to extract from the premises. I got out of the truck and attempted to open an old metal gate. The kids started yelling for Meemaw. The gate was held together by bungee cords and rust. I shook it gently until it fell apart in my hands. I disconnected the broken doors, setting them aside carefully and getting back into the truck to begin backing into the yard. An old brown hound dog growled menacingly but did not move in my direction. Soon the whole family was on the back deck, staring silently as an eerie quiet descended with the sun.

No one spoke to me or left the back deck, and everyone settled into the darkness behind the house to watch the evening's entertainment from lawn chairs, something they were clearly expecting: The Repo Show, starring yours truly. Resting against the side of the barn, a long-discarded plastic swimming pool full of rancid green water sloshed over its sides, unleashing one hellacious odor of mildew and mold as I dragged it out of the way. I picked up the pace and quickly maneuvered the rig into place, attaching the chains to the front of the barn and dragging it up the hydraulically elevated trailer with the winch cable. It was getting dark now, and the golden blonde dye in Meemaw's cotton-candy hair glowed, backlit from the porch lamp behind her. From the backyard, the family looked like alien silhouettes with invisible features, animated outlines like the life-size cowboy cutouts leaning against so many country homes, their bandanas around their necks, their ten-gallon hats tipped.

My wife was riding with me on this particular occasion, responding to my periodic need for company and solidarity, a companion with whom I could share my struggles in real time, somehow validating the spectacle that was daily barn hauling. Sometimes I just needed a witness to the insanity. Normally at this point in the day, I was thinking of four things: lovely wife, hot shower, hot meal, cold beer. With the wife already with me, these priorities were shuffled. This may have bumped cold beer to the top of the list.

In the dark now, I hastily engaged the loud gasoline engine that powered the trailer and winch and began dragging the barn toward the end of the trailer nearest the truck with the chain I had wrapped around the runners underneath the barn's front door. The bottom edge of the barn then proceeded to catch on the lip of the trailer, but I kept pulling with the winch, assuming that, as so often happened, the barn would pop up over the edge and smoothly drag itself into place. Because of the thick grass, dwindling daylight and the incline of the yard, I didn't notice that the edge of the trailer never touched the ground as it usually would on a relatively flat spot when fully extended, so when I kept pulling with the winch cable, I caused the chain to pull the front edge of the barn against the sharp edge on the far end of the trailer, thus ripping the bottom of the barn apart.

This was fantastic entertainment for Meemaw and the brood; I am about 20 miles out of town. We shook hands, and the next day we were winding down the country road toward the site in Harold's beat-up truck.

We spent the next several weeks together digging out the foundation for his house by hand, measuring depths and marking off sections with a laser level and string. I dug a lot of trenches, carried and cut a lot of wood, learned to use an acetylene torch to cut steel re-bar that would go into the concrete, and built the wooden forms with plywood and two-by-sixes. We didn't have a construction crew. It was just the two of us working on the extensive foundation for what would be a large, two-story house, so the work was tough and repetitive. I dug those trenches over and over again with pick axes and shovels because we could only go out to the property late in the afternoons and on weekends. When it rained, the trenches filled up with mud, so I dug them out all over again. And again. And again.

While working on the house, I also had an on-again off-again gig with Harold on various odd jobs at businesses and houses around town. I carried tools and held flashlights. I listened to stories, drank a few beers and sometimes worked my ass off. I learned a little about plumbing, carpentry, drywall, electricity and flooring with Harold. I also learned how to cut corners. Jobs didn't have to be completed perfectly with Harold, as long as they looked good enough and seemed to function. As Harold was fond of saying,

"This ain't no million-dollar home."

He knew how to do all kinds of things, which had impressed me to no end, but gradually I began to get the impression that Harold wouldn't ever admit that he didn't know how to do something if he were ever stumped. Instead, he'd act like he knew exactly how to proceed, improvise, hope for the best and argue to the death with the resulting unsatisfied customer if the work proved faulty.

"You ain't no country boy, I'll tell yuh that fer one thang."

This was another comment he often liked to direct toward me in a teasing way. He was right. I'd grown up in the South, but I was used to city life and had never really experienced a lot of what Harold had. We got along well, but his occasional racist jokes or meanness toward customers would bother me, and at first I'd speak up about it, but I learned soon enough to just let Harold be. Who did I think I was to try and enlighten him? Harold was my elder and set in his ways. He wasn't going to change because of some college city boy's speech in the truck. I had to take the good with the bad. I needed the money, generally enjoyed his company and felt like I was learning things. Besides, he was right. I weren't no country boy nohow. He also liked to say

"Life's a bitch 'an then ya die…or ya marry one."

It didn't make much sense grammatically, but I caught his drift. Harold was not above taking digs at his wife one moment and singing the singular importance of family above all else with the next. He was unhappy with his employer but happiest when he was working. He spoke highly of African-American and Mexican acquaintants but told racist jokes at their expense. He loved his family but seemed to feel more at home when he was away from them.

Though I despised many of his tendencies, I accepted these contradictions in his character and despite our differences appreciated the connection we shared. I was happy working outdoors with Harold. I loved to work hard and sweat, exercising under the sun. It reminded me a little bit of the beach. Overcast, rainy days always depressed me; I felt sluggish in the gray gloom, which made it harder for me to work. I told Harold that I had diagnosed myself with seasonal affective disorder, and he laughed at how I worked a lot harder than he did when the sun was beating down, but that he'd work circles around me when it was rainy or cloudy.

As we rode around in Harold's little beat-up truck, he'd entertain me with stories about growing up in Jacksonville, Florida and brawling at Lynyrd Skynyrd shows. He told me the stories behind the many scars he had accumulated over the years. Harold spoke of braving alligator-infested waters to hunt and catch huge catfish underwater with his bare hands and had seen a gator tear the scalp from a friend of his. I wouldn't have wanted to be on Harold's bad side. When he'd get into abusive arguments with people who had contracted him for work, I was surprised at first. Usually he'd been drinking—he never went anywhere without a half-case of Busch beer in the back, one can open between his legs, and a pint of Jim Beam under his seat. I usually looked the other way, but the drinking got worse, as did the quality of Harold's work and his moods. People noticed. Soon he was arguing sloppily, clearly drunk, with clients who had hired us, telling them (in their own homes) that they were "fuckin' idiots" who didn't know what they were talking about, and it was getting pretty embarrassing to be associated with him.

One day I went to the mall with Harold and wandered through the Sears tool department. After unleashing a slurred barrage of insults at the man behind the counter, he tried to pick a fistfight with the poor salesman because Sears didn't have a particular brand of lawnmower in stock. I decided then that maybe I didn't want to hang around Harold anymore. I wish I would have done more to help him, but I'm not sure what I could have done. I had long since learned that I couldn't change the man. He was who he was. I no longer lived near him, having moved in with Lena in an apartment of an old house in another part of town after she had graduated and moved to be with me, and eventually I stopped staying in touch with Harold. I did invite him over once when Lena and I had a keg party to celebrate moving in together. He showed up drunk and tried to pick fights with college kids half his age, hit on several of their girlfriends, got even more wasted, and knocked people over as he toppled into the bushes in the backyard to pass out until the next morning. Harold had a hard life, and I felt bad for him. I believed that deep down he had a good heart, and I wish I could have been a better friend to him. I heard that his wife died of cancer and that his kids grew up away from him after he lost custody, though I don't know for sure what happened to him. I haven't seen or heard from Harold in years, but I wish him well. We had some good times.

* * *

Still a full-time college student and in need of regular income, I was at a bonfire party soon after deciding to cut ties with Harold and learned of an opportunity to work as a valet, parking cars at various downtown restaurants and events in a nearby metro area. Thus began a four-year period of working off and on again for a guy named Patrick who basically put together a few wooden lock boxes to hold keys, hired a handful of college kids to work part-time, ordered a bunch of hideous XXL, bright bile-colored polo shirts with the company logo on the chest, and convinced several area restaurants to hire his valet service under a monthly contract. Multiplying these services with the addition of costly, intermittent private events and a steadily expanding roster of restaurant clients, it was truly a stroke of entrepreneurial genius.

Sometimes I'd work the private parties, and those gigs, while they were more work—I was constantly running back and forth from the parking lots or fields, fetching cars—were really the best moneymakers. Rich folks who lived in mansions on enormous plots of land would throw huge parties and hire the valet company to manage the looping stream of traffic arriving and departing from the party, which usually would last for several hours. We'd turn a front or a back lawn into a relatively well-organized parking lot and sprint back and forth to park another incoming car and grab the next outgoing one. We'd get a flat fee for working, plus tips from partygoers, and sometimes free catered food and a final tip from the host, if we were lucky. The majority of my time as a valet, however, was spent at restaurants.

During most shifts, I'd stand outside these restaurants during lunch or dinner shifts and read a book until people actually stopped and waited for me to help them get out of the car and park it for them. Sometimes homeless people would chat me up or demand money or mistake me for their long lost ex-husband and scream curses at me. Other times people would drive by and whistle or shout or even throw fast-food bags at me. It was amazing how often people's cars would line up, overwhelming me with business, especially considering that the parking lot was just around the corner at most of the dining establishments I stood in front of.

I guess people felt a sort of prestige when some kid in a stupid shirt parked their cars for them. I'd give them each a claim ticket, park the car and then run back to the front of the restaurant to either grab the next car or get back into my book. I was in another band at the time, so sometimes I'd use the time to write lyrics for songs. One day I was reading in front of a restaurant at the valet stand when Al Gore drove by with his entourage of block-long, bulletproof black limousines. One inconvenient truth was that those heavy limos probably got about seven miles to the gallon and spewed their carbon emissions all over the city, but perhaps these emissions were offset by the hundreds or thousands of cars that were not allowed to drive on the roped-off city streets when Mr. Gore was in town. Anyway, I'm glad he was around to spread the scientific truth in a region packed with climate-change deniers.

Years later, still stuck in Barn Land and unable to make productive use of my education, becoming borderline desperate for a real job but inspired by my grandfather's military service and the allure of government benefits and job security, I applied to the Secret Service. An old friend, former roommate and skateboard buddy had embarked on what has become a successful career in the uniformed division, but the Secret Service turned me down too. Just like the Naval Officer Candidate School did after seeing my test results. Sorry, Granddad. Too much math, I guess. Or maybe it was too much dope. I told the truth on the applications. I was no wasteoid but had definitely smoked some weed as a younger man, even though I hadn't touched the stuff for over a decade by the time I applied. At least the Secret Service and the Navy hadn't completely ignored my applications, like my local fire department and even Mr. Gore had. So much for public service. Now what?

The valet job paid eight bucks an hour, but only if I didn't make that in tips. Tips were unpredictable, as they usually are. Sometimes a guy in a Porsche would give me a buck, and the next guy in a piece of shit Nissan would give me $10. Once a famous NFL quarterback tipped me $50 to park his Lincoln Navigator, while a star running back gave me $20 to park his Mercedes. One extravagantly attired businessman, a regular customer at one of our best restaurants—a Japanese sushi bar and hibachi grill—owned several different but always new and meticulously detailed Corvettes. He was well known as a douchebag who liked to throw his money around, sometimes wildly, depending on his current mood, and many valets for our company did their best to suck up to him and give him special treatment. Sometimes it worked. He had been known to tip in the hundreds of dollars from time to time and nothing at all on others. Sometimes he wouldn't even bring a car but would arrive in a stretch limousine Hummer with 10 or 15 young women in sparkly short skirts and high heels, but I wasn't going to kiss his ring. I made it a point to treat him exactly like I treated every other customer and was friendly, prompt, respectful—Porsche or Yugo—and he didn't like it. I never got anything beyond $20 from the guy, but $20 (an insult in his mind, I think) was still a pretty damn good tip.

Depending on how amiable the management was at these places, I'd sometimes enjoy visiting with servers and staff. One maître d' for a five-star restaurant would yell at me for sitting down and studying when I had nothing to do and would try to get me to sweep the parking garage. Other times he was in a good mood and would ask me about how my classes were going while he took a smoke break. Valet parking itself seemed to me to be an inherently ridiculous extravagance anywhere, but it was even more so at this particular fancy-pants eatery because the entrance to the restaurant was *inside* a parking garage, *between* actual parking spaces. It was impossible to attend this restaurant without being surrounded by what Lena liked to call "rock star parking." Naturally I was required to block off all the most convenient, accessible spots with orange construction cones, so that no customer could actually park his or her own car.

I would walk to the driver's side of the incoming car, open the door, leave the car running while I moved one of the orange cones out of the way, get back into the car and park it in the spot as the customers walked a few steps to the door. It was snooty idiocy, but it was ritualized before I ever came along, and most of the customers seemed to understand and even appreciate the routine. It was my source of income, and I definitely felt out-of-place in the elite culture that created and accepted this grandstanding.

The rumor was that in order to maintain some recognized five-star rating, the restaurant was required to provide valet parking, as if parking has anything to do with the quality of a restaurant. In demonstration of this ridiculous policy, I was required to spend one New Year's Eve sitting in the back of a limo until 3AM with a friend and fellow valet, doing nothing but sitting there, keeping out of the cold due to the kindness of the driver who was also spending his New Year's Eve simply waiting to take care of the drunks as they filed out of the piano bar. The fact that we were there, available, doing nothing, maintained the five-star rating of this hardwood and bronze-laden bar featuring a silver-haired, polyester-suited crooner who was belting out Sinatra and Jimmy Buffet covers, accompanying himself on a miniature Casio keyboard.

One of the most ridiculous places I ever worked as a valet was a popular nightclub called Tonics, and its patrons definitely considered it The Place To Be Seen for a year or so. I made the most money there, but I worked harder than I would in three or four nights at a similar restaurant. People who went to Tonics were going To Be Seen, and they didn't let me or anyone else forget it. Every customer who arrived thought he or she was a VIP and deserved to be treated like one. Many sharply dressed night-clubbers would drive up to the front door of the club in a gigantic SUV and proceed to block four parking spaces and exit the vehicle, leaving one or more doors open—engine running, stereo blasting at mind-numbingly loud volume—completely blocking the traffic that spilled out into the busy avenue behind the car…and strut into the club. Customers expected me to know who everyone was and what everyone drove.

I would usually be sprinting from the parking lot far in the back and return to the front to see the next car "parked" like this, having no idea who had left it for me. I would save the keys in the key box because I didn't have time to wander into the packed, deafening, smoky club with my big dumb yellow shirt to try and figure out which VIP had left his or her car running outside in order to give the customer a claim ticket for the vehicle. Empty SUVs were often backing up into the street, several at a time, waiting to be parked. I'd scramble to get them out of the traffic, hoping to avoid being yelled at by a passing cop. In this way, I built up a huge inventory of claim tickets with my own cursory descriptions of the vehicles written on the back of the ticket, attached to the keys, so that I would (hopefully) be able to match the keys to the car without the benefit of a matching claim ticket that few of the customers had bothered to wait to acquire.

At unpredictable intervals, groups of patrons would decide to leave the club, and several impatient, intoxicated people would approach me at once, swaying awkwardly in their sparkling finery, outside the club at my little valet stand. Each would demand simply but urgently,

"Where's my *car*?!?!"

Of course I had no idea who most of them were, and not many of them had a claim check to give me.

"Could you describe your car, sir?"

"Huh? Come on man, you *know* me!"

All of these club patrons were irritated that I didn't recognize them or immediately know which car was theirs, though they had never seen me before either, having just walked into the club, leaving their obnoxious, thunderous, gas-guzzling monsters running behind them without even glancing to see who would attend to them. I might recognize someone from a previous night, but our boss rotated valets around local restaurants, and I couldn't begin to keep track of what everyone drove. Some people showed up in a different car every time. Everyone wanted me to serve him or her first because everyone thought of himself or herself as a VIP, of course. So, I ended up sprinting back and forth between the parking lot in the back and the front of the club, alternately trying to appease VIPs and assure them that we would find their cars in turn, and trying to calm each self-identified celebrity as he or she grew impatient.

HARDBARNED!
One Man's Quest for Meaningful Work in the American South

I fought the recurring temptation to suggest that certain privileged characters simply employ their own personal vehicle attendant in order to assure the level of service they were clearly accustomed to. Invariably, this pattern would continue for several hours throughout the evening, at times punctuated with drunken brawls or spectacular crashes, like the time several fashionable, meticulously made up women came to blows over who knows what, when I had brought one of their cars up from the back lot. I just got the hell out of the way as they actually knocked each other onto the hood of the sleek new Mercedes I stepped out of, bludgeoning each other with their broken high-heeled shoes and handbags, tearing blouses and hose, and drawing blood with their sculpted claws until their amused male companions reluctantly broke them up.

One night not long after the fight, I was jogging back to the club from the rear parking lot when I heard screeching tires. I looked over to the gas station next door to Tonics and saw a truck slam into the curb, flip upside down into the air and smash into a street lamp. The truck rocked back and forth on its roof, smoke rushing from underneath the crumpled hood. I started running toward the wreck, along with other pedestrians and onlookers. The first to the scene was a slender young woman who grabbed the passenger door and tried to open it. The male driver and the woman with him were trapped, pushing against the windows, visibly disoriented and distraught. Before I could reach the truck, the slight woman had planted her foot against its side, hauled back with all of her strength and what little weight she had, and nearly ripped the door off its hinges. She pulled out the bloodied and disoriented passengers one by one. I stood nearby, trying to think of a way to help, but by this time, paramedics had arrived and were taking over for her. I could already hear the VIPs screaming for me next door:

"Where's MY CAR?!?!?"

Tonics was a bloody mess. Whether drunken VIPs were screaming and beating each other up in the parking lot or crashing vehicles next door, whether NFL players were fighting with prostitutes or demanding special treatment from the valet, it was usually a chaotic night. Near the end of my stint as a valet, I went bar hopping downtown with a bunch of other valets, and we ended up at the apartment of the most senior guy in our group. We drank beer and told our favorite stories about our adventures in Valet Land. Later that evening, the guy who had originally gotten me the job climbed onto the handrail and pissed from the balcony onto someone's shiny new Hummer while yelling insults at the monster truck at three in the morning. It was a fitting end to my years of parking SUVs for VIPs.

* * *

Yet another job I held during my last two years of college was as a member of my university's light and sound crew. We weren't much more than semi-skilled laborers (undergraduates studying the recording industry) who knew how to set up a stage and sound system, needed some extra income and were willing to move a lot of heavy things around in hot weather. We set up audio equipment, lighting systems, and staging for indoor and outdoor concert performances on campus with occasional travel to other states as contracted laborers. As a crew member with this group, I once helped set up a Goo Goo Dolls show on campus and watched from backstage as the manscaped frontman was pelted with bras and panties from screaming fans at the edge of the stage. After the concert, we were tasked with collecting the scattered lingerie in a pile in order to take down the equipment without tripping over bra straps or accidentally tangling panties into the miles of cable that had to be wound up for transport.

We had one semi-regular gig at a floating casino barge in another state that paid well and put us up in a hotel for a couple nights over a weekend, but the job consisted of 18-hour days of hauling massive speaker cabinets around, setting up gigantic stage rigs for lighting, and building the colossal stages themselves. It took twelve of us to erect the lighting trusses that hung over the stage. We'd gather around on the field—most of these concerts took place on football fields—and line up with a rope that had been secured to the sectioned aluminum lighting towers we had assembled with nuts and bolts, four-tiered structures comprised of two-foot sections and designed to secure expensive, remote-controlled lights, which would ultimately hang horizontally over the stage, two or three stories high.

Though none of us wore kilts, I felt like a participant in the Highland Games as the team of dudes, most of them much brawnier than I, would engage in a heated tug-of-war with the heavy 60-foot truss tower until we were able to secure it in place, the rope flexing, the dudes flexing back, yelling

"RRRHHAAAAAARRRRGGGHHH!" in unison.

This antiquated Highland-Games method has since been replaced by powerful motors and servos that drag the trusses and heavy lighting rigs into place high over staging with remote-controlled consoles and fewer hernias. Mainstream country and pop acts would play these outdoor shows to an audience of mostly older casino patrons and families who required seating. We converted the huge parking lot into a live-music venue with hundreds of pieces of metal scaffolding and wooden floor sections, which we used to build a stage under the lighting rigs we had assembled and hoisted. We trucked in thousands of steel folding chairs, which we set up and took down, just like we did with everything else. The casino fed us, and the food was tolerable. We were basically construction workers who happened to be in college. The days were long, and the heat was oppressive, but we were energetic and needed the cash.

Once we were contracted by another university in a neighboring state to work on a show featuring a popular country music star. The set-up was similar to what we did at the casino, but this school had an outdoor stadium with bleachers, so this time we didn't have to install and remove chairs. Band members angrily yelled at me to move cables or drums or amps for them, which was a totally foreign concept to me, having been in crappy DIY bands that no one had ever heard of and never once expecting anyone to move my amps around for me, but if you're famous, you get to be an asshole *and* get people to set up all your crap for you.

Once we were finished putting everything together, several of us were cut for the evening and a few of us, myself included, were instructed to remain at the wings of the stage, ready for anything. T-shirt and confetti cannons were blasted at the screaming crowd, and this particular singer liked to change outfits for different songs in his set. He apparently thought it would be great to change the stage setup to match his outfits, which matched the lyrics of the songs—which he probably didn't even write. I was assigned to work on a mid-set number that evidently celebrated his love for vacationing in the Caribbean. We scrambled in the dark behind the curtain and quickly made the stage look like an elaborate Julie Taymor-designed theatrical rendition of Jimmy Buffet's "Margaritaville." I was stationed behind a brightly colored, 30-foot inflatable palm tree on one side of the stage. The tree was held aloft by a monstrous fan that blew hot air straight up from the bottom of the stage and into the trunk of the absurd decoration, though the tree was so top heavy (not exactly a marvel of modern engineering) that it tended to flop over to one side or the other, which could potentially obscure or even fall on top of the band.

Having the widest wingspan, I was told to stand behind the tree on an elevated platform for the duration of the song, wrap my arms around the tree trunk and do my best to keep the thing upright. The song began, and I was at work immediately. The flopping fake tree was kicking and bucking and burning with the hot air blasting through its trunk, but I held on to it as if I were taming an unruly mutated anaconda, 30 feet tall and angry.

Directions were being yelled at me by a stage manager from somewhere, but due to the band's onstage volume and the furiously blasting heated fan on the floor in front of me, I heard nothing. The tree bucked and pitched, the trunk buckling periodically, sending the heavy treetop and fake coconuts toppling in one direction or another, threatening to muss the frosted highlights in the prickly guitar player's $200 haircut. He shot me a threatening look, his Chicklet-white teeth contrasting with his crispy, dark-orange fake tan. I spread my arms and legs, struggling to control the monster tree like a greenhorn cowboy attempting to saddle a wild giraffe, the metal coils of the tree trunk hot from the air funneling through like elements on a stove, burning into my chest and arms as I held tight.

At this point, I had another internal moment of existential ennui, mentally retreating from the situation, zoning out from my immediate reality, revisiting the bigger picture and wondering how in the hell I had gotten myself into such a ridiculous position. Little did I know how many more reflective moments of *how and why the hell* and *what the fuck* were in store for me over the next several years of stupid jobs.

I'd be going it alone, however. Lena and I had broken up and gotten back together a few times and had lived together off and on over the last year and a half of nearly five years together. We couldn't get our timing right, wanted different things and had grown apart. It hurt a lot for a long time, a deep loss like I'd never felt before. It was hard to let go, but it had to be done.

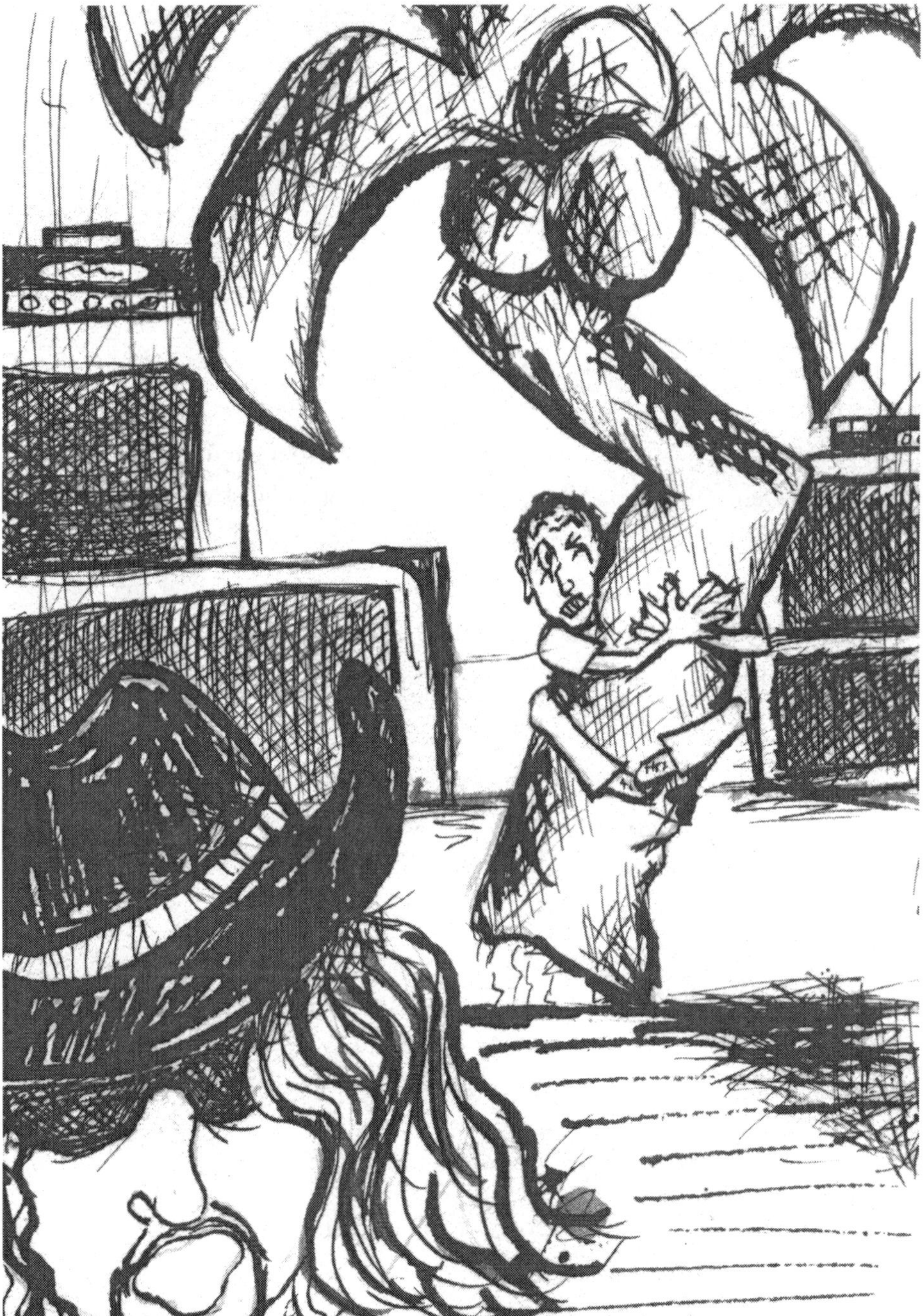

Sweet Old Piss Town and Muddy Bitter Barn Blues

It was the worst of times; it was the worst of times.

—Bill

Working in Barn Land for three years, Bill and I encountered a wide variety of gut-wrenching aromas on a daily basis, not only olfactory assaults attributed to (or caused by functions of) human bodies, but also smells borne of a variety of creatures of the animal kingdom. Food stenches, mildew stenches, rot stenches…chemical, excremental and death stenches were omnipresent, but I didn't think it was possible for a whole town to stink of urine.

At first I thought it was cat piss, and maybe somehow a cat had relieved itself on the mat inside my truck, but I didn't start smelling it until I drove into one particularly small town where I had often delivered barns. I would have noticed the smell in the morning when I got into the cab of the truck, but this sour bouquet began to percolate only as I entered the city limits of the wee rural town. I rolled the windows down for a while and rolled them back up again. No difference. Maybe the smell wasn't actually feline in origin, but human after all. I had smelled some awful smells throughout my barn-hauling tenure, but as I flipped through my mental backlog of funky fumes, I couldn't place it. This stink was unique. Though I was in a familiar town, I began a routine attempt to follow pitifully handwritten directions from the sales lot to the customer's home. Of course the street signs were all missing. Why wouldn't they be?

There were more mobile homes and trailers than actual houses, and I wondered about the septic tanks in their yards, and the various aromas unleashed upon the nostrils when the inevitable happens and a tank is breached, either intentionally by the septic-truck-driving man (I want to read *his* memoir) or unintentionally by people like me, or the UPS guy, or uncle Jimmy and his RV, visiting from West Virginia, when either of us accidentally drives a heavy truck over a soft spot in the lawn barely deep enough to protect a septic system. I tried to focus on the delivery, but everywhere I drove, windows down, or windows up with AC, all I could smell was urine, from one end of Piss Town to the other. Was there an epidemic of broken septic tanks? A roaming army of alcoholic stray cats on a bender? Had a plethora of port-a-johns been toppled by mischievous middle-schoolers, tired of cow-tipping?

    I was lost, so I called the lady whose barn I was trying to deliver, and she offered to come and meet me. Of course I didn't want to waste more time aimlessly wandering the unmarked roads of Piss Town, so I gladly accepted her offer, describing a shabby, deteriorating country store I had spotted nearby. I pulled over and turned on my emergency flashers, as there was no room to park my truck and barn anywhere else without blocking part of the narrow road. Frustrated locals drove around me with ESD and FUMF looks as I attempted to direct traffic on either side of the oversize load with SRWs, managing to avoid crashes between cars and trucks heading in opposite directions along the slender asphalt path. The woman arrived and parked her car, though I was hoping she would just wave, drive on and expect me to follow, getting all this over as quickly as possible. Shuffling slowly across the street, a tiny old woman in grey slacks, a pink turtleneck sweater and short, silver hair combed straight back, leaned into my driver's side window to give me detailed directions. Her kind eyes and genuine concern melted my frustration in an instant. She was the sweetest, cutest little old lady I had ever seen, with the most endearing smile. Just being in her presence was calming.

    I followed her home and realized the delivery would be a challenge. The woman pointed to a steep slope behind her driveway and a large pile of gravel, which sat in the middle of the slope. She wanted the barn to be placed on this slope, atop the small, high mound of gravel. I explained that in my experience, placing barns on the most level ground available was usually the best plan for safety, stability and aesthetics, and she agreed to trust my professional judgment. I quickly attended to leveling the barn in another part of the yard as she stood nearby, regaling me with stories about various people in her family and their comic antics. Though her stories were hard to follow, I liked having her around. As it turned out, there was a little bit of sweetness in Piss Town, and as Brian pointed out in *Vanilla Sky*,

"Without the bitter, baby, the sweet ain't so sweet."[1]

It was pretty easy for me to focus on the bitter—obviously—and on another cold, wet day when I had managed to immobilize the whole truck, trailer and barn, axle-deep into the mud beneath a thin layer of deceptively dry grass in a customer's finely manicured yard, I was livid. Wasting my day away in the middle of nowhere, spinning my four-wheel-drive tires to no avail, two years into a barn-hauling adventure that seemed inescapable, hopelessly ignored by every employer I ever contacted about writing or editing jobs and then helplessly stuck in the mud, I felt I understood the concept of bitter. Having been assured over the phone by this customer that his backyard was dry and suitable for delivery, I had driven the 10 miles to his house and entered the yard. Things had gone smoothly until, as I neared the barn drop-off point, the grass transformed into mud, aborting the delivery in sheer futility. After waiting a couple hours stuck there, I went toe-to-toe with another grizzled old tow-truck driver who finally arrived on the scene in another rust-bucket truck from a bygone era, only to spew vitriol at me for his perception of my inability to drive my own truck. I wanted to punch the guy but kept my mouth shut. After attaching his tow cables to my truck and trailer in an attempt to dislodge me from the deceptively dry section that had morphed into Dagobah, his quaking rust bucket of a tow truck shook so hard I thought it would collapse before it moved my rig an inch.

---

[1] *Vanilla Sky*. Dir. Cameron Crowe. Perf. Jason Lee, Tom Cruise. Paramount Pictures: 2001.

Feeling deja-vu, I ducked for cover from his ancient, gnarled winch cables as they snapped back, twisting through the air like a whistling bull whip, close enough to decapitate me. Enduring a tirade of curses from this vile man, as though it were my fault that his decades-old truck wasn't strong enough to pull mine out of the mud, I was indeed bitter, but no punches were thrown. And yet, after the old man grew tired of cursing and spewing spittle at me and drove away, the kind folks who lived at the delivery site insisted that I come into their home, apologized profusely for having assumed that the yard was dry enough for delivery, fixed me hot chocolate, offered me snack cakes and helped me find the number for another local tow truck driver, even after I had completely torn the hell out of their back yard, battled the angry old man as his truck disintegrated, ruined their nicely manicured lawn and drawn several nosy neighbors to the brouhaha. People with kindness and patience of that magnitude were incredibly rare and thoroughly appreciated in Barn Land. On these rare occasions when a little sweetness seeped in, right at the moment when all the constant chaos threatened to overwhelm, it was pretty damn sweet and a little less bitter.

* * *

One beautiful fall day, I was on a mission to deliver a little 8X8 barn with Bill. We almost always hauled separately but happened to be working together that day, enjoying each other's company, and we were lost down a long series of narrow, winding roads that were nearly overgrown with kudzu and vines and weeds on both sides of the unmarked, intermittently paved path. Without street signs and with massive vegetation everywhere, it seemed as though we were tunneling into a plant planet—a vortex of rural green nowhere from which we might not return.

At one point we turned down an overgrown road into a cul-de-sac and were instantly surrounded by a pack of a dozen random canines, most of them friendly variations on a Labrador, and we found the place.

It became apparent that all of the roaming dogs resided at or near the house where we were delivering the barn, and the entire block and yard had become minefields planted with their assorted leavings. A giant aboveground pool sat dormant at the side of the house on this early fall day, still full of water, now dark green with algae blooms, breeding a legion of mosquitoes for us to do battle with as we danced around awkwardly, swatting the bugs and dodging the poo all over the ground. A yo-boy[2] appeared in the doorway as Bill and I surveyed the scene. Squinting at us from underneath his sideways ball cap, scowling under a peach-fuzz mustache as he murmured to someone on a cordless phone, the young man lazily addressed our general direction.

"She in da house. Dunno where she want it" was his opening line, shouted from across the yard.

"Hi!" I shouted back in reply with a smile and a wave. Shortly thereafter, a clearly intoxicated bottled blonde stumbled from the house in glasses, baggy black sweat pants and a stained yellow tank top. She mumbled in a staccato blend of country accent and slurred speech. All I could discern before she disappeared was something about the dogs and the general vicinity that she wanted the barn to be placed in, mostly discerned by disinterested gestures. Of course this area was on a 45-degree slope that would require several feet of concrete blocks to level. Bill and I set to work, carving a sizeable chunk out of the hill with our shovels in order to create a flat spot for the concrete blocks, motivated to get the job done and get the hell away from this place. At least it was a small barn. It would be over quickly, we thought.

Backing the truck down the sharp incline from the road and into the front yard, our truck quickly carved through the seemingly dry layer of grass and spun its tires in the wet mud beneath us on the steep slope.

---

2 According to the Urban Dictionary site user IhateAkon's April 30, 2007 posting, a "yo boy" is a "white male youth…who wants desperately to fit into the urban 'gangsta' lifestyle in his grammar, musical taste, clothing and attitude but who only serves to irritate everyone, including real gangstas…a very annoying white male youth that desperately needs to be dropped off in Compton for a day or two and be taught a lesson."

Sweet Old Piss Town and Muddy Bitter Barn Blues

Bill and I spent nearly an hour trying to maneuver ourselves out of the predicament but only sank deeper into the ground and managed to wrap the rig around a telephone pole that happened to be in the yard as we slowly slid sideways down the hill, rendering ourselves completely immobile.

Way out in the sticks as we were, neither of us could get a cell phone signal, so we began a series of trips on foot between the truck and the house, borrowing the cordless landline telephone, making calls to various towing companies and receiving calls in return. Nobody seemed to want to drive a tow truck out to our extreme backwoods location, if they could even find it. Bill and I declined to go into the sketchy house and preferred to wait in the yard. We spent the next several hours sitting in the truck on the slope as we waited for a tow truck that we assumed would have as much difficulty finding the remote address as we had.

Darkness descended, and we watched from the truck's cab as several cars and kids came and went. Sometimes the costumed characters (strutting, skinny Caucasian teens in XXXL urban hip-hop-styled clothing and awkward swagger) would leave their vehicles and knock on the door of the house, entering briefly and emerging shortly thereafter to return to their cars and leave. Sometimes the young man who seemed to live there would run from the house to a particular vehicle and lean into the driver's window for a long conversation. Sometimes a young woman with minimal clothing would emerge from the house and spend 20 or 30 minutes in a series of opaque-windowed, lowered pickups or blinged-out Hondas before she'd skip back into the house and await the next visitor. Clearly a variety of transactions were taking place on the premises.

Sitting in the truck as the hours passed, Bill and I wondered aloud how we had ever gotten ourselves into a situation like this. Neither of us ever could have imagined a fate such as this. In post-graduate debt like this. Without hope for a career...other than this. Tasked daily with madness in the mud...just like this. Finally around nine that evening, the bright headlights of a shiny new tow truck emerged from the foliage-encrusted country road. Securing itself to the pavement above the lawn with a heavyweight counter balance/control arm, the tow truck's powerful winch slowly dragged us over the steep slope in the muddy front yard below the pavement. Each tire on our truck and trailer ripped tarp-sized, gaping swaths of grass from the lawn, like so much skin from baked chicken breasts. Bill and I got home around midnight after a quick stop at Taco Bell.

As I had anticipated, I was required to return a few months later to the very same home to repossess the wee barn that had already wasted so many hours of our lives. It had been filled with discarded old insulation. I wondered why a customer would go through so much trouble to order a barn from so many miles away and have trucks and trailers and tow trucks tear her yard apart in order to get it into a very specific and difficult-to-access place on her steep front yard, which was completely inappropriate for a barn, only to fill it with discarded scraps of flammable cotton-candy style insulation, refuse to pay for it and have it repossessed. Why? *Seriously.* WHY? It always took a few months of missed payments to warrant a repossession. Maybe this was the customer's plan all along. A free garbage disposal service, courtesy of the barn seller and the hauling company. I left the old insulation in the barn and returned it to the sales lot to be sold and delivered yet again.

On another occasion, I was in the yard behind a customer's trailer home trying to deliver his 8X12 lofted barn. Though with the loft it was taller than the yo-boy insulation barn, this one was still pretty small compared to many others, but sometimes the smallest barns turned into the biggest headaches, much like the 8X8 barn debacle just described. I guess it didn't occur to this man, who rented a trailer with his teenage daughter and her baby, that because someone was bringing a *building* to his place that he might want to clear a path and move at least a few of his four broken-down cars, his three trucks, his van or his boat, all in various states of immobile disrepair. With much effort over nearly an hour of maneuvering, somehow I snaked the truck and trailer around the various obstacles including the vehicles, assorted lawn jockeys, ceramic confederate soldiers, plastic wise men, deflated inflatable snowmen, rotten railroad ties and several yapping rat dogs who refused to calm down, despite my best efforts to befriend them.

"You'd get outta thar if you had some four wheel drive on 'at truck," the idiot blurted as I spun all four tires (obviously in four-wheel-drive), throwing mud against his shins and carving deep, wide trenches through the grass.

"Gall damn. Willie's gon' be pissed," said the rent-to-owner.

"He's my landlord, at's his trailer, an' he's a gal dang pain in my ass *ever* damn *day*," said the man as he took another gulp from his breakfast beer.

"Don' chew worry none, I got a track-der cummin' soon an' he'll git you out. Jus try not to make it worse 'ar hit my field lines."

I was furious, all the while wondering why the hell this guy hadn't told me the truth on the phone in the first place when I had specifically called to ask him if the yard was dry enough to deliver his barn, but this was par for the course. He had assured me that conditions were appropriate and encouraged me to bring the barn over immediately. I had hoped to avoid the current situation by waiting for a day or two until the ground was dry, but I had relied on the word of this man, half drunk at nine in the morning. It didn't matter that I remained suspicious after arriving on the property and walking around on the grass that felt a little soft. I had already driven out there, and the customer insisted that I attempt to get the barn into place.

Ultimately, the tractor showed up and was able to pull my truck and trailer out of the two-foot, axle-deep mud trenches I had created for myself behind his double-wide, but not before my truck, trailer, and the dude's tractor absolutely tore the man's yard to shreds. The next customer that day, a hairy, semi-intelligible man in camouflage, could not manage to tell me how to get to his own house and would not cease reminding me (literally at the end of every sentence) that he was a disabled vet. I'd had better days on the job, and I was seized once again by the old familiar grip of the muddy bitter barn blues.

Magazines, More Movies, Meatball and *MAXIMUM ROCKNROLL*

Oh, you hate your job? Oh my god, well why didn't you say so? You know there's a support group for that. It's called EVERYBODY. They meet at the bar.[1]

—Drew Carey

In 2000, I finished college and was planning on hitting the road with the punk band I'd played in for the past couple of years, but we had decided to wait two more semesters for our drummer to graduate. I had earned two bachelor's degrees: one in music business and one in English. I'd realized while studying recording engineering that my brain wasn't wired like the technical manuals I was required to memorize in order to operate the multitudes of recording consoles, software, gadgets and devices I would need to master. I preferred literature and film studies to ProTools and signal-flow schematics, so I opted out of yet another career possibility. Hesitant to waste a lot of credits I'd already earned, I switched the recording degree emphasis from audio engineering to music business but decided to stick around a little longer to complete an English degree too.

I had started to realize that I wanted to write, and if I could write about music, even better. In fact, I'd been writing record reviews for a zine that a friend of mine ran and briefly adapted into a website, and I loved it, but it didn't pay anything other than the free CDs that I could occasionally sell for money to buy instant noodles. I had a year to work before the band left town. The problem was that I looked everywhere after graduation and couldn't find a job as a writer (the same problem I had five years later

---

1 Carey, Drew. "In Ramada Da Vida" *The Drew Carey Show*. Season 4, Episode 2. ABC, 1998.

after finishing graduate school). The first thing I found that even remotely related to writing was a job as an "account executive" (I didn't know what that meant) at a magazine distribution company. Magazines! It had to at least tangentially involve writing. Nope.

For nine months I sat in a gray cubicle under a fluorescent light and learned to manage a distribution database for hundreds of magazine publishers. I found out later that I was hired because I looked the interviewer in the eye when answering questions; he thought I had "gentle eyes." I had admitted that I sucked at math but had mentioned I was a scuba diver, so from all of this he had concluded that I was an honest, detail-oriented and responsible person. The only writing I did on the job consisted of short email messages to clients—publishers who wanted to negotiate the margins of their distribution contracts or confirm sales data—and an occasional snail mail letter on the company stationary. I crunched numbers in Excel. I decided how many copies of *Maxim* needed to be shipped to a particular chain bookstore in Little Rock, whether or not *Mother Earth News* would sell well at another new store in Boulder, and how many copies of *Newsweek* were needed in seven chain stores in Atlanta. I tried unsuccessfully to secure a major distribution deal for *Chunklet*, a hilarious indie rock magazine that I loved. Sorry Henry, I tried.

By studying spreadsheets of sales data, I had to decide whether hundreds of other independent and mainstream magazines could sell in any number of corporate stores across the country. I spent long days deciding how many copies of this or that should be added to or taken away from one store or another, shuffling through an infinite loop of sales numbers in search of the most efficient ratios of shelf space versus single-copy sales history versus title popularity in any given market. I was never provided with any helpful demographic data whatsoever, so I had to make educated guesses about what would sell where. This meant spending every day hunched over Microsoft Access databases, drinking a lot of coffee (I didn't even *like* coffee), eating vending machine Pop-Tarts or doughnuts for breakfast, negotiating distribution contracts over the phone and living for the nights when I could re-enter my real world, hang out with my friends, and practice or play shows with my band. With almost zero opportunities for writing, my job was really focused on numbers, with a little over-the-phone customer service and sales negotiation thrown in.

After nearly a year of this, I only had the summer left before leaving to go on tour with the band, and again I felt the pull of the summer sun and the out-of-doors. My friend Donnie owned a landscaping business with his Dad and was happy to offer me something temporary for the summer. Donnie had finished a degree in anthropology and spent a summer cataloging artifacts as an intern at a state park, alone in a dank cabin in the woods full of spiders and scorpions. Afterward he had decided not to pursue anthropology and joined the multi-generational family business as a landscaper instead. I was done with the climate-controlled cubicle and ready for some serious physical activity in the summer sunshine again. Donnie would be a lot cooler to work for than Harold, I thought, and I was right.

It was a small crew—I was one of two other employees of Donnie and his Dad—and I was happy to ditch the office environment in order to dig ditches with a pick and shovel in the sun, making way for the irrigation systems in new suburban homes. It was a welcome contrast from the depressing office space; I was overjoyed to leave behind the monochromatic spreadsheets of endless calculations, business casual attire and masochistic coffee injections. I spent hours picking rocks from new suburban yards as we graded acre lots by hand and prepared them for new sod. I rode on the back of the work truck and fed bushels of straw into the enormous machine attached to the bumper hitch that shredded and blew the coarse, dried pieces out from the other end like a grass-seeding bazooka. I picked itchy little bits of prickly straw from every crevice in my body, and my constantly irritated skin developed a rash in all the wrong places. It wasn't so bad though. I loved being outside and enjoyed the work. I had a good time working alongside Donnie and his Dad; their witty banter made the day go by quickly, but I had made another stupid mistake.

HARDBARNED!
One Man's Quest for Meaningful Work in the American South

I should have held on at the magazine distributor gig for the rest of the summer before leaving for a three-month cross-country tour. It would have been easier to save more money that way, but I was young, impulsive, perpetually restless, more focused on the band than anything else and simply eager to Get In The Van. Not long after I started working outside, I learned of an opportunity to make nearly twice my landscaping wages at a video warehouse. I'd also be able to carpool with some other friends who already worked there, and it was all temporary anyway. I didn't want to leave Donnie and his Dad, but I needed the extra money I could make in the warehouse before the tour, so I explained the situation to Donnie, thanked him and his Dad profusely and moved on.

* * *

The enormous video warehouse distribution center happened to be right across the street from the magazine distributor I had recently left. I needed to earn all I could in the couple of months before tour, so I signed on. Movies, I thought. How bad could it be? My group of friends carpooled from the duplex we shared in our little college town and worked on our feet from 4:30PM until 2:30AM and drank beers and played videogames after we got home.

We stood on the concrete floor in a deafening production complex on thin rubber mats and furiously fed VHS tapes and DVDs into thunderous, roaring machines that chewed them up and spit them out, either with more or less wrapping material on them than before we had crammed them in. We competed with other employees and were pushed to set speed records by our supervisor, a guy we called "Meatball," an Andre The Giant-sized dude who addressed us like a high school gym coach, lumbering around and constantly barking at us to stop talking, work harder and speed up production.

We tried to see how fast we could process the most product without jamming the machines or accidentally feeding them our fingers. Often we

Magazines, More Movies, Meatball and MAXIMUM ROCKNROLL

would spend an entire shift standing at a table with a mountain of DVD cases, either peeling off or putting on little security stickers until we lost all the feeling in our fingertips, or we'd simply build boxes from flattened stacks of cardboard until our brains dissolved into Play-Doh. We would take our breaks together in the parking lot outside, buying junk food from the lunch truck that stopped by to sell us greasy vending machine burgers, chips, candy and sodas.

Meatball wasn't so bad, but he somewhat resembled a meatball on two chopsticks with a football jersey, and he would waddle around and yell at us with his good ol' boy twang if he caught us talking, but we had to joke around with each other on the job to avoid becoming insane, mannequin-like automatons. Meatball would attempt to entice us to work harder, quieter and faster with "incentives," like being able to listen to some shitty commercial radio station for a couple hours during one day of a 50-hour work week, or a coupon for two dollars off the regular employee price on an overstocked VHS copies of films nobody wanted like *Space Jam* or *Speed 2: Cruise Control*.

One of the other supervisors seemed a lot more human and took an interest in me, complimenting me on my work and inviting me to what I thought was a party but turned out to be a pyramid-scheme recruiting seminar. I showed up at the house and was ushered into a room where a guy in a dress shirt and tie was standing in front of a white board with a magic marker, a pointer, and a drawing of a pyramid.

"If you can convince ten of your friends to buy these products online, and they can convince ten of *their* friends, think of the money that will be in your pocket! What about the boat you've always wanted, or that European vacation?"

Everyone was nodding and smiling as the dollar signs multiplied on the board. It creeped me out, and I told my manager it wasn't for me. He protested gently:

"I get *everything* my family uses online through this company, via my own website, even meats and milk! I'm my own best customer."

"Great."

I was wondering why I had wasted my Friday night on this.

Pretty soon it was time to leave for my real priority—nearly 12 weeks on the road with the band—and I told this supervisor what I had planned. He said I could come back and work at the warehouse anytime I wanted, which was exactly what I needed: a flexible job that I could return to between tours. Finally, I was ready to hit the road and realize a dream, visiting both coasts on a punk rock tour. I was super stoked, ready to get the hell out of town and see the country doing what I had long felt I was supposed to do. Writing original songs, screaming and yelling and playing guitar in a touring rock band that nobody had ever heard of. It never seemed like a job, but looking back, maybe that's because I never earned a living! I thought that one day I might at least earn room and board with this gig or enough to simply keep at it. Most nights we were happy if we could afford something to eat, a couple beers and a tank of gas.

* * *

I've never had a problem with work. Working is healthy. Being productive and creative is satisfying. The tough part for me has always been finding that balance between meaningful work and a satisfying job. Doing something worthwhile and still making ends meet. Earning a living from something dependent on a tangible engagement with personal artistic impulses and acting on those interests, skills and values, simultaneously. Feeling like there's a point to all of it, a positive impact. Feeling like I was doing something real and productive at the same time. In the band, I felt like that. It only lasted a few years, but it felt right in a lot of ways that haven't quite fit together as well for me before or since. Punk rock touring deserves another book, but the brief synopsis is as follows:

There were only three of us: guitar, bass and drums. Our drummer was known as The Bear due to a combination of his excessive body hair and gentle, teddy-bear personality. In contrast, when he occasionally contributed vocals to a song, we called him The Pterodactyl because he sounded like one. Our genial bass player was quick to mediate conflicts and always wore a self-described shit-eating grin. Inspired by Fugazi and other trailblazers that preceded us, we wrote our own songs, booked our own tours, carried our own equipment, and drove our own van and trailer. No managers or record labels or booking agents or A&R guys or lawyers. No tour support or PR or marketing.[2] Very few paying audience members either, as it turned out. Luckily we played some well-attended shows back home, both before and after most tours, which helped us pay for the trips. We were also lucky to often have our friend Stan along with us.

Stan is a jack of all trades: an actor, artist, musician, mechanic, and a very funny guy. He was one awesome dude to have along on tour. He'd carry things, take pictures, fix the van and play his banjo. Industrious as he was, Stan had installed a restroom of sorts in one of his two vans (though it wasn't the one we used) that consisted of a hole he had cut into the floor of the van and a PVC pipe that extended to the tailpipe region under the rear bumper. All one had to do was position oneself on the floor, insert the necessary parts into the appropriate receptacles, and then rinse the pipe with a little water, but I never had the opportunity to experience this unique men's room. Stan, while prepared for just about anything and intimidated by no one, was not a big fan of showers, but none of us smelled particularly good on tour. Showers were not always available. Our bassist said that Stan smelled like a baby's diaper, but I didn't really notice.

Though we'd played a few shows in other states on short jaunts here and there, on this first significant tour we played 46 shows in 27 states over 76 days and 15,000 miles on the road. When stuff broke, we fixed it. When two people showed up to see us play, we played anyway. We ate cold SpaghettiOs from a can, lots of beans and rice and Ramen noodles, and

---

[2] "One aspect of Do It Yourself is that you really have to do it yourself. It's work! We manage ourselves, we book ourselves, we do our own equipment upkeep, we do our own recording…we don't have other people to do that stuff. This is what we do and it takes time…I think there's a lot of infrastructure work that we do that people are unaware of." Mackaye, Ian. Interview by Daniel Sinker. *We Owe You Nothing: Punk Planet: The Collected Interviews*. Chicago: Punk Planet Books, 2001.

we slept on strangers' floors or in the van. We experienced temperature extremes and we got sick. We frequented the Wendy's 99-cent Super Value Menu. We lost weight. The van broke down.

We played a show at a hippie college in Vermont with a band called Vomit Dichotomy who passed around a frying pan and took turns making themselves puke into it as they performed, dumping the pan onto the drums and cymbals and incorporating their puke into the show. We backed away. We were interrogated for three hours at the border north of Detroit and ultimately were not allowed to enter Canada after pleading with them for hours that we just wanted to play rock for a few kids and make enough gas money to get back, if we were lucky. The border guards were a little touchy—it was just after 9/11/01, and they threatened to put us in jail if we tried to cross at another checkpoint.

Our trailer axle fell apart as we arrived in Mobile to play a show with another band whose members miraculously happened to work day jobs as professional welders and spent the entire next day repairing our rig. We played shows with rappers at city parks, for punk kids in their parents' basements, with synth pop and goth bands, stand-up comics and Metallica cover bands. We even performed for a police and firefighter fundraiser with balloons and hot dogs. We shared stages with rock star wannabes in frat boy clubs, old VFW[3] halls and dirty punk dives, in living rooms, basements, and outdoor sheds, stages and rock clubs, wherever and whenever we could get a show together. We played with some fantastic bands and some horrible ones and made some great friends too. As luck would have it, a friend of ours from the recording program back at school was working as an engineer at Steve Albini's Electrical Audio studio in Chicago, and we ended up recording an album and staying there for a few days, which was surreal for me, having been so influenced by Albini's editorial years before. We discovered Mike Judge's comic masterpiece *Office Space* in Albini's extensive video collection. I loved it immediately, having recently left the cubicle life.

---

3 Veterans of Foreign Wars: Drinking clubs for old military dudes.

HARDBARNED!
One Man's Quest for Meaningful Work in the American South

We went on other tours between 1999 and 2002, playing in a total of 37 states, around 180 shows (actually not that many for three and a half years as a band) but we came home and worked crappy jobs in-between tours to save up for the next ones. None of our other trips surpassed the length and intensity of our initial three-month journey across America. We weren't the only ones trying this approach, of course. We were no pioneers, just one of many bands having a go at it. Many of them had it a lot tougher, went at this a lot harder and for a hell of a lot longer than we did. Though all three of us played in other bands after ours split up in 2002, only one managed to earn a real living at it for the next decade. I was just stoked to have the chance to travel and perform original music with friends for a few years when my work life and creative passions converged. Smartphones and the Internet have changed the methods, but a vibrant underground network of independent punk rock bands still tour on their own, DIY-style.

It took some sacrifices. Sometimes we'd question why we kept doing it, and sometimes we didn't get along, but I think we all realized that we were privileged to have had the opportunity. We loved to play music and were able to travel and share it with different people and experience new places and have an adventure. It was a job unlike any other, and overall it was a completely fantastic experience. We never made any money and spent a lot from our own pockets. Any money we did make was channeled back into the band's expenses. We sold most of what we owned before we went on tour. To keep going, I even parted with my comic book collection and all my old *Star Wars* toys. First-world problems, right? Maybe that's what I should have titled this book.

The only place people really showed up en masse to support us was in our small college town, but that always felt good and helped us get where we were going. It had its ups and downs, but looking back, it was an overwhelmingly positive experience, all built on art created collaboratively with two friends who remain dear to me to this day. I wouldn't trade those experiences for anything.

HARDBARNED!
One Man's Quest for Meaningful Work in the American South

The Barn-Land DOT... and Deer Semen

You might be a redneck if you own a home that is mobile and five cars that are not...or if you cut your grass and found a car.[1]

—Jeff Foxworthy

As a trucker, I was rarely harassed by the Department Of Transportation. I think most DOT employees are probably responsible people trying to do their jobs well. There were, however, exceptions that stood out. They were not always professional or well organized. It seemed that many state troopers who pulled my truck and loaded barn trailer over to the side of the road, or stopped me at a weigh station for a shakedown, had their own specific and individualized understanding of state laws. Sometimes these interpretations varied so widely that I figured they must have passed out blank motor vehicle regulation guides like *Mad Libs* and encouraged new troopers to get creative in those little black leather books.

One day a particularly unfriendly trooper waved me over at the weigh station for a 90-minute shakedown. I understood the concept of ramped-up law enforcement paranoia and overreach in a post 9/11 world, but this was beyond ridiculous. Was there not a law related to probable cause? I have no idea what he could have been looking for. Maybe it was just a random, routine search, but that day I felt like I got a tiny dose of understanding of what Hispanics in Arizona or Alabama must be feeling today, or what African-Americans have put up with in this country for decades when they are pulled over and harassed for no reason. Not that

---

[1] Foxworthy, Jeff. "You Might Be a Redneck If...". *You Might Be a Redneck If...* Burbank: Warner Bros. Records, 1993.

I have any claim to an understanding of the experience of daily life as a minority experiencing institutionalized racism. White dudes are usually the perpetrators of such idiotic behavior, but as a white dude who had never experienced undeserved, state-sanctioned harassment quite like this, I caught a small glimpse of perspective...but I never feared for my life. Had I been a minority, I may not have been so lucky. America can be a dangerous, divisive place, but the concept of race itself is just another ignorant way we label and ostracize each other, just as we do with religion and nationalism. It's going to take a hostile alien invasion to snap us out of it, most likely.

The officer literally shuffled every piece of paper I had on board and inspected every detail of every section of the truck and trailer, inside and out. He threw my stuff everywhere and made a mess of the cab. He made a point to contradict, provoke and dismiss me from every possible angle, as if I were a criminal, although I was initially careful to be friendly and polite. He didn't care who I was or where I came from and wanted me to shut the hell up so he could rifle through all my stuff in search of a broken rule. I gradually made less of an effort to be accommodating, realizing I wouldn't be granted the same respect I afforded him, and my answers got shorter as I minimized my responses. His pointed accusations and threats based on imaginary violations his selected interpretation of regulations produced nothing concrete with which to punish me and only resulted in his mounting frustration and deteriorating civility.

I have no idea where this particular trooper came from or why it felt good to belittle, badger and insult a compliant and friendly weigh station regular like me. I can't say what convinced him that I was in violation of any number of stupid, random rules when the trooper running the show the day before or after wouldn't even mention a single one of them. Why one female trooper would wave me by the scales with a friendly smile when another male officer on a different day would drag me from the truck and into the interrogation room, acting like I just keyed his squad car, is inexplicable. Probably it was a random hassle based on one otherwise evenhanded officer's desire to trust his instincts and intercept a possible drug smuggler. Maybe it was that suspicious beard of mine. Or maybe dude just had a bad day and took it out on me, the next random driver in a long line of truckers waiting to get on with their business. Maybe the barns are what stood out. Why not? I blamed them for everything else.

Perhaps barn hauling, to the DOT, is truly an enigma, an immeasurable wild card, unquantifiable by the powers that be. Maybe they all secretly hate barn haulers because there is no defined section about us in their rulebooks. Our custom rigs and oversize cargo are anomalous to them, so they are thrown off their game a little when we drive past. Maybe this section of the rulebook is still being fleshed out. The old rules don't apply, and they have to guess. The chapter hasn't been written yet; perhaps DOT officers are on the front lines in a new war that hasn't been explained to them and all they can see in their thousand-yard stare is chaos on the steep, potholed highways choked with oversize loads, barns hanging off both sides of trailers, taking up too much highway. A select few of these officers sure seem to be making up the rules as they go along, abusing friendly folks who are just doing their jobs. But I have to believe that many others are decent folks, trudging through their own unsatisfying jobs like the rest of us.

What does the DOT have to do with deer semen, you may find yourself wondering? Well the answer is not much, but after one extremely long delay involving this overzealous highway patrol officer, I received a call from Mitch and learned that after finishing my scheduled deliveries for the day, which had already been pushed back a couple of hours, I would then need to stop by the site of a previous delivery in order to appease a dissatisfied customer. The man to whom I had delivered a garage-style (12x30) barn the week before had convinced himself that I was coming back to set it up for him again, this time on concrete blocks, though when given his choice of setup options in person upon delivery, he had agreed to have it set up on the wooden blocks that we provided free of charge. It wasn't Mitch's fault. I was in the area that day, and we had to keep our customers happy. I wouldn't have time to do whatever it was that I had planned for after work that night anyway. I called the customer.

"He towd me y'all be comin' up issa way with somebody whose gohn wipe that stayne on 'dis buildin' an' then level it up with some uh them concrete block."

"Well, sir…again, we level the buildings with pressure-treated wooden blocks and charge extra for concrete blocks if the customer requests them."

"He put it up on them wood blocks and it ain't no level. It ain't no pressure treated neither. He missed some them spots with that stayne too. It ain't been nothin' but trouble since I's bought this buildin'."

"Sir, I'd be glad to come out there this afternoon with some stain for the spots the builder missed. Also, I can level the building on concrete blocks, but I'll have to charge you 75 dollars for the labor and two dollars each for the blocks."

"I done got them blocks. That uther one I's talkin' to said it'd be 50 bucks."

"Well, sir, if you have your own block, I'd be glad to use them, but the labor charge for me to come out there again and level the barn again is still going to be 75 dollars."

"Well. Awright. I shore wouldn' do somethin' for nuthin' neither."

I arrived at the man's house several hours later in the cold gray afternoon, weaving through the broken-down rusty vehicles partially concealed by tall weeds on the man's front lawn, the sun barely peeking from behind the mountain that loomed over the rural suburb. When I had first delivered the garage to this man during the previous week, he had asked me about our policies regarding concrete block, and I had explained them to him then, just as I did for a second time on the phone before this second visit to his property.

I had never expected him to call not only the salesperson at the lot who had sold him the building, but also my boss who owned the trucking business, and even my boss's contractor, due to his frustration over not having the building leveled on concrete blocks, despite the fact that he had agreed when I initially delivered the building to have it leveled on pressure-treated wood blocks. Even though he had told me he was happy with it when I left his house the first time, he had changed his mind, and his complaints had run up the chain of command. It was cold enough to wear my black Carhartt coveralls, which meant it was damn cold. I pulled on my warm winter hat, left on my sunglasses, grabbed my work gloves, and stepped out of the truck. No one appeared, but I started to unload my tools as I usually would: jacks, hammer, hatchet, level, etc.

Just a week before, I had been ripped off by a customer who had refused to pay me for the 60 heavy concrete blocks I had brought to his trailer home and used to level his gigantic barn on the steep slope where he lived, although he had lied and agreed to leave the cash he owed me at the sales lot before I got there the following day. I called and harassed the man a few times, though he never answered the phone. He cheated me out of my time, labor, and money and then stooped to a new low, having his children answer his phone and lie for him. That time, I had barely resisted the temptation to return to the man's trailer home and smash the blocks I had stacked under his barn to tiny bits with a sledgehammer, causing the building to crash to the ground from its extreme slope and roll over into his mobile home. So this time, I was determined to receive payment before I started crawling around on the ground underneath the barn in the dog shit and dirt in the descending darkness to level a barn for a second time after explaining our policies to the same man for yet a third time.

Suddenly I noticed the man across his back yard. As I started to walk toward him, he turned and walked away from me.

"Howdy!" I shouted in his general direction.

He muttered something in response and shuffled away. A driver doesn't paint or stain the buildings he delivers. It's not part of our job, but this man had complained about a few spots that were missed by the builder. For the first time ever, I had brought some stain to a customer's home for touch-ups. I got out the steel bucket and prepared to touch up the places that had been missed (the only time I ever did this in three years of barn hauling), and the man reappeared. I didn't know how angry or difficult he would be. As I've testified, some barn customers try to be as antagonistic as possible in an attempt to play the role of the dissatisfied customer, to whom everything is supposedly owed. Exploiting this outdated "customer is always right" business philosophy, some customers go to absurd, excessively stupid and occasionally insane lengths.

I started by asking the man if he would like me to apply the stain to the missed spots on the window frames of the barn, or if he would prefer that I leave the stain for him to handle at his own discretion. He spouted a pouting protest that indicated his expectation of retaining the services of a more qualified stain-applicator-specializing professional than my scruffy-looking barn-hauling appearance would apparently belie. I replied that I would be happy to apply the stain for him and began moving in that direction with bucket and rag in hand. The man continued muttering under his breath about all the trouble caused by the entire experience of purchasing the portable garage. I lowered the bucket to the ground and, in a friendly tone, attempted to call his bluff by offering to return the building to the lot and refund his money, thus relieving him of all his troubles and frustrations.

"Aw hell naw! I'm keeping the dag'um thang now. Yall better believe it. You kin jes leave 'at stayne. It's too cold now anyhow. I'll do it myself later on sometime."

I agreed and left the stain and rag. The next order of business was to receive my cash fee for the service of returning to the man's house and leveling his barn for the second time, this time on concrete block, which he had provided. As I mentioned before, I wasn't going to do the work without getting paid first, and so I told the man this exactly.

"It's nothing personal," I said.

Again, he turned on his heel and walked away without a word, disappearing into his house. I sat on the narrow edge of my trailer, watching my breath evaporate in the cold air and staring into the sky at what little was left of the evening sun. As I had done so many times before, I wondered how my life had taken such a turn. How was it that I was in this foul man's back yard, on this nowhere country road, responsible for this heavy equipment, demanding a cash payment, representing a barn company…I *never* could have predicted it. Not for a second. A moment later the man appeared again, this time with a freshly printed sheet of paper with one sentence at the top which read: "I have received $75 to level this barn on concrete blocks."

There was a line for me to sign, and the man handed me a pen. As I signed, I smiled and said,

"You don't think I'd just drive off with your money without leveling the barn, do you?"

I waited for a response, but there was none. It was obvious to me that neither of us trusted the other; this was the natural progression of such an absurd situation, yet somehow, a repo wasn't even involved. After the paper was signed, the money changed hands, and as my work began, the man's entire demeanor shifted. He began regarding me as an old buddy who had stopped by for a beer and a little help with the new garage. He followed me around the building as I jacked it up and placed the concrete blocks, crawling underneath with hammer and shims, and gradually completing the process of leveling the garage again. Unprompted, he regaled me with anecdotes about loud car stereos in the neighborhood.

"Mah daughter, she runs around with a boy who does 'at shit with his radio. Ah tol' her when he gits in 'at driveway, it's off with 'at noise or I's coming out! She don' want me tah come out! My wife used ta work at Wal-Mart and theys this boy who had one 'a dem radios and he plum vibrated the windows off when he drived by."

And his neighbors, whose barn I had recently repossessed.

"At was yew who jes' come up right next door and repo'd that one barn jes the other day, weren't it? Them people over there ain't worth a shit."

191

And his ex wife.

"She done tried to run me over one time! She's damn crazy. It was three years 'fore I found out…what I found out. Then I took her to court. She SOLD me our little girl! Four years old an' I *bought* her off her. That woman had the damn devil in her, no lie."

And his cousin.

"Her and her husband sells deer. 30 thousan' dollars each. Ta hunters! They buy 'em and set 'em loose and shoot 'em. They been breedin' 'em up 'ere too. She sells 'at deer semen. They got this contraption goes and jerks 'em deers off. Must be nice. Ha! Ain't no bad moods or no complainin' or nuthin. Big business, 'at deer semen."

The Barn-Land DOT… and Deer Semen

An Alaskan Ogremonger

Try to smile as they devour our youth.[1]
—Sunny Day Real Estate

There was a time when I thought that a man named Ogremonger might devour more than just my youth. When my band went on hiatus in early 2002, I decided to fly to Alaska for an adventure with my old friend Joe. Though I had been in and out of town with the band for the last couple years, Joe and I had remained good friends, and since my Mom was living in Alaska at the time and had invited us to spend the summer with her, we figured it sounded like a great adventure. The previous summer, Mom had FedEx'd me two huge boxes of enormous, wild Alaskan salmon steaks on dry ice for my birthday—over 60 pounds of the best fish I'd ever eaten. Maybe the best *food* I've ever eaten. I do know that one vegetarian friend started eating salmon regularly after that first amazing evening of grilled fish. My buddies and I called all our friends and fired up three grills for three hours in the backyard for probably 30 people and still had plenty of huge salmon steaks left. All we added was a bit of olive oil and Paul Prudhomme's Blackened Redfish Magic seasoning—it was phenomenally delicious stuff.

For a couple weeks over the holidays during the previous winter, I had visited my Mom in Alaska. During that visit I'd worked in snow up to my waist, shoveling it from the roofs of tour buses in a parking lot, trudging from bus to bus with a ladder and shovel over my head, for some extra cash. Standing alone in the snow in a deserted parking lot on the roof

---

[1] Sunny Day Real Estate. "The Shark's Own Private Fuck." *How It Feels to Be Something On.* Seattle: Sub Pop Records, 1998.

An Alaskan Ogremonger

of a bus with only a couple of bald eagles soaring far above for company, I was enveloped in the quiet and seduced by the magnificence of the panoramic landscape that surrounded me. The immense mountains and incomprehensively gigantic glaciers made a big impression. It was beyond beautiful, and while it was fun to navigate snow up to my midsection for the first time, I thought I might like to visit Alaska in the summer when there would be a lot less of it to dig through. Joe and I had both heard about how we could make good money on a fishing boat or in pipeline construction, and we were sure we'd come home with great stories and enough money to pay off our student loans and then some. At least we were right about the stories.

We lived in one of several tiny fishing villages in the Prince William Sound, near where the Exxon Valdez had made her infamous unscheduled deposit of nearly 11 million gallons of crude oil in 1989, and these hardy locals were no strangers to tragedy. Rewind about a century into the village's calamitous history, and you will discover records of the 1898 Gold Rush Stampede. Some 4,000 prospectors, survivors beaten into submission by successive mining accidents that had claimed the lives of scores of their less fortunate peers, had returned to the Lower 48[2] from this spot with great stories and no gold, just like Joe and I did, just over a century later.

In 1964, an earthquake registering 9.2 on the Richter scale—the strongest quake ever recorded in North America—hammered the same village. Survivors were quick to band together and rebuild, winning national recognition as an "All American City" the following year. Anyway, 1989 turned out to be another pretty rough year. The winter following the Exxon Valdez oil spill disaster, the cleanup effort still going strong, oil still soaking into the shores, our little town received a record 47 feet of snowfall. Perhaps as a result of all these struggles through the years, perhaps as a genetic predisposition, or perhaps as a general rule, Alaskans are tough-ass people who are used to getting the shit kicked out of them and getting back up, again and again, with vigor and vinegar.

---

[2] Alaska became the 49th U.S. state in 1959.

HARDBARNED!
One Man's Quest for Meaningful Work in the American South

When Joe and I arrived in the late spring of 2002, the weather was overcast and cool, rainy and dreary. On the one or two glorious days when the sun came out from behind the clouds that season, Joe and I hiked up a mountain overlooking the city. We spotted a few black bears on distant hills with our binoculars, but we never ran into one up close. After getting a brief feel for our new surroundings, we set ourselves to the task of finding jobs, which was a lot more difficult than we had expected.

After visiting a few local watering holes and being discouraged by various locals' many stories of evil, drunken captains, lost arms, severed legs and fingers, missing toes, eyeballs, paychecks and lives, we soon gave up our initial idea of working on active fishing boats around Alaska. All the remaining work in the little town (population still hovering around 4,000) seemed to either be highly-paid, unionized construction jobs with the pipeline company or gory jobs in the cannery for minimum wage. Because we had just moved to town, we didn't have a year of established residency, so we were ineligible for the pipeline union. We didn't want to stand around in the noxious cannery all day, up to our knees and elbows in fish guts for six bucks an hour, so we hit the pavement in search of more attractive and lucrative employment.

We soon discovered that with few exceptions, small-town Alaskans didn't look kindly on interlopers trying to steal jobs from hard-working local folk. As in my North Carolinian summers, Joe and I fit into neither the "tourist" nor the "local" categories, so in Alaska we just didn't fit in. We were surprised to find that outside the bars, we could barely get anyone to give us the time of day, much less a chance at a decent job. Employers were consistently dismissive of two young men from Down South. Perhaps they were shocked to see that we still had all our teeth, wore shoes with socks and lacked straw hats, but none of them seemed shocked enough to hire us.

Having mentioned a few southern stereotypes, I feel another digression into my experiences with them is called for. I grew up Down South, but my parents were college degree-holding Yankees, for the most part. We lived in a southern city that was full of highly educated people, boasted a nationally ranked school system, offered quite a bit of cultural diversity and subsidized the arts. My folks divorced when I was five, but they remained friends, and I was extremely fortunate because they both played an active part in my life. We were never even close to wealthy, but I had everything I needed and a lot of what I wanted. I grew up in simple homes and apartments. I'd say we were middle class, but we didn't live far from areas with polar extremes of poverty and ignorance, wealth and privilege.

In my home town, if you knew where to look, you could find what qualified as a fancy suburb for rich people just as well as you could spot a poor area populated with shacks, but most homes were modest and fell somewhere in between. Plenty of people who grew up nearby lacked many of the economic and educational opportunities I took for granted, but I didn't realize how insular an environment my home town was until many years later when I really got to know the rural South through my job as a barn hauler and saw the roots of many stereotypes of southerners that I had never truly understood or related to, up close. Though I grew up in the South, I had lived in a city, and as Joe and I searched for jobs in Alaska, I had yet to fully experience the southern rural culture that seemed to be working against me.

While there is an element of truth to southern stereotypes, of course they can be incorrect and hurtful, and they are only a small fraction of the story of what it is like to grow up Down South. Any exercise in assumptions about entire groups of people is generally unfair, usually inaccurate, and always ill-advised, but we make judgments about who people are and where they come from every day, within seconds of meeting each other. It's innate.[3] In a certain sense, I had been raised in the South but did not identify with many of the standard assumptions about southerners.

---

3 A research study by Phil McAleer, Alexander Todorov and Pascal Belin, entitled *How Do You Say 'Hello'? Personality Impressions from Brief Novel Voices,* published in the international peer-reviewed journal PLOS ONE in March 2014 found that we all make judgments about personality traits like trustworthiness, likeability and aggression almost instantaneously, at the sound of a person's first word of hello.

It was difficult to be on the other side of a stereotype, feeling as though assumptions were being made about me as soon as my home state was revealed, which wouldn't have bothered me nearly as much if it had not been standing between me and a paycheck. Like most people, neither of us liked to be placed in a category before we'd had a chance to prove ourselves worthy employees, and every individual deserves a chance to prove his or herself.

I can't hold a grudge against Alaskans, though. The national media has not traditionally been kind to the South, reinforcing southern stereotypes routinely, some of which are rooted in reality, as I discovered daily throughout my adventures in Barn Land. My most memorable example is a time when my home state made the nationwide evening news. I believe I was in high school at the time, and still watching newscasts on TV, back when nightly network news programs featured actual news instead of cat videos and shopping updates. We were surprised to see our state featured at all, until we saw the footage they chose to broadcast. It must have been a slow news day.

Swarms of loud, intrusive cicadas had infested large portions of our region, and locals were dealing with the infestation in unique ways. The national news producers decided to show clips from an interview with a barely intelligible woman who was living on a floating mobile home in the middle of a lake, grilling the thumb-sized insects on her charcoal grill like kabobs and demonstrating how tasty they were with a bit of mustard. Facing repeated rejection as we wandered the streets in search of gainful employment, I flashed back to the televised image of this woman, a cackling sort of Tolkien-esque hag, crunching down on her steaming Cicada-bob with a gap-toothed grin and a thumbs-up, and I marveled at the power of television, southern stereotypes, and their tangible consequences for me and Joe in our present moment of desperation in this small Alaskan fishing village.

Sure, in plenty of cultures it is perfectly acceptable to eat insects. They're packed with protein, but this spectacle, beamed across the nation

An Alaskan Ogremonger

years ago, wasn't helping anyone improve their innate assumptions about the intellect of the average southerner. Or maybe it was all in my head and stereotypes had nothing to do with our unemployment, but what else could we blame it on? We bathed, smiled, looked folks in the eye, offered firm handshakes and spoke clearly. It wasn't enough. It had been weeks, and we had no offers of employment.

After losing much of our initial job-hunting enthusiasm, we hit a few of the bars again. People were more welcoming and talkative at the local watering holes, but things weren't looking up. Wondering what to do, our delusions of financial freedom dashed on rocks like so many lost ships in the Prince William Sound, we wandered aimlessly around by the docks, watching the squealing seagulls fight over the fish remains tossed aside by boat captains and admiring the magnificent bald eagles as they swooped in to claim their shares, scattering the terrified gulls. At times the gulls would gather the courage to gang up on a solo eagle and chase him away, but it took at least four of them to budge the eagles, massive and intimidating beasts that they were.

We grabbed an occasional breakfast at the hunting-lodge themed restaurant or the diner at the dock, keeping to ourselves and learning to drink unsweetened ice tea. We finally found work scrubbing blood and fish guts from a charter boat down at the dock every night, but that was only an hour or two of work for each of us and didn't pay much at all. We enjoyed listening to the classic rock station on the boat's radio and drinking cheap Icehouse and Ham beer, scouring the boat at dusk with mops, sponges and sprayer nozzles, laughing at our circumstances, and yet still in awe of the beauty of our surroundings. We'd stop by the video store on the walk home and pick up DVD copies of *Cemetery Man*, *The Burbs*, and the *Evil Dead* trilogy. Eventually we found an ad in the paper placed by a guy who owned a construction company and needed laborers. Though Joe and I had both worked for Harold and had a little experience in various areas of construction, we had *no idea* what we were in for.

Ogremonger, our employer, was one intense dude, but intense is an extraordinarily inadequate adjective. The man was built like a juvenile gorilla, powerful but agile, of average height but exceptionally strong. His hands were three times the size of ours. He moved very quickly at all times. He was incredibly focused. The man did not stop or rest. Ever. Like a Terminator. Physically, he resembled a slightly shorter, more sinuous and muscular version of the relentless, mustachioed biker/bounty hunter in *Raising Arizona*. We soon realized that with the exception of an occasional, unpredictable visit by a petulant 16-year-old boy whom Ogremonger tolerated once a week or so in a fleeting effort to instill some discipline in the lazy kid or perhaps impress his mother, Joe and I made up the entire Ogremonger construction crew.

Of course there was Ogremonger himself, a force of nature. There were to be no more employees, though we could easily have used 10 more guys. Despite the fact that everything in the grocery store was at least twice as expensive in Alaska as it was at home, he only paid us 10 bucks an hour to work harder than either of us had ever worked in our lives. Harder than either of us may ever work again. He kept his tools in an old yellow school bus that he had converted into a mobile tool shed, which he would drive to each job site and park for the duration of the job. He took out all the seats and replaced them with shelves for the tools. He had Joe cut rebar for 10 hours straight (with a pair of bolt cutters as tall as a man) and then stack and order it for four more hours, while I dug up rocks with a pick and shovel and threw them out of the trenches of the foundation we were building for a new house. It was a lot more fun with Donnie and his Dad.

There was no actual soil in Alaska. There was merely thin, black, sandy silt and a bunch of rocks. After I'd dug out most of the decent-sized rocks and chucked them out of the four-foot-deep trench that was to house the foundation, we were asked to pummel the ground into submission with a shuddering, gas-powered contraption that bounced up and down like a robot bull in a cowboy bar. The main difference between this device and a jackhammer was that its business end had a flat, metal surface, about the size of a sheet of paper, instead of a sharp tip. This ultimate challenge of power tools was designed to tamp down or flatten and compact the rocks inside the footer in preparation for the concrete foundation, instead of breaking them apart as a jackhammer would. We were expected to hold onto the bare metal handles as it slammed into the ground, relentlessly hammering the silt and rocks into a muddy stew, as Ogremonger stood above the deep trench and squirted the ground around us with a garden hose, an effort that may have helped the soil to compress in preparation for the concrete to come but nonetheless transformed the trench into a slippery, soupy, dangerous mess.

Trying to hold onto—much less control—the machine as it slammed up and down and pitched in every direction must have looked ridiculous. Spectators couldn't decide whether to laugh or fear for the safety of the operator. Joe wisely refused to operate this awful machine after a short attempt, fearing the inevitable shattering of bones inside his thin running shoes. Stuck with it, I managed to finish the job without smashing my feet, though I did earn plenty of bloody knuckles as the thing pitched and kicked me into the sides of the rocky trenches I had dug, while I struggled to hold the bucking bastard steady. Eventually Joe finished cutting the rebar, and I finished scooping out and pounding down the trenches, and together we built the wooden forms to wedge into the trenches that would hold the concrete foundation and walls.

Mosquito season began, and we had never seen such insects—the size of houseplants—in our lives. We were forced to roast in the heat of beekeeper's hoods and endure endless bites on our exposed flesh or forego the hoods and face the constantly dive-bombing bugs in our eyes, noses, mouths and ears. If we stopped work to swat at the bugs, we faced Ogremonger's wrath or his attempts to joke about how we didn't work hard enough. He figured that 20 minutes a day for lunch was plenty of break time in our typical 14-hour days of intense physical labor. We finished the forms for the concrete foundation while battling the bugs. The day the concrete truck came, we were running from end to end of our foundation, either desperately trying to hold one makeshift wooden form together while another burst open with overflowing wet cement, humping two five-gallon buckets of wet concrete from one area to another to pour into a hole that the truck missed, or smoothing out a section on top of a form that actually held. We finished the foundation and five-foot concrete walls and got to work on framing the house. We had only spent a few days framing when, for reasons we never learned, we left the site of the new house and began work on replacing the roof of another one.

    Joe and I were exhausted and sore all over, lacking any other appealing job prospects, still making 10 bucks an hour after several weeks, despite early talk of a pending raise, and we were really sick of this Ogremonger guy. We started to talk about cutting our Alaskan adventure a bit short. When we began the second assignment with our taskmaster, we spent a couple days tearing off an old roof, throwing shingles into the yard, ripping up the tar-coated paper, and finally, on our hands and knees, prying every one of thousands of tiny staples from the plywood sub-roof with pliers.

    Then the weather took a turn for the worse. Ogremonger was unfazed. He had us cover the exposed roof with gigantic sheets of clear plastic because he didn't want the wood underneath to get wet before we were able to re-tar and re-shingle. We assumed we would then leave and wait for the weather to improve so that we could finish the job. No. We were expected to work in the driving rain, on top of the plastic sheeting that we had covered the steep roof with, exposing and finishing small sections as we balanced precariously on the plastic while carrying huge walk boards that easily weighed hundreds of pounds. The walk boards were designed to allow us to access various sections of a roof sloped and angled in many different directions, but what kind of maniac would force his employees to walk un-harnessed on plastic sheets on a steep roof in the rain, struggling with hundreds of pounds of walk board? We protested this decision and pointed out that we would certainly slip on the wet plastic and fall.

    "No you won't. Just be careful."

    At this point, we knew he didn't like us, and he knew we didn't like him. He owed us a few weeks of back pay, and since he paid us in cash, there were no records of us having worked for him. We would have quit right then, but we didn't know if he'd pay us the money he owed us, and if that happened, we wouldn't be able to afford to fly home. Joe and I resolved to finish this job, get paid and walk away for good. Each of us had at least one extremely close call, slipping and coming very close to falling off the slippery plastic-covered roof in the rain, but we always managed to catch each other before either of us fell. We watched each other closely and had each other's backs as we always had. Either of us would have fallen off without the other. Ogremonger laughed when we slipped and complimented us on our "performances."

There were times when we half-heartedly discussed attacking him from behind with shovels and 2X4s, but we were pretty convinced that he would have killed us both without really trying that hard, and we sure as hell didn't want to be stuck there without money to get home and a murder rap, if we even survived. Finally, the day's work came to a close. The next day I went to meet Ogremonger and collect our cash. I didn't need to say anything for him to know what we had decided. Our barely restrained rage the day before on the roof in the rain had made our intentions clear.

"Guess you guys've had enough, huh? Heading back down south?" He sneered victoriously.

I told him I didn't know what we were doing next, but that he was right about one thing. We'd definitely had enough of working for him. He paid up in cash as promised, and I never saw him again. I like to think that we impressed Ogremonger a little, but I'll never know for sure. He worked the hell out of us for months, and we never complained until that last day on the roof in the rain. He must have known that he got more than his money's worth out of us. Of course I realize that there is only a brief window of weather each year in Alaska in which construction work is viable, and this was part of Ogremonger's reason for working so hard and fast, every day and into the night. He had to make as much money as he could in the short time that he had for contract work. Living up there is hard. I understand that. What I don't really get is how or why his judgment became faulty enough to endanger his entire workforce with an unsafe and clearly ridiculous situation that drove us to quit. Only Ogremonger can explain the actions of Ogremonger.

We made friends with some neighbors—union pipeline workers—sharing beers in the backyard after work, and one night they invited us to drink with them at the local Moose Lodge, where we were treated like honored guests, a welcome contrast with what we were used to. We learned how to drink a "Duck Fart," a uniquely Alaskan concoction involving Bailey's Irish Cream, whiskey, amaretto, and a deep post-shot inhalation. Joe tried a "Waterfall," which involved at least three kinds of liquor, three shot glasses, a mess and a lot of laughs. Joe has since speculated that the Waterfall was merely a joke waiting to be played on a willing participant, preferably interlopers like us. We walked home in the middle of the night, but it wasn't dark, which took a little getting used to. After working for Ogremonger, however, despite the bright nights, we were out as soon as we hit our pillows.

Before we left Alaska, we were finally able to arrange one glorious day of deep-sea fishing, thanks to the kindness of one local halibut fisherman who seemed to enjoy our company and probably felt sorry for us. A salty sea captain with a thick, dark beard, a sailor's cap, squinting eyes and an easy smile, Biff was in the middle of a drawn-out lawsuit after an accident that had broken both his legs and left him hobbled and reliant on a steady stream of painkillers. Joe and I had never been deep-sea fishing before, and we were beyond stoked. Biff's old, arthritic chocolate lab named Cindy joined us on Captain Biff's tiny fishing vessel one morning. We left early, brought sandwiches, and drank beer all day on the water.

Halibut fishing was something like fishing for a catfish: the Drop Your Line and Wait method. A deep-sea vacuum cleaner, the opportunivore known as the halibut can grow to nearly 500 pounds. Not a pretty fish, the halibut is a bottom dweller of the flounder persuasion, nearly flat with a white belly and brown topside with two bulging eyes like muddy marbles. They are delicious on the grill, though—a dense white meat akin to swordfish. We'd cast our lines out close to the boat with heavy weights and let them sink. From then on it was a waiting game, watching the little floats and keeping an eye out for movement on the line. If we detected something, we'd stand up, seize the huge pole from its holder on the side of the boat and jerk the line mightily to one side, hoping to set the hook in whatever giant monster of the deep we had managed to hook. Throughout the morning we caught several bait fish and even a few stingrays, which we reeled in and tossed back. Sometime before noon, Joe stood up suddenly and started yelling.

"I got a BIG one! This thing's a MONSTER! Man I'm gonna need help!"

I jumped to react, grabbing the fishing belt with the plastic pole-anchor, wrapping it around Joe and buckling it around his waist as he struggled with the fish. Together we got the pole into the belt, and I watched as Joe excitedly wrestled with this fish for the next 30 minutes or so. Finally dragging the monster to the surface, Joe's expression changed quickly. The fish was 20 pounds at best—a certifiable monster if pulled from a lake Down South—but by no means large for an Alaskan ocean-floor-dwelling halibut. It was a keeper, though, and we all enjoyed teasing Joe for the rest of the day about his little monster. We caught a few other random baitfish, and I managed to pull a 68-pound halibut aboard, which was definitely a thrill for me, having caught no more than a few small bass or bluegill in freshwater lakes in my limited experience as a fisherman. Still, we hadn't yet seen a big halibut. A few hours later, something flinched on Joe's line, and he grabbed the pole. Right away he started yelling,

"THIS ONE IS THE ONE! IT'S REALLY A MONSTER THIS TIME! OH MAN THIS THING IS HUGE!"

We laughed and let him struggle.

"Oh *yeah*!" we said.

"Another *monster*! Be *careful*!"

An Alaskan Ogremonger

We laughed again and had another beer. After 20 minutes or so, however, we began to get curious, and Joe clearly needed help. The fish was pulling him left and right, and he was struggling to hold on, even with the belt. I reached to help, and together we hefted the fish to the surface. It was immediately clear that Joe was right. This fish was five feet long and as wide as we were. We fought it to the side of the boat and tried to figure out what to do next as the monster beast smashed itself into the side of the boat. Cindy, roused from her slumber by the ruckus, prepared to attack the demon from the deep in our defense, barking ferociously though unsure of how to help. Before we knew what was happening, our boat captain had drawn a chrome revolver. He reached down beside us and put four bullets point blank into the fish's head. That did the trick. Joe, Cindy and I looked wide-eyed at each other for a moment, and Captain Biff returned with a huge gaff, which he hooked into the prone corpse, lugging it aboard.

Joe's halibut weighed 128 pounds. Nearly 13 hours after leaving, sunburned and exhausted, we returned to the docks to take pictures of our catch. Joe and I stood proudly on either side of his colossal halibut, the snow-capped Alaskan peaks at our backs, a triumphant end to a glorious and memorable day at sea. We watched our generous host clean our fish and pack the huge steaks of thick white meat into the coolers we had purchased at the local grocery.

We didn't know how to thank our rare friend, the boat captain Biff. How did we deserve an all-inclusive free day on a chartered fishing boat with Biff and Cindy? He even cleaned our fish. Biff's generosity was overwhelming and had come at just the right time, when Joe and I had had about enough of our little Alaskan adventure and had just about given up on getting a chance to do some real deep-sea fishing. We couldn't afford to pay for what he had given us, but the least we could do was treat him to a steak dinner, which he graciously accepted. Though I have since tried to contact him, I lost touch with Biff, but Joe and I still owe him a debt of gratitude for making the best Alaskan fishing trip I could have hoped for. Thanks Captain Biff, wherever you are. I hope you got the big settlement and the spectacular yacht you so richly deserve.

Our Alaskan adventure at an end, we headed back home, two coolers full of frozen halibut steaks in tow as part of our checked baggage. We were early for our first flight and drank a lot of beer in the airport bar. We were celebrating. Joe and I had wrapped duct tape around the coolers to keep the lids shut as the fish went from plane to plane. We had already been forced to open both coolers at one of the four airports. Despite our protests, a TSA employee donned rubber gloves, cut away the duct tape and emptied the ice and frozen fish into plastic containers, searching for contraband.

Upon arriving at our final airport Down South, exhausted after four flights with whiskey on the plane and beers in between, we waited at the baggage claim to pick up my trunk full of clothes and our coolers. I wasn't happy to discover that the metal lock on the front of my trunk had been broken off, and all that was left was a piece of jagged metal that cut a deep gash in my hand as I reached to pull it away from the rotating baggage carousel. Bleeding heavily, I then noticed the two coolers, now wrapped inadequately with the reconstituted duct-tape, just as they tipped the edge of the steep baggage-claim ramp. They both came crashing down and popped open, spilling cold water, frozen fish and crushed ice all over the luggage carousel, which I promptly decorated with the bright blood that spurted from my hand. Joe and I chased our bloody frozen fish around the carousel, scrambling to refill our coolers with the prized and edible trophies from our Alaskan adventure. It was finally over, save the three-hour drive ahead of us.

Our pal Austin had driven out to pick us up and was ready to haul us home in his old punk-rock minivan. We were a scraggly-looking mess when he found us at the baggage claim, and Austin put up with our crazy stories until we both passed out in his van. Upon returning to our hometown, we immediately called all our friends and grilled a massive feast of halibut. Austin still cites that particular treat of grilled Alaskan halibut as the best meal he's ever had.

An Alaskan Ogremonger

No Asphalt, No Fiction and "Naw, I Ain't Got No Message."

Masochism is a valuable job skill.[1]
—Chuck Palahniuk

I arrived at the builders' lot to pick up a special-order barn. This happens sometimes when a customer can't find exactly what he's looking for on a sales lot and has particular features in mind. Orders are supposed to be completed within two weeks, but it doesn't always work out that way. From time to time, albeit rarely, builders screw up. They're only human. Sometimes the windows are on the wrong side, or the walls are too short, or the wrong type of door is installed, or they use the wrong kind of shingles. In general, the barns I delivered were extremely well built, but perfection is impossible, and random errors occurred on occasion. Some people are more particular about their barns than others, so sometimes these little errors didn't matter much, but of course it's all subjective, and everything depended on the customer.

This time I jumped out of the truck and was greeted by a loud SPLAT as my old steel-toed boots (with the steel toes falling out from kicking Hi-Lift jacks into place underneath barns far too many times) sank into the soupy gray mess that was once a gravel lot. At this particular manufacturing lot, the ground conditions were either a sloppy morass of muck or a dry dust storm, the likes of which would give Luke Skywalker flashbacks from Tatooine. A driver could usually expect one or the other:

---

1 Palahniuk, Chuck. *Choke*. New York: Doubleday, 2001.

mud or dust. It seemed that things would work a lot more smoothly for everyone if the lots were paved, but they never were.

Ah, how nice it would have been if the forklifts the builders used didn't get stuck in the mud, spinning their wheels and requiring rescue by trucks. And oh, how those builders might appreciate it if drivers didn't kick up dust typhoons that blow directly into their open garage-style building areas every time we passed by on the lot with truck and trailer, but such was the situation when I was hauling barns. Sadly, there was no asphalt.

On this particular visit to the manufacturer's lot, I quickly spotted the colored tag I was searching for and just as quickly discovered that the special-order barn had been built incorrectly. I called the builder via cell phone and realized he was standing a few yards away from me in the mud. Owen: large, hairy, jolly. He smiled in his peaceful way and addressed me by my full given name, like an angry parent or Jay from the Brown Horse restaurant might've, but gently. This was his usual manner of greeting me. I asked about the barn and he made a call to the sales lot, confirming that the barn had not been built according to the customer's specifications. He assured me that the rebuilt barn would be ready in a few days. Then Owen surprised me with a compliment about my attention to detail, and I thanked him, though I wasn't convinced it was really a compliment. I inexplicably blurted that I was burned out on the barn-hauling job and planning on getting out of the business to try my hand at being a starving writer and hack musician for a while. That brought a chuckle. He asked if I liked fiction.

"Of course!" I said.

He went on to say that in his experience, any writing that wasn't based in Profound Truth wasn't very interesting or worthy of his attention; therefore, he only read "educational" works and non-fiction,

"Except for Arthur Conan Doyle and Shakespeare, of course."

I had to admit I had never read any Sherlock Holmes stuff, but I liked *Hamlet* and *Macbeth*, *Othello* and a few others. I told Owen that he

HARDBARNED!
One Man's Quest for Meaningful Work in the American South

was missing out by refusing to read fiction. I pled my case with what was probably an ineffective argument on how fantastic Cormac McCarthy's novel *The Road* is. I talked about how it was the most visceral, desperate and beautiful illustration of the power of a man's love for his son—any person's love for another person, really—that I had ever read, Shakespeare included. I doubted I could have convinced Owen to read anything that I'd suggest to him—not that he wouldn't at least hear me out—but he was a stubborn guy. Of all the wonderful fictional characters to enjoy, why would only Hamlet and Holmes make the cut? How could Owen disregard the entire international canon of fiction because according to him it isn't the Truth with a capital T? I could argue all day that it is. Owen went on to say something about mystical realism that didn't make any sense to me. He asked if I understood.

"No. Not really."

"Well bless your heart."

Maybe I'm wrong, but in my attempts to bridge our divide, I felt somewhat dismissed. I tried once more, arguing that good fiction is made great by its innate ability to reveal profound truths about real people and real lives. I don't think that affected him much either. So I loaded up a couple of barns for inventory without incident and hit the road for the sales lot. I had about an hour and a half ahead of me in the truck, and I had a stack of audio books—fiction and nonfiction alike—to keep me occupied and at least take my mind far away from Barn Land.

* * *

Barn hauling dug into my psyche like the mud, grease and oil I could never seem to remove from under my fingernails. One day I was sitting in the truck in another mud-and-gravel used car (and barn) sales lot in a steady rain, beneath shimmering, flickering perimeter flags indicating perpetual sales and desperation. Surrounded by purple and blue 1980s stand as the salesman shuffles through his many stacks of papers to locate a phone number, one I know he doesn't have because there is only one on my work order, and if the customer had offered a second contact number, any sales person would have added it to the work order with the first.

My problem is that I'm trying to deliver a barn to a lady who has ordered the barn, agreed to the delivery date and been reminded to expect me today, but she doesn't answer or return any of my calls. I'm trying to confirm that she's home and ready for the delivery, so she can show me where to put her barn before I leave the lot. I don't want to waste my time. There is only one phone number on the work order. The spaces for work phone and cell phone are left blank. Maybe she doesn't really want me to deliver the barn. Maybe it's buyer's remorse combined with a general disregard for the plight of the unfortunate man tasked with delivery of her building in the midst of a storm, but it's probably not that complicated. A lone customer appears in the sales bunker, attempting to haggle with the owner over a used car on the lot, and it's obvious that the random gathering of old men in the room is convinced he's a fool. He doesn't give up though, offering to trade in a gun.

"I'll take fifteen fer it."

"Fifteen dollars 'ar cents?"

The room erupts in laughter.

"Fifteen hunderd's what I said."

"They don't make no gun I'd pay that fer."

The salesman keeps the keys to the doors of all the empty barns for sale on his lot in his safe, and the logic in this escapes me. No other sales lots do this.

"It's not like somebody's gonna grab the keys and drive the barn away,"

I say with a smile.

"You know we got little kids runnin' around here sometimes and if they see's 'em keys, they grab 'em."

"Oh."

I decide not to point out the obvious—that there are probably only three or four different patterns for barn keys, or that the builder leaves each set on a screw inside the top of the barn's doorframe, far higher than any little kid could ever reach. Why would anyone take the keys to an empty barn for sale on a lot anyway? I might personally congratulate a thief determined enough to pick out a barn on the lot by day, sneak on to the lot after hours, take the keys from inside the empty barn, stake out the lot for the next month or however long it takes to sell the barn, lurk around until I deliver the barn, follow me to the customer's house, and hide in the woods until the person fills the barn with a bunch of crap, so he can finally steal it and go home. That thief really deserves the bag of used clothes, the holiday decorations, the box of old computer parts and the broken yard sale junk he ends up with, but why complicate things?

I keep my mouth shut and follow the salesman's All Purpose Employee (APE—I had been one in my restaurant worker days, so I knew one when I saw him) back out into the raging thunderstorm. We try each of the keys on his gigantic key ring—which, it turns out, contains lots of other keys to other things as well—on each of the locks on all of the empty barns on the lot. Attempting to prevent the APE from climbing onto my soaking wet trailer to try and find the right key to the barn that still sits on it ready for delivery, I encourage him to let me climb up and try the keys. We can't have him slipping and falling and breaking an ankle, I assure him. The APE consents and I climb on, trying one key at a time, getting thoroughly soaked. I finally find the right key and break for lunch.

Saturated and dripping in my tractor hat, fuzzy beard, muddy sweatshirt, ripped jeans and torn-up boots, I get a few sideways looks at Subway when I stop in for lunch amid the small white-collar crowd of bank tellers and teachers awaiting their sandwiches, but I'm in deep cover, and it's not like there aren't other scruffy-looking blue-collar dudes around these rural outposts. I look the part for the gig, and I talk like it too; when I get my change back from my sandwich, I *preeshiate* it. I can use *ya'll* and *ain't* and *yes ma'am* and *aw hell yeah* with the best of 'em. As Mitch put it, explaining why he'd often adopt a deeper southern accent while hauling barns,

"A lot of times, I'll just talk like they do. It makes things easier."

My beard was long enough that on hot summer days it felt like a sweaty squirrel was trying to pry my lips open and climb inside my mouth. It was unpleasant but somehow appropriate and satisfying. To hell with business casual. At least I wasn't stuck in a soul-sucking fluorescent-lit cube somewhere. I finish the sandwich and head back to the lot. Still no word from the barn lady who had made the appointment for today's delivery.

Almost two hours pass, and I'm still sitting in the truck, listening to NPR predict that the rain will soon begin freezing. It'd be nice to get home before that, I think, but the one and only reason I am in this remote rural town is to deliver one lousy barn. I have nothing else to do here but watch the clock and imagine my fantasy of a relaxing evening's free time evaporate into nothing. My eyes fixate again on the sparkly plastic-fringed flags that line the crummy little lot in red white and blue. Even in this weather, they're just so sparkly. The woman who won't answer her phone still hasn't answered, and I leave another message on her machine.

At this point I hear from Mitch and learn that the customer has marked the spot for the delivery, crucial information, which for some reason was neither mentioned by the salesman nor added to the work order, meaning that I've wasted several hours and that the customer doesn't even need to be there when I deliver the barn. I never needed to talk to her on the phone in the first place. Details like these are elusive, precious and infuriating. Now I can finally leave, and yet I could have left hours ago. The salesman didn't bother to write directions on the work order either. The lady won't answer her phone, nobody knows where she is, and I'm still soaking wet, wasting my day away in the used car lot, and now a storm of freezing rain is imminent.

I almost never get furious anymore; at this point in my pre-smartphone, pre-GPS life of barns, I just expect this dysfunction, but I can always make an exception. I get directions from Mitch's wife over the phone via her computer's Internet connection, and I venture out. It's still raining, getting foggier as I head up a mountain in rural nowhere. Now it's starting to get really dark, and there are, of course, no motherfucking goddamn street signs. I punch my trip odometer at every turn, guessing and hoping that these unmarked streets correspond with those listed in my newfound directions, and that the distance measurements between turns are somewhat accurate because that's all I've got to go on. Swiftly I become lost and even angrier. I decide to try calling the woman again. For the first time all day, she answers, barely.

"I'm trying to deliver a building to your house."

"Yeah?" she replies, disinterested and mildly irritated, as if I've interrupted re-runs of *Murder She Wrote*.

"I guess you didn't get the messages I left on your machine. I've been waiting for hours for you to return my calls with directions. You made an appointment to have your barn delivered today and left this number for us to call upon delivery. There aren't any directions on the work order. I've been sitting at the sales lot for hours, hoping that you'd call me back, and since then, after finding a route online through a friend, I've been driving around in circles in your general vicinity with this oversize load that blocks most of both sides of the road, but there are no street signs anywhere near your house. Your barn is the only reason I drove to this town today. Now it's getting dark and the rain is starting to freeze. I need to know how to get to your house."

"Naw, I ain't got no message."

The answering machine debuted sometime around the year 1935. It is phenomenal that after more than seven decades in production, people purchase it, install it and still don't know how the fuck it works. The answering machine takes on essential significance when one doesn't own a cell phone and is expecting a driver to deliver a building on a date previously agreed upon while living in the middle of nowhere without a single street sign in the vicinity, in the middle of a rapidly darkening storm of freezing fucking rain, but what do I know?

Much later that night, after finally parking the truck, hanging my head and trudging toward my apartment, I noticed a yellow, plastic pellet stuck to my car amid a white puddle of bird poo. Neighborhood kids around our low-rent apartment complex often hurled themselves, shrieking with glee, up and down the outdoor stairs like herds of small elephants, wild with ADHD and their regular rations of soda and McDeath, shaking framed pictures from our walls as the iron staircase quaked under their stomping pudginess, shooting at each other with toy Airsoft pistols, dodging bright pellets the approximate size of rabbit turds. Apparently a bird had eaten this colorful plastic projectile and actually passed it. It reminded me of *Terminator II: Judgment Day*, when John Connor says

"We're not gonna make it, are we? Humans, I mean."

"It's in your nature to destroy yourselves,"[2] the Terminator replies.

I felt so sorry for the poor bird.

---

2 *Terminator 2: Judgment Day*. Dir. James Cameron. Perf. Edward Furlong, Arnold Schwarzenegger. Carolco Pictures, 1991.

Lawnmowing, Luggage Toting, Love Connections and Job Rejection

When you can't create, you can work.[1]
—Henry Miller

Just before I returned from Alaska at the tail end of the summer of 2002, my band broke up, eliminating our plans for another fall tour of the US followed by Europe in the spring, and I wasn't sure what to do next. I went back to looking for work as a writer and editor, but my luck hadn't changed much. Nobody was biting, and I had to do something. This time, my friend Brenner suggested that Joe (who was also looking for work) and I try our hands at landscaping with him. He thought his boss could use a couple extra workers.

"Ron's a real jackass, but he means well, and he'll probably hire both of you," said Brenner, a live sound engineer who had toured with my band and had worked with me before, on the fake palm tree and casino gigs, and on several others when we were both under the employ of our university's live sound crew. These days he runs sound equipment on tour with country music stars, but at this point he was looking for his first real job in music as he cut lawns and planted shrubs for Ron between semesters. Thus began several sweaty, late-summer months of messing about in the dirt, mowing grass, weed-eating, planting shrubs, digging drainage ditches and trying to convince Joe not to attack our new boss, Ron, with a shovel to the back of the head, which he came much closer to actually doing with Ron than he had with Ogremonger.

---

1 Miller, Henry. *Henry Miller On Writing.* New York: New Directions, 1964.

Ron, while nowhere near as tough or demanding as Ogremonger, was more like his antithesis, disorganized and infuriatingly absent minded. Brenner liked to refer to him as "the moron." Though Ron claimed decades of landscaping experience, he didn't appear to have learned much from it. Every day he would insist that Joe and I arrive at his house in the early morning, where we would invariably wait around for an hour or two while he figured out what the hell we were going to do for the day. We often suggested to Ron that he spend a little time at the end of the previous day to figure out what we'd be doing the next day, instead of paying us both for standing around twiddling our thumbs for a couple hours every morning, but this logic was lost on him. Often Ron would leave us at a job site without a design plan for installing a bunch of new plants he had just left us with, or without all the right parts for the installation of an irrigation system, or without tools. Eventually, Joe got angry and decided to show up later in the morning. Ron would yell at him for it, and their working relationship deteriorated further, but Ron knew that Joe was easily his most skilled worker and wouldn't dare let him go.

One day I was stuck on weed-eater duty at some rich guy's house. His permagrin and ultra-bronzed look reminded me of "America's Favorite Game Show Host," Guy Smiley from *Sesame Street*. This guy lived on a multi-acre spread with a three-story mansion and a mile-long driveway. Usually Brenner and I would spend a few hours cutting the grass, trimming hedges, spreading pine needles and generally maintaining the property once a week. Mike May or Ray Hey or John Jay—or whatever his annoying, rhyming name was—always had a revolving assortment of approximately four shiny new SUVs, sports cars, and luxury sedans in his driveway, many parked in front of his four-car garage, all with TEAM HEY (or whatever) on the novelty plates. I usually got to drive the X-Mark zero-degree turning radius riding mower, which could spin on a dime and was actually kind of fun, but on this day Brenner got the X-Mark. I was slumming it on foot, trimming weeds around Guy Smiley's pool with the weed eater and blowing leftover grass around with the leaf blower, an obnoxious, noise-polluting invention I thoroughly despise, much like the car alarm.

As I made my way amid the scores of carefully manicured evergreens, the weed-eater suddenly jammed up in knots, and I had to take it apart to untangle the thick plastic line from the spool, which resulted in my hands being covered with a thick green slime, leftover from the cut grass and weeds that had gummed up the works of the handheld machine. By the time I'd untangled the mess and put the weed-eater back into service, the green slime had dried on my hands. I rinsed them off at the spigot behind the house and kept working. The next day I awoke with skin gloves on fire with a fierce case of poison ivy/sumac/oak/dark-green Spooge of Satan. The worst part was the itching between my fingers, which was impossible to alleviate. I found myself repeatedly hunched over like a supervillain's disgusting sidekick, compulsively threading and unthreading my fingers, a maniacal grimace peeling across my face, as I struggled in futility to relieve a merciless, unscratchable itch. Neither cortisone cream nor medicated spray could alleviate the maddening effects of the seemingly innocuous demon elixir in which I had dipped my unsuspecting hands. I just had to take it for two weeks until they started to dry out.

I was getting sick of putting up with Ron and his bumbling, and I still wasn't having a bit of luck in my perpetual search for writing and editing jobs. I heard from another friend about a job at a somewhat fancy hotel, downtown, about an hour from where I lived. I thought it might be fun to work indoors in a nice clean place for a while, instead of in the dirt with a shovel and a weedwacker. Indoors always seemed nice after a stint at an outdoor job in the hot summer, and the out-of-doors often looked equally attractive to me after a few months of sitting at a desk in business casual attire in an air-conditioned cubicle looking out the window at trees and greener grass. If *only* I could find a job writing about something I was interested in and make a living at it, I thought. Maybe then I could finally hop off this merry-go-round of unsatisfying work.

* * *

HARDBARNED!
One Man's Quest for Meaningful Work in the American South

Lawnmowing, Luggage Toting, Love Connections and Job Rejection

The hotel job was a bellman position, and I was stationed at the guest services desk in the vast, open hotel lobby. I stood posted on the polished marble floor in a fancy black-and-gold monkey suit with shiny buttons and shoulder pads. Though I was not required to wear a stupid hat, I looked a bit like Tim Roth in *Four Rooms*, or an affluent scarecrow. Much as they like young men in goofy golf shirts to park their cars for them, rich folks like to have these same young men dressed as showbiz monkeys carry their bags, it seems. I was expected to stand at attention with a shining, seven-foot-tall brass luggage cart, which I had most likely just finished polishing. Poised on the gleaming marble floor of the ornately decorated lobby behind the mahogany guest services desk, I greeted customers as they arrived. I would roll the lustrous cart up to the guest and offer to help with her luggage. If she accepted, I'd escort her to the elevators and to her room, sometimes telling her about room service, the bar, the weight room and pool, the massage therapist, etc. Other times, I'd make small talk or be quiet, depending on my impressions of the mood of the guest. Some looked as though they would prefer that I stared straight ahead and kept my mouth shut, so in these cases I would.

Occasionally I'd meet semi-famous people, usually actors, athletes, or country music stars, like Lee Greenwood, who is really short and bald and sings "Proud To Be An American," or Ronny Cox, the guy who plays the guitar in *Deliverance* before he gets all twisted up like a pretzel on the river. He was also blasted out the window in a hail of bullets at the climactic ending of *Robocop,* and he was a good tipper. I was once tasked with delivering chocolate-covered strawberries to the Rolling Stones, but they weren't in their room. From time to time, an entire NFL football team would stay at the hotel. It was a spectacle to see these massive men file in the front door in tracksuits with headphones and then leave a few hours later, this time in expensive suits of every pastel color imaginable. They looked like gigantic, millionaire cartoon bodybuilders, all spiffy on their way to a celebrity gala Easter-egg hunt for the March of Dimes.

HARDBARNED!
One Man's Quest for Meaningful Work in the American South

The hotel was connected to a convention center, so we would often host and provide guest services for conferences and conventions, everything from the Baptist Leadership Conference (the largest assembly of fur coats and extravagant peacock feather hats I had ever seen) and the Tractor Supply Company (TSC) vendors convention (tool show) to the National Embroidery trade show (very quiet, lots of blue hair) and the Kiwanis Club Regional Assembly (more funny hats...or were they Shriners?) to the Gospel Music Association Conference (most expensive male haircuts I'd ever seen) and the Society of CPAs Accounting Fest (suitsville).

There was the Folk Festival, which filled the building with various fragrant herbal aromas courtesy of scraggly-looking, excessively friendly baby boomers in overalls and flowered skirts leftover from the '60s who would meet up for impromptu jam sessions throughout the hotel and convention center. Banjos and guitars could be heard twanging away with mandolins and singers at all hours and on all floors for days at a time. I felt like I was backstage at the rehearsals for *A Mighty Wind*. Sometimes we'd get free stuff, usually pens and tote bags and the usual crap, but once I got an axe from one of the TSC guys. I got some funny looks from guests as I walked around the convention center and hotel in my monkey suit with a four-foot, double-bladed axe.

This time I had a really cool boss, Katie, who was funny as hell and great to work for. Katie was short, feisty and hilarious. She always dressed in a business suit, sported a spiky shock of red hair and reminded me of a cardinal; she also reminded me (fondly) of my old boss back home, Jay from the Brown Horse Restaurant. They had the same haircut and both yelled

"Oh Chris-to-pher *DRI*-ver!"

when they were looking for me. Like many of us there, Katie had aspirations beyond guest services, and I think she ended up teaching kindergarten. There was an eccentric, bald, hunched-over old black man named Cletus who worked with us at the guest services desk and reminded me of a friendlier Igor, responding when greeted that he was

"Cool, calm, and collected!"

Cletus had an enormous, toothy Steven Tyler grin and always carried a wad of cash six inches thick, which he loved to flash to whomever would look, bragging about how he was

"Runnin' those numbers!"

He had gnarly vampire fingernails and actually drew blood when accidentally scraping them across my arm a couple of times when we were really busy juggling luggage, but he usually had a good sense of humor. We gave the old guy a hard time sometimes; I remember making homemade "wanted for number running" posters featuring Cletus and posting them in the bellman's closet. That annoyed him a little, but he teased us too. We got along pretty well and had a lot of laughs along the way.

One evening in late 2002, at a house party I was attending with some rowdy friends, I ran into a young woman I had met the previous spring, prior to leaving for my final tour with the band and three years after I had split with Lena. I had noticed this beautiful young lady at a rock show and realized instantly that I'd hate myself the next day if I didn't at least introduce myself. We had ended up talking late into the night, until the bar closed. She was as intriguing as she was stunning. An artist and student of fine arts and psychology, she wanted to combine her talent for both, head to graduate school to become an art therapist and work with young people. She loved rock and roll, motorcycles, the ocean and sushi, and we hit it off right away.

When I asked for her number, she declined. She was seeing someone. I was disappointed but glad that I had met her and given it a shot. I had seen her around a couple of times since, and we were friendly, but we hadn't crossed paths for many months by the time I ran into her again at the party. This time she immediately let it slip that she was single and said yes when I again requested her phone number, writing it on my arm with a permanent marker. Though neither of us were fans, I scored free tickets to a pro hockey game, and our first date was for dinner at a nice Italian place where I had worked as a valet, followed by the hockey game. We've been happy together ever since. Three and a half years later, we were married.

That New Year's Eve on the job at the hotel, I ate some bad chicken in the employee cafeteria on my lunch break. Or at least I suspect the chicken. I was running to the bathroom with urgency 20 minutes later and asked to leave early. I felt desperately ill and fought to control the car on the interstate, in gastrointestinal agony, swerving with a large plastic bag in front of me on the steering wheel. I pulled over twice and leaned out the window, barely onto the exit ramp and swerving erratically. Somehow I made it home and spent the entire evening crawling from bed to bathroom every 20 minutes for the next eight hours. I truly thought I might die and realized that I'd rather die at my apartment in bed than in the waiting room of the ER on New Year's Eve. I made it through the night and told a couple managers about my experience, eventually discovering that it must have been the chicken, but apparently no one else had been sick, and the grumpy cook behind the counter didn't want to hear about it. He just glared at me with his wiry gray scraggle of a mustache and Coke-bottle glasses. Questionable, rubbery chicken was an occupational hazard for hotel employees brave enough to devour whatever this perpetually aggrieved gentleman served, I supposed, and I'd either have to toughen up or brown bag it.

After nearly a year of carrying around luggage in the monkey suit, I started getting antsy again, and my now occasional applications for writing jobs still got me nowhere. I enjoyed working with friends, but I felt that old familiar feeling of longing for something more, that nagging voice telling me that I could and should aspire to something more challenging and satisfying than another customer service job.

Toward the end of my guest services stint, a guest angrily criticized me for placing his dress shirts in the closet while somehow gripping the plastic-covered hangers in a manner that was displeasing to him, and I laughed a little to myself and probably shook my head. That set him off. Instead of tipping me, he said, he had now decided to give me his Ten

Commandments Penny, which I "needed more" than he did. This was a penny that had been run through one of those novelty machines, flattened and stamped in tiny print with the Ten Commandments.

"Gee, thanks," I said as I left the room. It was time to move on.

Barn Mud, Blue Blood, Detours and Dinars

I don't want to hear any more about money.[1]
—Ian Mackaye

I once delivered a barn to an absurdly wealthy man who had a private outdoor basketball court—regulation size—on the side of his house (in the middle of an average-looking middle-class subdivision), and an entire football field in the back yard, goal posts and all. I had to push a button on the intercom so that the remote-controlled gate would open at the top of the slowly winding driveway on the hill, high above his massive estate. I had to drive my truck across the football field to get out of his yard after dropping the barn.

Construction work had sent me on a confusing detour through various suburbs, knocking over bright orange barrels on either side of the truck with the corners of my oversize barn, but I finally found the place. Once I did, it was hard to miss the elaborate, wrought iron fence, twisted into the shape of the homeowner's last name. He seemed like a nice enough guy, but I didn't recognize him—not that I'd recognize very many professional football players up close anyway. He was an enormous man, and he did have on some sort of jersey, so I asked him what he did for a living. Turns out he played for a West Coast NFL team. His family was from the South, hence the mansion on the other side of the country. No tip.

Ah, tips. Statistically an unlikely occurrence in Barn Land, tips I received over three years included cash, sports drinks, teas, sodas, offers of

---

1 Embrace. "Money." *Embrace*. Washington D.C.: Dischord Records, 1987.

Barn Mud, Blue Blood, Detours and Dinars

adult beverages I had to sadly decline, homemade bread, backyard honey, T-shirts, work gloves, and even four Iraqi dinars from an Iraq war veteran. I have a deep and sincere respect for service members who have volunteered to put their lives on the line for their country, but given a choice, I would have preferred a currency I could spend at the gas station on the way home. I keep those dinars in a little box with my other assorted bits of international pocket change. This box will sit under my desk for the rest of my life, most likely. I will never put it on display. I will never spend it.

Maybe one day I'll sell it and all my other global petty cash on eBay to a currency collector. Some people do collect money and are quite serious about it, but I don't understand why. I get that it can be rare and that unique artwork is involved, but other than that, what is so special about money? Why do people collect bicentennial quarters or special edition nickels? I just don't care. It causes enough problems in the world already. Why turn it into trophies?

As much as I hate to make a fuss about money, *a necessary evil, the root of all evil*, and all of its other clichés, I went through a lot for the bloody necessary green stuff. At some point during my tenure in the truck, a man ordered a 12X36 barn from one of the sales lots I regularly stocked with barns and delivered from. This was a gigantic, garage-sized barn, not quite approaching the maximum-sized 14X40 monstrosity I delivered a couple of times and yet still sure to strike a profound fear into the hearts of pedestrians, cyclists, mailboxes and street-parkers everywhere, not to mention the drivers who have to haul the big bastards around Barn Land.

I was delivering the garage to a proud new rent-to-owner. Around 40 years old, about five foot nine, medium build with a big beer gut, he sported a dark Billy Ray Cyrus-style mullet with a trucker hat and a flannel shirt, unbuttoned halfway, sleeves rolled up and un-tucked. Rusty was outgoing and friendly, approaching me on the sales lot while I was working and telling me all about his recent open-heart surgery, pulling his flannel apart to proudly reveal an enormous vertical scar. Barn customers who realize they are going to ruin your day with absurd delivery situations and over-the-top expectations often begin with strong overtures of friendship and sympathy-eliciting schemes, like, oh, telling me about their recent heart surgeries. I knew then that a rage-inducing quagmire was likely awaiting me at Rusty's place.

I found Rusty's residence deep in a Barn Land hollow—what is typically referred to as a "holler"—an unkempt area cut off from the rest of civilization, often found at the end of a narrow, dead-end road (you guessed it—no street signs), a sort of rural, unpaved, overgrown cousin of the suburban cul-de-sac. Holler residents often appear related in some familial sense.

Basically a huge sinkhole containing multiple mobile-home trailers precariously perched atop tall stacks of cinder blocks and wedged all around the steep slopes of a circular, forested area, the holler ends in a central, semi-level sector that has been cleared of trees and collects the rainwater from the surrounding slopes on the sides of the road leading in and out. This perpetually muddy area in the middle is typically used for partying, muddin', garbage-burning, wrestling, and for storing flattened beer cans and broken-down vehicles, which appear to melt into the landscape and become part of it over time.[2]

I was unsurprised to find Rusty ill-prepared to receive the barn when I arrived on his property and found my way blocked by two junked Nissans: a green Pathfinder and a white Sentra. Though we had agreed on a time for me to arrive with the huge building, no path had been cleared for delivery and no one was there to meet me, so I waited outside my truck as various screen doors opened around the holler and a series of yapping dogs and suspicious stares gave way to women screaming at their husbands to come out and size up the intruder.

---

[2] Muddin' refers to the popular practice of drinking beer while driving cars, trucks and motorcycles around in a circle in the mud behind the trailer in the holler in which at least some of the participants typically live. Participants and observers scream with delight at the spectacle and throw their beer cans into the mud, where they are flattened, impacted and create a sort of beer-can mosaic, as seen in Jacob White's classic documentary, *The Dancing Outlaw*, which appears to have been filmed in Barn Land.

Eventually, Rusty emerged with a 40-ounce beer in one hand, his lanky father in tow. It took three of us to get the broken-down Pathfinder to move. We pushed and pushed until we got the thing to roll away down the hill, Rusty clumsily chasing it and jumping in to pull the emergency brake before the useless thing crashed into a ditch. The Sentra wasn't having any of it, however. As soon as Rusty, his skinny old Dad and I started pushing it, the wobbly front axle snapped and the wheels twisted sideways. The car protested once with a loud screech of rusted metal before collapsing with a thud on its front end, effectively immobilized.

All that was left for me to do at this point was to drag the barn between the tree line on the right and the Sentra on the left. It was going to be a tight squeeze, and it was obvious that some tree limbs would have to be cut, as Rusty had done absolutely nothing to prepare the site and had no chainsaw. If someone didn't cut the branches, they would tear the edges of the new barn's roof and shingles to pieces. Since he had already brought out his ladder, I decided not to unload, unfold and set up my aluminum one. Remaining calm, keeping my mouth shut and tempering my rage, I reflected on how Rusty had had several days to move the cars and trucks and limbs out of my way because he had selected the day for delivery of this building, a barn easily as big as his mobile-home. I thought of the paperwork he had signed clearly stating the customer's responsibility to prepare the delivery site. I thought of the other deliveries I had planned and would have to cancel today due to Rusty's lack of foresight. I laughed as I caught myself getting angry, recognizing by now the futility of anger at barn hauling in general and choosing to forget it all, oiling, gassing and pulling the ripcord to start the chainsaw.

I was stuck in the job, and this was what the job entailed. Why waste my energy being angry anymore? I climbed up Rusty's rickety old ladder with the rumbling, sputtering chainsaw. Lifting the spinning blades over my head, I cut into a limb with the circumference of a compact disc. The sawdust showered over me, sticking to my sweaty neck and grimy T-shirt as the rubbery ladder jiggled as I struggled for leverage. Though I managed to turn off the chainsaw and hold on to it without injury, I couldn't get out of the way as the limb fell from the cut point over my head, and it landed directly on my shin, nearly knocking me from my precarious perch on Rusty's ladder.

"Dang, man! You okay?" Rusty asked from a safe distance.

"Yeah," I said, grunting through clenched teeth, my jeans stuck to my bloody shin. After clearing several more limbs, I managed to squeeze the barn between the tree line and the Sentra, making it to the center of the holler, the only remotely reasonable place to leave the barn, only to learn that Rusty wanted me to back the building out of the relatively flat clearing and up into the steep, sloping grade of the holler's walls, which would require lifting the front of the building higher than three feet (our standard limit) in order to make it level with the back end, which would be elevated by the steep wooded slopes of the holler above and around the clearing.

This maneuver would mean I'd have to swing a tight 360-degree turn with the building and back the truck right through an inexplicably still-smoldering campfire in the center of the holler, sending the rear of the barn upward into a muddy hillside between tight clusters of trees. Then, assuming I could even back the five-ton building up the forested slope and into the trees, managing not to melt the cab's tires in the campfire coals at the front end and still pull the truck and trailer out from underneath the 12X36 barn somewhere near the impractical slope that Rusty demanded, I'd still have to jack the barn's front porch up four or five feet from the ground, requiring maybe a couple hundred cinder blocks to level it. Perfect. Why the hell not? I could just set the damn thing on fire right now and make it easier on all of us, or just take it back to the lot now, where it would end up anyway after a few months and its inevitable repossession.

"Cut 'er *this* way! Naw, cut 'er back '*at* way," Rusty yelled.

All barn customers "yousta drive a truck."

As I tried over and over to back the garage into Rusty's preferred spot, forcing the weight on the back of the trailer as far up the hill and into the trees as I could, spinning my truck's tires in the softer ground at the bottom of the holler, my cab started filling with airborne ashes and smoke from the campfire under the truck. Hoping like hell that my tires weren't melting, I drove back and forth across the glowing, smoky remains of his fire, trying to get the barn exactly where Rusty wanted it without getting mad at him. Coughing as the cab filled with campfire smoke, I got out of the cab a couple times to look around, and though I mostly avoided the hot coals, I stepped in dog shit twice. I finally got the barn in place, and it didn't look good to me at all. I tried one last time to convince Rusty to let me unload the barn in a more level area, but he was adamant. I conceded and drove out from underneath the barn. I had to hammer on the gas pedal to build enough momentum to propel my heavy truck and trailer out from underneath the 10,000-pound barn and escape the soft, muddy earth beneath the tires. I revved the engine several times, finally caught traction and lurched out from beneath the building.

The solid barn crashing into the holler floor sounded something like a tall, heavy tree, attached to a wrecking ball, smashing into the side of a wooden house. Due to the considerable difference in elevation from the rear of the barn (which Rusty had insisted I back up the steep slope into the woods), and the front of the barn (which was sticking out into the clearing in the middle of the lower part of the holler near Rusty's old campfire), the porch that had been added onto the front end of the 36'-long building snapped and broke in half when it hit the ground.

"I can't do anything about this now," I said.

Somehow I began to find humor in the accumulating madness yet again. Like a bad movie that's so bad it starts to become good again, I was so angry that I eventually found things funny. What could happen next? I assured him I'd return as soon as possible and left as quickly as I could. Ultimately, Mitch and I returned on another day to fix the porch and level the barn, and this time we spent over eight more hours working on the thing, half of that on our backs in the dark with flashlights, our fingers numbing in the cold. Rusty wasn't there this time, but his kind father did bring us an extra light and a couple Honey Buns and Cokes. I don't think we even charged Rusty for the extra trip, or for the outrageous amount of time spent on delivery, but of course it was all a waste of time and effort, as—you guessed it—I was back out there in fewer than six months to repossess the barn after Rusty had cut the thing full of holes, installed his own pink "towlet," and stopped sending in his monthly payments.

HARDBARNED!
One Man's Quest for Meaningful Work in the American South

All Hail The Retail King (and Customer Queen)

Rental sting
The customer is king
Waste your life
Waste your life
Little things can cost you everything
Save your life
Save your life[1]

—**Archers of Loaf**

One office job involving periodical distribution, a field that I had worked in before, required a double set of interviews. I was enthusiastic but tempered my optimism with a healthy dose of restraint. Not so long ago, I had been after a copywriter position and had driven to another city, a few hours away, twice, for extended interviews that seemed to go exceedingly well. Having been introduced to the entire staff and CEO and asked when I could begin working, having been granted the time off from the new job for my forthcoming honeymoon already, having looked at houses with my wife in the area and spoken with a realtor and mortgage officer, I was then ignored for weeks until I was able to pry a curt rejection email from the lead interviewer stating that they had decided not to hire *anyone* for the position I had been virtually assured was mine. My job-hunting skin had since thickened.

This time I wore a suit and tie and projected a lot of confidence when attending the interviews for the magazine distribution executive position. I could do this job—no problem. I'd done it before. I could do this job again, and I could do it well. The only catch was that I didn't want to. I had no real desire to crunch sales numbers, even if I would be working for a book publishing company, which, with my record of job applications and

---

1 Archers of Loaf. "Rental Sting." *All The Nations Airports.* Alias/Elektra, 1996.

interviews, would be a pretty huge deal. At least I'd be in the right industry with a foot in the door.

The vast majority of writing jobs that I encountered when searching online were technical gigs that required years of history in the role already, working as a technical writer, describing network schematics or automotive drivetrains or medical record retrieval systems. I might rather scuba dive for lost balls on golf courses. People do that for a living. But this was different. This was a prominent company in the world of book publishing, and I thought I had a shot at getting started on a career. I figured that maybe, just maybe, if I played my cards right and worked hard on the corporate ladder with this company, even crunching periodical sales data for a while, at least I'd be in a house of books and meet people. I could prove myself capable and worthy, and maybe somehow I could impress someone important enough to find my way into a job that could *mean* something to me, perhaps even work my way into the editorial department.

One day I might read manuscripts, share my opinions with editors, be part of the process of discovering great writers and making them successful, actually reading books for a living! But it didn't happen this time either. Yet again, I had to pry another icy, curt, impersonal, form-letter email rejection from cold electronic fingers after two interviews that had left me feeling good about my prospects. All I wanted was the chance to show someone that I could write something relevant and useful and do it well.

Searching for a full-time writing gig just wasn't working (big surprise), and my bills and student loan payments were looming, so out of absolute necessity I temporarily acknowledged defeat and redirected my search from professional to retail, which I thought would be easier to accomplish, but I was wrong again. The economy was in bad shape, and despite my failure to find a job relevant to my skill set, I still thought it would be much easier to find a job at a supermarket, a bookstore, a sandwich place or maybe a video game shop. Again, I was wrong. I applied multiple times to all of these places and more and got nowhere fast. I was trapped in limbo between two worlds: possessing the education but lacking the required experience as a professional writer *to land a job as a professional writer* and starting to wonder if my education was working against me as I struggled to find work in retail. I'd heard the phrase *overeducated and underemployed*, and it was starting to resonate.

I discovered to my great disappointment that most national retail chains—even groceries—had begun using an online hiring exam primarily focused on a licensed, software-based personality inventory.[2] This now disturbingly ubiquitous[3] multiple-choice questionnaire presents approximately 100 questions with zero context, like:

"I feel nervous around other people: A. Always. B. Often. C. Sometimes. D. Rarely. E. Never."

Well, maybe one of those other people is a disgruntled postal worker, Ebola carrier or Tea Partier. Maybe we're all naked. It's Sartre's perfect little vision of Hell. Yeah, I'm nervous. Perhaps one of us is getting a raise and the other three are getting fired. Concerned? Wait, that's not a choice.

"I get angry when other people do things incorrectly: A. Always. B. Often. C. Sometimes. D. Rarely. E. Never."

Do things? What things? Brush their hair? Design skyscrapers? Yeah, when people treat me like a robot and force me to answer context-free questions like these that make no sense whatsoever, I get angry. A. Always.

"I don't like being around large crowds."

---

2 The personality exam trend is brilliantly skewered by Barbara Ehrenreich in her excellent book on working low-wage jobs, *Nickel And Dimed: On (Not) Getting By In America*.

3 "As the class of 2015 heads out into the workforce this summer, they are going to have their heads examined by the companies they hope to work for. Convinced by the gurus of Big Data that a perfect workforce can be achieved by analyzing the psyche and running the results through computers, hundreds of employers now insist that job candidates submit to personality tests. The phenomenon spans the pay scale from burger flipping to high finance. And the questions range from the intrusive ('I dislike the high taxes we pay in the country') to the positively bizarre ('Sometimes I'm not sure what I really believe')." Gray, Eliza. "How High Is Your XQ? Your next job might depend on it" *TIME Magazine*, June 22, 2015.

What kind of crowd? Are there blindfolds and gunshots? Are we all lined up to take a flu shot? Are we at Lollapalooza? Are we talking Wal-Mart on the day after Thanksgiving? Is someone handing out free Thai food? Give me some fucking context.

One major electronics store chain required me to take a long, frustrating customer service-oriented personality exam when I applied online for a job as a delivery driver. How many customers will I really be interacting with as a delivery driver, I wondered? Probably fewer than I would if I worked in the store, but I had a clean driving record, and customer service is a complete joke, isn't it? It's a no-brainer, right? Just be cool to people—that's it. How hard is it to merely be friendly, efficient, polite and respectful while doing your job? This will be great, I thought! All I have to do is get through this stupid test. I didn't hear anything for a couple of weeks, so I made a follow-up call to the local store. I waited patiently as the woman at the other end of the line called up my application on her computer terminal.

"Hmmm. Yeah. We've received your application. Looks like corporate didn't recommend that we hire you because they didn't like some of your responses on the personality inventory. You're welcome to try again in 45 days. Thanks for calling."

What had I done wrong? My initial impulse was to tame my generally negative outlook on all things corporate, yet to be as honest as possible. Yes, I have emotions. Yes, I react to others and can occasionally be confrontational when necessary, but I am a polite, respectful, honest guy who expects the worst but is optimistic and gives everyone a chance to be cool. I work hard and do what I am hired to do as well as I know how. I try to treat people as I would like to be treated. That's all I ask from others and all I expect in return. Give me a chance to show you that I just want to be cool to people, people! I guess these sorts of responses didn't translate well in the personality exam.

I applied again at the electronics chain 45 days later. This time on the exam, I lied through my teeth. I tried hard to sound like the pliable automaton they seemed to be after. The opinion-free, emotionless cyborg—malleable and loyal, the blank slate that the corporation could tattoo freely with their slogans and acronyms, with programmed, twisted permagrin intact, like Smylex victims—*Love that Joker!*—in Tim Burton's *Batman*. I would be the corporate retail version of Ralph Fiennes' character in *Red Dragon*, but this version of me would be tattooed head-to-toe in corporate logos, drastically marked-down sales tags, customer interaction slogans, holiday coupons and OSHA acronyms, a grotesque, living embodiment of capitalism and effective retail branding. I reacted to nothing in the survey, erasing any semblance of problematic emotional reactions to the personality test itself and appeared not to have anything to offer but a strong back with two capable arms and legs. I called back again two weeks after finishing the application process for the second time. This time the woman put me on hold, and when she returned after several minutes, she said they were no longer hiring. I protested gently that the job ad was still on the website.

"Yeah…I don't know why they do that," she replied.

"But can you tell me why the job listing has been online for the last two months?"

"No. I think the guy who used to work here is coming back. Pretty sure."

"Really? It's just that I thought I was particularly qualified for –"

"Yep. That's right. He's coming back. Thanks, though."

CLICK.

At this point I had pretty much given up on trying to find work even remotely related to what I cared about or what I went to school for and was ready to call Taco Bell. I had to bring home some money. Somehow, over the phone, I convinced a manager of a sporting goods store I had applied to online to meet with me in person. The local bookstore had shown zero interest in hiring me after three applications, multiple phone calls and visits, including a personal recommendation from the manager of another branch in the same chain, a good buddy's older brother who was trying to help me out.

I entered the tiny office in the back of the huge sporting goods store for my interview. A friendly, reasonable man with glasses and a goatee shook my hand and offered me a seat. The florescent lights permeated the shoebox of a room. As the manager finished some work on his desktop computer, I looked around at the walls, noting procedural documents, scheduling folders and policy manuals. A framed message with a multi-colored magic marker drawing of a smiley face and a rainbow read:

"If we always do what we always did, we will always get what we always had."

A famous NASCAR driver looked down on me sternly from his life-size penciled portrait; his also famous son grinned from another frame beneath his dead father, each man decorated head to toe with corporate logos of sponsorship. From another frame behind glass nearby, a struggling fish leapt from a churning lake, hooked but fighting hard. A loyal dog returned to his camouflaged master, a large dead bird in his jaws.

"How do you feel about guns?" the manager asked. This store sold rifles and shotguns.

"I'm not a hunter, but I like to shoot at the range once in a while."

"Would you consider yourself a fisherman?"

"Not really, but I like being on the water for just about anything."

"What do you know about customer service?"

"I think I have a pretty solid grasp of the concept. Smile. Look the customer in the eye. Make him feel welcome. Solve problems. Be honest. If you don't know the answer, find out what it is."

I thought the interview went well. It only took about 15 minutes. I got a call back a few days later and returned to the same office for a second interview.

This time the manager interviewing me was the manager of all the lesser managers, including my previous interviewer. He had a spiked, slightly rounded flat top, with the sideburns trimmed almost to the top of his ears, high above his temples, like a coach. He had a coachstache too, and the regimented manner to go with it. He was more challenging with his questions and did not smile. He asked me about sales experience and talked for a long time in much detail about the intricacies of the "merchandising environment." I found it hard to get a word in. He said that my customer service experience at restaurants, groceries, clothing, souvenir shops and movie rental stores was "not exactly retail." He pontificated at length in monologue about "the intensity of the rapidly changing and constantly demanding world of retail." We were often interrupted by employees, phone calls and email. He left me alone in the office several times for long stretches. At one point, this manager of managers asked me to *sell* him the red magic marker on his desk, handing it to me and staring me down with real intensity.

I flashed back a few years to a previous unsuccessful job hunt, a second interview for a customer service position at a car rental company, when I was wearing a brand-new, black suit and tie, which I had just put on my credit card. I had been informed by the first interviewer at the car rental place that I might want to "consider dressing up" for the second interview, after wearing merely a buttoned-up dress shirt with slacks and nice shoes to the first interview. I figured I'd need a suit sooner or later for a wedding or a funeral anyway, so I had dropped a couple hundred bucks on a plain black two-piece suit and showed up snazzy for round two in the tiny office trailer in the car rental parking lot. I was asked on this black-tie affair—this second-round entry-level car-rental sales job interview—to *sell* the interviewer the stapler on her desk. I didn't immediately believe that she actually wanted me to give her an impromptu sales pitch for a stapler. I was wrong. I didn't take it very seriously, couldn't help laughing a little at her deadpan insistence, and I didn't get the job.

"Well, yeah, you see, this thing here is called a *stapler*. It's made of metal and designed to clamp sheets of paper together like *this*. You need it if you plan on clamping sheets of paper together, *like this*. Okay?"

This time, I sold that red magic marker with gusto. I offered the imaginary customer/sporting goods store manager of managers/gym coach from *Beavis and Butthead* my best description of this particular magic marker, the pros and cons of its design and the myriad applications for its use. I related my personal experience with the marker as well as improvised impressions offered to me by imaginary customers who had bought the same marker and returned to my fictitious calligraphy store to relate their own fascinating experiences with the marker, which had inevitably led to additional purchases of various other models, which I would of course have been glad to have gone into detail describing. The coach cracked a rare smile.

After an hour and a half, I was told that I would be hearing something soon. Another several days passed, and a third manager called me from the store, informing me that he wanted to set up a third interview with himself and a *fourth* manager, neither of whom I had met. What the hell can I say to these people to convince them that I can handle a part-time retail job, I wondered? The third interview proved to be a rehashing of bits and pieces of the previous two interviews, though this one was in a slightly larger room with two tall, skinny, younger managers closer to my age. Both retail professionals were friendly and reasonable, and though I basically repeated what I had said in previous interviews, it was over quickly and seemed to finish the process, as we discussed convenient times for me to start work. A week went by, and I heard nothing. Amazed, I started to think about calling to ask about what was going on. Would there be a fifth interviewer? Finally I received a call and went in for paperwork. After surviving three separate interviews with four different managers over several weeks of sustained uncertainty, I was officially a part-time retail sporting goods employee, earning eight bucks an hour.

I was assigned to the footwear department, instead of the guns and rods, having been informed that I seemed to be keenly in touch with the principles of "good customer service," and that this department was suffering from a lack of it. However, on my first day, I was introduced to the shoe warehouse behind the sales floor, where no customers ever ventured. I learned to navigate the shelves stacked three times my height. I spent hours organizing boxes of shoes, attaching security devices to shoes, labeling boxes of shoes, rearranging displays of shoes, fetching various sizes of shoes and discussing the merits of and problems with hundreds of models of shoes, but I never saw a customer. After a few weeks, with a pretty solid grasp on standard procedures in the footwear department, I finally began to interact with shoppers. Somehow I managed to handle the intensity of the "rapidly changing and constantly demanding" world of retail, for a while anyway.

While I believe wholeheartedly that every human being deserves to be treated with dignity and respect until he or she proves him or herself undeserving, sometimes in the course of commerce, the customer/employee relationship makes it easy for people to prove themselves unworthy of the bother. Of course, those infuriating times usually occur when I'm on the employee side of the relationship, but I always do my best to be a thoroughly friendly, reasonable and less-than-demanding customer when I'm on the other side of the transaction. I know well what it's like to be treated like a servant who deserves his fate of servitude and belittlement, and I vehemently resent that shit. Early in my shoe-selling stint at the sporting goods store, one of my co-workers in the shoe department was accosted by a dissatisfied, borderline hostile customer who was clearly perturbed and demanded the following aloud (twice):

"I AM THE CONSUMER! YOU ARE THE MERCHANT!"

Well, thanks for clearing that up, lady. As if emphasizing this glaring chasm of obviousness would somehow enlighten my co-worker into ignoring her other customers and responsibilities and approach the woman in a more revered way, perhaps bowing deeply at the waist, as is customary in some cultures. As if by re-defining the sales relationship with terms other than the pedestrian customer/clerk and instead using deity/peon terminology would somehow elevate this holier-than-thou shopper in the eyes of the clerk. Though Ben Affleck's character may have been on

HARDBARNED!
One Man's Quest for Meaningful Work in the American South

All Hail The Retail King (and Customer Queen)

the right track when he proclaimed—in response to the old cliché about the customer always being "right"—that

"The customer is always **an asshole**,"[4] I wouldn't entirely agree.

While there are always plenty of assholes to go around, the corporation itself is often the real source of the bullshit. Kind, respectful customers can be shafted by the retail milieu just as easily as service-minded employees. Ever try to figure out how much a cell phone actually costs, or endure a pitch for an extended warranty that you don't want or need? In the shoe department where I worked, there were at least two prices on the shelf for each pair of shoes, and another set of prices appeared in the weekly flier. They often did not align. Of course it was frustrating and confusing for the consumer. Plus, we were expected to try and sell warranties to each customer, complete with a brochure lathered in fine print and designed to screw them. Really? An extended warranty for sneakers? I can't blame shoppers entirely for their bad attitudes.

And yet it is still clear to me that a large portion of American adults have never worked in any sort of service-oriented position whatsoever, and these people usually act like it. What makes them look at people who serve the public in our daily work lives as if we lack intelligence, experience or self-worth? What gives them the right to make such judgments and act upon them? Maybe our country should have a two-year mandatory customer service stint for teenagers, akin to Israel's military service requirement. Maybe customers and employees would get along better if everyone had spent time as a service industry employee. I'm for increasing the empathy all around, and if you don't know what it's like on the other side of that counter, you may be less likely to care. Compassion shouldn't be dependent upon experience, but if this mandatory service experience could turn a few nasty customers around and reach a few people in dire need of compassionate enlightenment, I'm all for it.

In the shoe department, I did my best to answer any questions

---

[4] *Mallrats*. Dir. Kevin Smith. Perf. Ben Affleck. Gramercy Pictures, 1995.

that came along, based primarily on my decades of experience with wearing shoes, combined with what I gathered from my coworkers and other customers, but sometimes I couldn't answer every question. I still don't know what the hell an athletic shoe sole is comprised of. Ladies and gentleman, in the vast majority of cases, sneakers are neither vegan nor earth-friendly. Synthetic materials you cannot pronounce are chemically bonded with other nasty stuff in China or Bangladesh or Singapore or Vietnam by someone who makes enough to buy a can of American soda and instant noodles every day.

Does that help you decide which sneaker to buy? I didn't know the difference between a lot of the shoes we sold that looked almost exactly the same. They didn't tell us. Well sure, we had posters featuring a shoe or two that the corporate store wanted us to push harder for a particular week or so, but pairs of cleats don't come with a guide to materials, and even if it's football season, I don't know why we only carry one cleat in wide! Sure, I learned things along the way and wanted to be relatively well informed about the industry that employed me, but I didn't have all the answers. I didn't know why we only had a size seven and a half and a size 13 in stock, with no sizes in between. No, we didn't order more when we were low on Nike Shox or Reebok Easytones. I too found it frustrating, and it didn't make sense to me either, but it wasn't my asinine policy. Inventory was determined by a nameless, faceless, corporate algorithm, which controlled nearly everything in the store from afar, electronically, based on intangible sales data. It wasn't my damn fault. I'd much rather please the customer by providing what was requested, but that was often simply impossible, and some shoppers could never be satisfied.

One day, two women came into the shoe department together. I don't think it was intentional, but it rapidly became a good cop/bad cop scenario. The lady who wanted the shoes had questions about them, and the other lady didn't like my answers to her friend's questions. I tried to be as helpful as possible and answered in some detail. With considerable condescension, one woman asked if I "knew anything" about shoes. I smiled and told her all I did know about the shoes she had asked about, which wasn't enough. She asked if I had any socks with which her friend could try on shoes. The store didn't allow customers to open new pairs of socks for trying on shoes, so they provided little slip-on pantyhose booties. I was explaining this policy when the woman cut me off with a glare and a command,

"I NEED TO KNOW IF YOU *HAVE SOME SOCKS!*"

I raised my eyebrows and took a step back, clenched and unclenched my fists and jaw, waited a beat, took a deep breath, and the incredulous look on her face had not changed. Slowly and quietly I responded.

"Well, yes...ma'am, we...have socks. In fact, we have a whole wall of them right over there behind you."

I gestured to the wall of socks.

"THANKS FOR ALL YOUR GREAT HELP!" she spat at me with considerable venom.

Soon after that encounter, another woman came in with her husband. She was rotund, with short, gray hair and piercing blue eyes. Her husband was quiet and rail thin, with a foot-long gray beard and glasses. This time the man needed boots. She was calling the shots, however, and she made that clear from the start.

"How much do you *know* about these boots?" she asked as she held up two different models of a similar boot.

"One is waterproof—Goretex," I replied.

"What can you TELL me about these boots?" she demanded.

"Not much, really. One is an outdoor work boot and one is more of an indoor oriented work boot; different soles, but there's not much difference. One is waterproof."

"You don't do this *full time*, do you?"

"No. Part time, actually."

"BWAAAH HA HA HA HA!

"Well, I can tell! Listen, I have to explain. You see, we're from an *EXTREME* place, and we live in *EXTREME* situations. We're on our way to the West Bank for a construction project, so we very well may be dodging *MISSILES* and *BULLETS*. We need a very strong boot for less than $50."

Though it was immediately clear that our inventory did not include what she needed, and despite my doubts that battlefield-class tactical ballistic-missile-proof footwear existed in her price range, I helped the quiet, polite man find sizes for about four boots as he selected them.

"Ma'am, you probably won't find what you need here for the price that you are interested in paying. You might want to take a look at Wal-Mart."

"Oh yes, we might very well find what we need. That's why it's called *SHOP-PING*."

I felt my jaw clench again.

"I'm just trying to help you as much as I can with the limited selection available in the store."

Another customer then approached my footwear manager and asked her for a certain size of a certain pair of shoes. The manager agreed and was on her way to get the shoes when she stopped for a moment to answer a question that I had about the boots for my customer. The tall, awkward man my manager had been helping—all knees and elbows—race-walked over to us with the exaggerated posturing of Fire Marshall Bill[5], shaking his head vigorously as he stared at the floor between us with a jutted jaw, waggling a finger and tapping his extended toe.

"Your customer service is *just…*"

He stood there, shaking his head at the floor and tapping his toe, lost in search of a perfect, elusive adjective. My coworker opened her mouth to reply and he interrupted,

---

5 Jim Carrey's spastic, accident-prone character from the mid-90s sketch comedy show *In Living Color*.

"WHERE are my shoes? You were getting MY SHOES."

She began to reply, "I was just," and he cut her off again.

"You've been CHATTING. That's all you're both doing is CHATTING."

I started to interject.

"I'm sorry, sir. She was just explaining…"

"CHATTING. I don't want to hear it. That's all you're doing is CHATTING."

With that, the man withdrew his tapping toe, spun on his heel and stiff-legged it up front, where he tattled on us to the manager, telling him a blatant lie about how we had been "wandering all over the department for half an hour," ignoring the poor man and CHATTING.

In fact, we weren't chatting. We were working. If you're a customer, don't level accusations based on your assumptions at the employee who is serving you. You know what they say about the word assume. You may find the quality of your customer service deteriorating rapidly. While we're on the subject, it's not really that hard to phrase a request in the form of a *request*, rather than in the form of a command, and when you're working in customer service on the other side of the counter, it makes a big difference. If you are a service provider, waiting tables, selling hamburgers, ringing up groceries, stocking salad dressings or locating shoe sizes, you hope to be treated with respect and courtesy, and that's pretty much all you can hope for because you damn sure aren't making a living wage. When customers don't think about anything but what they want, they often simply make commands.

"Get me this. Give me that. Grab me one a' them."

No *please*. No *thank you*. Just *do this* and *do that*. It's the little things that count. Simple words, a smile, eye contact, body language, anything that makes a service employee feel like his humanity is being acknowledged rather than stomped on is significant. But isn't this obvious? At the risk of sounding like an advice columnist, sometimes such encounters can make a big difference in someone's day. Don't be a selfish scumbag toward employees at the stores and restaurants you find yourself in. Have a little patience. The next time someone serves you, be cool. I'm just saying.

Whenever I started an opening shift at the sporting goods store, another unlucky employee was scrubbing the bathrooms with a pungent array of manufactured cleaning chemicals. One morning, when I stepped into the bathroom to tuck in my requisite polo shirt, the cloud of noxious fumes almost knocked me over. For some reason, I thought of Robert Duvall in a helicopter with a drill instructor hat and cop shades.

"There's nothing like the smell of napalm in the morning!" I offered.

My ever-cheery co-worker chuckled, explaining that he didn't even notice the intermingling aromas anymore:

"Either I'm high or this crap has burned the sensors out of my nose!" he said amiably.

So be nice to people when you go shopping or out to eat. We, the legion of peon employees, have easy access to a wide variety of industrial strength chemicals. I'm just saying.

A song that popped into my head fairly often at the store (if I could manage to filter out the sports babble and country-pop radio drivel) is by the band Primus, and it's called "Here Come The Bastards."[6] Whenever the customers start surging toward the shoe department, there's just something about the cadence and lyrics that seems entirely appropriate.

Here they come, here they come…here they come, here they come…

A customer once approached me with a question I had never heard before.

"Ya'll got them fightin' necklaces?"

I didn't know what to say in response. Do we have *what*? Why would you want a necklace in a fight? Wouldn't it just get in the way at best or endanger your life at worst? Or were they some sort of toy necklaces that

---

[6] Primus. "Here Come The Bastards." *Sailing The Seas of Cheese*. Interscope, 1991.

fight each other? My best guess was that the recent surge in popularity of Mixed Martial Arts, the Ultimate Fighting Championship and the Tap Out brand (skimpy camouflage apparel we sold to steroid smugglers) had led to a merchandising campaign featuring topless meatheads wearing branded jewelry, but I just said that I didn't know and directed the young man to someone who could answer his question.

One hulking customer announced that he was a rugby player and asked me the difference between rugby and soccer cleats. We didn't carry cleats designed specifically for rugby. I said I didn't know exactly but pointed out that many rugby players used soccer cleats and showed him the difference between materials in a couple of them, pointing out that leather uppers were softer than some shoes made with synthetic materials. He exhaled dismissively, rolling his eyes at the young bleached blonde woman on his arm, saying,

"Oh, what's the difference? It's rugby, not a beauty contest!"

Well you asked me, didn't you, douchebag? Once I helped a grumpy old guy who was in really bad shape and seemed mad at the world. He moved very slowly, not happy at all to be in the store. He was dressed head-to-toe in black, with a skullcap and a ponytail down his back, a long black and gray beard to match—an elderly extra from *Sons of Anarchy*. He wanted something comfortable and cushioned and *black*. My first challenge was to determine what kind of shoe he needed.

"Just a regular one," he insisted.

Would he like a boot, an athletic shoe or a sandal, I asked, trying to narrow it down among the general categories we sold. We didn't sell loafers or dress shoes. Frustrated, the man said again that he wanted "a regular one." Stumped by his unwillingness to choose between the three generalized categories I had mentioned, I then tried another approach, asking what he planned to do with the shoe: would he run; play basketball, tennis or football; work in a warehouse; cook at a fast-food joint; hunt antelope, storm a crack house with a SWAT team; wade through a river or what? We carried shoes appropriate for all of these activities. Even more frustrated this time—and no, I didn't actually suggest each of those things—he said,

"It ain't nuthin' *ethnic* 'ar nuthin. It's just a comfortable shoe."

Ethnic? I paused, now thoroughly stumped, pondering that one with an eyebrow askew.

"Not a boot?" I tried again.

"Aw naw, not that."

Bewildered, I gathered the most comfortable black athletic shoes I could find in the shoe department and brought them to the man who was now sitting on a bench with no intention whatsoever of perusing our displays on his own. I placed the shoes next to him and somehow convinced him to try one on. He then began what became an hour-long episode of trying out each of our several types of special insoles, but, as he was accustomed to a higher level of service from ages past, first he wanted me to take out each insole from its packaging and insert various combinations of different insoles into each shoe, some with the insole that came with the shoe, other times without it, and *put them on his foot*. After working through dozens of combinations and configurations of insoles, the man turned his attention to socks.

"Do y'all have some real thick black socks?"

"Sir, we carry several kinds of black socks. Some of them are very thin liners, some are slightly thicker running socks, some of them are pretty standard thickness (athletic socks) and some of them are pretty thick hiking socks."

"Yeah, but do y'all have some real thick black socks?"

"Uh...here are some that we have."

Meanwhile, other customers were staring wide-eyed at me and my obviously most dominant of customers, some having forgotten that they even needed help, so mesmerized were they by the spectacle of the retired Hell's Angel who was demanding the entirety of my attention and patience.

I managed to slip away a few times to help some of these other customers, and one guy exclaimed over his shoulder on his way out,

"I hope you have a better day than you're having! SHIT man, your job SUCKS!"

The job didn't always suck, and the customers weren't always jerks. The money was lousy, but the hours were decent, and sometimes funny things happened. I still wasn't having any luck with my writing job search.

One day, I had a memorable encounter with an inanimate male mannequin from the athletic apparel department. The heavily muscled, larger-than-life-sized plastic man stood immobile and stoic, covered head to toe in a popular brand of perpetually advertised athletic wear. He was tall, dark and looking as perfectly chiseled as any growth-hormone-fueled all-American athlete could. On his size 13 injection-molded plastic feet were the last pair of football cleats in the size that my customer, an also gigantic but actual, living teenager, required for his impending high school game. I tried to pry the plastic athletic giant's cleats from his feet but got nowhere fast. Instead I hoisted the entire man from his steel display base by the waist, propped him horizontally over my shoulder and headed back to the footwear department, enlisting the mother and son to hold the pretend man down as I wrestled the shoes from his stiff feet.

The customers were laughing, clearly entertained. I finally got the first cleat-boot from the plastic man while accidentally breaking off his arm at the shoulder. He didn't seem to mind, but on further examination of the football shoe, I discovered a perfectly round hole in the bottom of the cleat. I learned from my manager that the store had received this pair of cleats at no cost, and so they were legally unable to sell this particular pair, which was only for use on display. They had drilled a perfect, 50-cent-piece-sized hole in the bottom of one of them. Why they couldn't just pay for them and sell them like any other pair on display in the store is a mystery. The annals of corporate retail policy are not rife with logic. As I mentioned earlier, they expected associates to push warranty plans for sneakers on every customer. Seriously.

Another customer asked me why we had such a poor selection of shoes, and I told her that I had wondered the same thing and had asked my supervisors (to no avail) why we'd keep one or two pairs on the shelf for months but neither put the last pair or two in the store on the clearance rack nor order a restock, while customer after customer would request sizes of the shoe that we did not and would not have available. This made no sense to me either, but again, we didn't even determine the inventory of our own store.

"Don't you realize that you are just the smallest peon?" she said with a wry smile.

"Yes, of course I do," I replied.

In fact, most of my job consisted of telling customer after customer that I didn't have what they needed in inventory but that I didn't order the shoes or determine how many pairs we would keep in the store. Whether this was a natural consequence of the national economic situation, a tendency to keep stocks low—as one very soccer-centric Dad pointed out to me—or not, I don't know. It was simply the day-to-day reality that I experienced as a low-level—*smallest peon*—retail representative of a national corporation, on a local level. On busier days, I hurried back and forth between the sales floor and the storage warehouse looking for different sizes of shoes as customers accumulated around the warehouse doors and twitched with anticipation like predators circling for a cooperative kill. Was it really too much to hope for a smile, eye contact and a simple *thank you*? That's all I really wanted from a customer. A bit of human dignity. I know I'm a peon, but don't treat me like it. As the late, great Bill Hicks once put it so eloquently, "We are a virus with shoes."[7]

Jobs are just where we must go and what we must do after putting on the shoes.

---

[7] Hicks, Bill. "People Suck." *Rant in E-Minor*. New York: Rykodisc, 1997.

Barn Dogs and Lousy Humans

The more people I meet, the more I like my dog.
—**Anonymous**

Dogs are truly noble beasts, and I've loved two of them. We had to give the first one away when I was a little boy. I don't remember the details but it involved a lot of pee and poo and my Dad being angry, I think. I had the second dog for nine years, until he committed suicide by running in front of a car. At the time, I was away on a long tour with my band, and I like to think he missed me and couldn't go on without me, not that he was too stupid to have learned that the road was not a good place for him to be, after I had tried to impart that bit of vital knowledge for several years. He was a great dog, and I still miss him.

I like most dogs better than most people, really. You don't ever have to wonder where you stand with a dog. They're not going to bullshit you. It doesn't take a genius to figure out how a dog is feeling about you. I saw every kind of dog imaginable on the job, hauling barns. Well, maybe not the mythical three-headed Cerberus, but a lot of different dogs. The overwhelming majority of these canines were friendly, but there were still quite a few dogs that I couldn't manage to win over. These were sad moments for me because it is quite a satisfying thing to win over a dog, showing him that you are a friend when he is initially suspicious. It's just not always possible.

While on duty in Barn Land, there were only one or two occasions when I felt truly threatened and decided that there was going to be certain violence between myself and a canine. Thankfully, I was wrong every time. On one of these occasions, I was trying to find an address and deliver a barn, and of course I couldn't find any street signs or mailbox numbers, so I had to park the truck with trailer and barn on the side of the road and walk up the street, trying to figure out where I was. A muscular, angry mutt was loose in a yard as I walked up the street, and he ran right at me, barking and lunging, closer and closer with snapping jaws. I stood my ground and tried to win him over, but it wasn't happening. I kept moving and kept my eye on him, making it past the house without contact. On the way back down, he was waiting for me. This time I was convinced he would attack, so I opened the knife on my belt and walked by with it in hand, and the same thing happened. He came close but didn't actually attack. I was relieved, but I was ready to use the knife if I had to.

The last thing I'd ever want to do would be to hurt an animal, but I would defend myself or someone else if it came to that, of course, and sure, I'd kill animals for food if I had to as well. A buddy of mine once called me a hypocrite for being a carnivorous non-hunter. I see his point, but until I decide to stop eating meat, or until society breaks down, grocery stores become extinct and hunting becomes a necessary part of everyday survival, I will continue to remain omnivorous and feed upon the flesh of fallen animals that others have dispatched for me.

It's not that I'm unwilling to hunt, but why should I? Hunting is expensive and bloody and boring. I like being outside, but not because I want to stalk and kill prey. I'd rather go for a hike and admire the view, dive in the sea to observe the fish or paddle down a river. Covering myself in camouflage fatigues, face makeup and deer piss and sitting around all day waiting for an unsuspecting animal to walk by so that I can shoot it, skin it, carve out its stinking guts out and drag its bloody body back to my car is not my idea of a good time. I will make an exception on occasion to share a day of hunting with my father-in-law simply because I respect him, enjoy his company and the out-of-doors. Call me what you will. One of my fellow barn haulers was attacked by a vicious dog once and had to kick the thing, crushing its throat and killing it. He too is a dog-loving non-hunter who happens to favor meat lover's pizza, but he only did what he had to do.

That said, I cannot believe how cruelly people treat simple canines who strive only for our approval and affection. In Barn Land, I've seen scores of squealing dogs climbing over each other in cages full of mud and shit mixed in with kibbles and bits and spilled everywhere, without any water in sight, and actually been asked if I'd like to buy a dog. I've seen multi-acre properties with 50 or more dogs on two- or three-foot chains attached to stakes in the ground with sick eyes, covered in flies, without enough to eat or drink. I'd hate humans and probably want to kill them all too if I'd been treated like that for my whole life, but many of these neglected dogs are remarkably friendly and simply desperate for attention. The saddest thing to see is usually the neglect. It's often one or two dogs that have obviously lost their enthusiasm for life because they are alone in a cage, or on a chain, or both, sometimes so sick they can barely move. I've called the animal control offices and called the people who lived in these homes and tried to tell them that their animals need help. They usually plead ignorance. Lousy excuses for human beings.

I once delivered a barn to a tiny house on a large plot of mostly level ground that looked like it had once been farmland years ago. I backed onto the property, approached the area where the barn was to be placed, and promptly got stuck in the mud. I got out of the truck and walked around to see what I was up against. Then the barking began. I had sunk the rear tires of the trailer deep into the mud, nearly equidistant between two pit bulls that were chained near each other. One was a friendly female, the other an angry male who was obviously enamored of the female. The barn on my trailer was just outside the nearly concentric circles that the dogs had carved out as perimeters, roaming the dirt in their confined spaces. I went over to the friendly female and assured her that I wasn't a threat. She was placated and stopped barking, content to watch me roam around my truck, as I tried to figure out what to do. The male, however, continued barking at a variable volume level according to my proximity to

HARDBARNED!
One Man's Quest for Meaningful Work in the American South

his established territory. I tossed him an oats and honey granola bar, which he sniffed and ignored, resuming his tirade. I found some pretzels in my truck and discovered that despite his lack of appreciation for granola, this stout beast was easily silenced, as long as the pretzels held out. Without the salty, crunchy snacks, he went right back to his barking. I managed to pry my truck from the mud by lifting my trailer at an angle with its hydraulic power and extending it into the ground, thereby pushing the truck out of the hole it had created for itself in the mud—a trick I'd learned long ago from Mitch. I unloaded the barn and left it at an odd angle in the yard, unable to maneuver further without getting stuck again. It was not a surprise when I was asked to return several months later to repossess the barn due to lack of payment. The pit bulls didn't seem to mind at all when I stopped by a second time for the repo.

On another day, I delivered a barn on top of a mountain. There were two friendly, energetic young dogs in the yard, and they playfully chased me while I was there. I enjoyed running around with them as I worked. Sure enough, several months later I returned to repossess the same barn, and as far as I could tell, no one was home. In the back yard next to the barn I found a cage containing the corpses of two long-dead dogs, partially decomposed. A neighbor showed up and begged me to intervene. She said that if I thought this was disgusting, I should see the inside of the house. I got the neighbor lady's number and called the cops. I called her back a few days later to find out what happened, and she said that the people living in the house had told the cops that the dogs had been buried elsewhere, but that roaming neighborhood dogs had dug them up. They must have been a well-organized tribe of highly educated and discrete roaming dogs because they managed to dig up the two dog corpses, keep them in one piece, and place them inside a locked cage. It was obvious that these two dogs had died from neglect in backyard cages. What the hell is wrong with people? Lousy excuses for human beings.

Another time, I repossessed a barn from a trailer park with my boss. We took a quick look inside the barn before chaining it up and dragging it onto our trailer. Noting an awful stench but only spotting what looked like a few piles of the usual random junk, we were proceeding with the repo routine, which means moving quickly so as to avoid detection or confrontation, when suddenly the barn doors burst open and a huge Great Dane jumped out and ran around behind the mobile home. We went around and tried to approach the sickly, skeletal thing, but he wouldn't let us get close to him. We went into the barn to see what else we might have missed. The stench inside could've killed a man, and there was a metal pail half-full of rotting food—someone's leftover table scraps. Whoever had rented this barn had moved away long ago and decided to lock their animal in a dark, cold barn with a pail of compost to eat. I could barely believe it was happening. *Lousy excuses for human beings* doesn't quite cover this one.

I can't tell you how many times I've come across abandoned, hungry dogs on the side of the road in the middle of nowhere while on the job with barns and how hard it was not to bring them back with me. The last time I had my own dog, he died when I was thousands of miles away. I don't even know where he's buried. Are you depressed yet? Well just remember that for every miserable story like this, there are many other happy, friendly, fantastic animals that have chased me around barns, licked my neck while I was crawling on the ground, jumped up on me and snuggled up to me, easing my creeping barn madness and improving my day immeasurably.

Temp Agency Trials, Insurance Office Bile and the International Lunatics of Logistics

I don't want to sell anything, buy anything, or process anything as a career. I don't want to sell anything bought or processed, or buy anything sold or processed, or process anything sold, bought, or processed, or repair anything sold, bought, or processed. You know, as a career, I don't want to do that.[1]

—Lloyd Dobler

Bored with the status quo and not getting any luckier with my constant barrage of writing-job applications, I thought I might give a temporary recruiter a try. I'd never availed myself of their services before, and obviously I needed professional help to find a decent job. Maybe they could find me something other than warehouse work. Surely there were companies out there that relied on temp agencies to staff at least some of their skilled, professional gigs.

Based on what I was told in an email, I was under the impression that I had scheduled an interview at a temp agency. I was wrong. I put on my car-rental-interview suit and tie and showed up at the employment office, a little surprised to get in line behind a bunch of dudes in denim shorts and wife beaters. I figured that I could find a temp job that bested my $8.50 an hour retail job (yes, I had received a 50-cent raise at the sporting goods store), which barely allowed me to pay off my already adjusted-for-personal-financial-hardship monthly student loan bill. I had a folder with my resume and references, scratch paper and a pen. I strapped on my one decent watch and laced up the dress shoes. I was led through a small room packed tightly with job hunters in flannel shirts, trucker hats and jeans, hunched over clipboards full of paperwork, and into another tiny room, this one bisected by a tall section of cubicle.

---

1 *Say Anything...* Dir. Cameron Crowe. Perf. John Cusack. 20th Century Fox, 1989.

I squeezed my legs underneath a child-sized school desk and was handed a thick stack of paperwork to fill out. After an hour of signing employee consent forms, tax information forms, drug, alcohol and sexual-harassment-awareness forms, acceptable behavior, information release, work history and insurance forms, I turned my packet in with driver's license and social security cards, added my resume and references and was told to sit back down. I sat alone again at the small table in the tiny room and waited. Almost another full hour passed, and I didn't want to be late for my shift at the shoe department, so I was about to give up and leave, but just before I stood, a woman showed up—not the woman I thought I had scheduled an interview with—and she said that her name was Dawn. Bright orange from some sort of artificial tanning product or lamp, Dawn smiled unconvincingly, saying that she was going to "interview" me. She proceeded to sit down and catapult herself through my stack of previously filled out forms, locking her eyes downward on the paperwork as she asked me inane questions about my previous employment, each of which was answered in detail on the pages she was staring at, as she intently learned nothing about me.

I think the entire "interview" lasted all of two minutes, after my two hours of filling out forms and staring at the wall. Dawn had clearly not absorbed one bit of my resume or any of the information I had filled her forms with; she made cursory comments about one job or another and never asked me anything whatsoever about my education, experience or background. She wrapped our brief meeting with another fake smile and a rapid-fire endnote.

"Well we don't have anything, but we'll be in touch if we do…Thanks!"

I never heard another word from the place.

A month or two later, during a routine Internet perusal of employment ads, I happened across the website of one of our nation's most well known shipping companies. As with the electronics chain, I'd often thought that (in the absence of a writing job and when I inevitably walked away from barn-hauling) driving a box-shaped delivery truck in my local area might be a decent way to earn a living. I could work for an industry leader that was widely recognized as a great place to work, receive good benefits and decent pay, and drive a route close to home with regular hours…if I could pass the inevitable personality inventory.

I applied online. No personality test. Nice! I got an automated email response, asking me to show up at an address 40 miles away, but the day and date listed did not match the day and dates on the calendar, so it was unclear which day was intended for the "application session." I replied to the email and received an automated "no reply" response. If I had any questions, I would have to discover the answer by weeding through the endless fine print on a contracted third-party's Frequently Asked Questions page, which I did, of course finding no useful information related to my question whatsoever. I attempted to call the shipping facility where the application session was to be held, but this proved to be a dead-end as well.

The company didn't list a contact phone number on any of its correspondence and would not even divulge through the toll-free number what any given facility's phone number might be. The impatient operator of the toll-free number nearly shouted at me after I explained in detail how her company, one of the world's most respected, and one might assume, best-coordinated outfits in all of the international business logistics community, was sloppily attempting to screen applicants on Wednesday the 12th when that date did not exist. Wednesday was the 13th. Should I show up on Tuesday the 12th? Wednesday the 13th? Thursday the 14th?

"Well you'll just have to show up for both days that you think it might happen on and hope for the best!"

The next day at work in the footwear department, I spotted a delivery driver from the shipping company I had just applied to and asked her about the application process. She said that the way I was pursuing it was indeed the only way to be hired, but that I might want to think about showing up a few hours early. According to her, the last time the company had offered an application session, "more than a thousand" people had shown up for four or five job openings.

I decided to arrive an hour and a half early on the first day that I thought the application session might occur on, and I seemed to be the only person there. Surely I wasn't the only one here. Where were the other 999-plus hopeful delivery drivers? I was let in by a guard who was very friendly but had no idea what I was talking about. I stood around for a while, the guard and I hoping that someone who knew about the application session might arrive. A second applicant appeared and stood next to me, having apparently just arrived from his duties as Dungeon Master in the basement of the comic book shop, a massive, quiet man dressed head to toe in black, with dark glasses, a thick goatee and a long single braid down his back to his belt. I greeted him and discovered that he'd had the same difficulties discerning the date and time of the session as I had.

Eventually a strutting, skinny, short young man in oversize clothes sauntered in, somehow in charge. I would learn later that Reggie was the regional hiring manager for the company. The guard mentioned to Reggie that we were waiting and gestured toward the Dungeon Master and me. We were leaning against the wall, as there were no chairs, and we had not been allowed inside yet. Surprised, Reggie said something about not being sure about what day or time he had posted online for the hiring session. The DM and I were then given access badges and led to a snack bar/waiting room, where we spent the next hour and a half watching the intermittent squawking satellite feed of the Weather Channel and listening to Reggie lecture about basketball, his family's restaurant and his numerous athletic exploits, though he did mention the job we were applying for occasionally if we interrupted and pressed him.

Approximately 10 other applicants appeared over the next 90 minutes; we were given pencils and got started filling out scores of pages of background paperwork in tiny little bubbles with Scantron forms I had not seen since college. Meticulous details of our whereabouts and exploits over the last 10 years of our lives were required. Four hours later, Reggie was so determined to talk about basketball that I literally stood in front of him, my completed paperwork in hand, for nearly 20 minutes as he held another applicant—a charming older woman—in check ceaselessly, making her quite sorry for having made a friendly interjection about how her grandson liked to play basketball. Before we left the basketball coach and restaurateur extraordinaire, he took pains to stress two points: first, his honesty, and second, his accessibility. He wanted us to know that we'd always be able to reach him on his personal cell phone number if we had further questions, which he recited to us all aloud.

"If you don't get me," he said, "I *WILL* call you back."

We shook hands and parted ways. Reggie the regional hiring manager even called me the next day and gave me an address, a phone number and a name. Encouraged, I was to show up at 10AM the next morning at a second location for a formal interview for my position as a delivery driver. I decided to be professional but not executive-like and wore a suit and dress shirt with no tie and didn't shave. Reggie had assured me that my tidy beard was acceptable, even telling a story about an executive at the company who had decided to grow one and had changed company-wide policy because of it.

I arrived at the shipping facility for the interview and was ushered into another break room. I was greeted by a few friendly employees who spoke highly of the company and the job and wished me good luck. After a few minutes, I faced off with two managers, one male, one female, both stone-faced, on the other side of a narrow table wedged into a cramped, closet-sized office by an open door to a busy hallway. Pleasantries were skipped, no emotions were betrayed; corporate interview questions and hypothetical scenarios were read to me aloud from forms the two managers held before me. I responded confidently, and my answers were rapidly scribbled down by both interviewers. I would hear something within two weeks, I was told.

I didn't. Two weeks came and went with no news. I called the number Reggie had given me for the interview location and asked for the branch manager who had interviewed me. The manager informed me that the position had been filled but that my application was "still active." I called Reggie twice, asking for advice about applying at other locations or for other positions. Reggie The Reliable and Accessible did not return my calls. At this point I allowed myself to get a little depressed, adding an entirely new sort of defeat onto my already omnipresent failure to convert my education into a career. What was I supposed to do? At least I still had my retail job.

A few days passed, and suddenly I received another automated email from the corporate website of this global paragon of shipping and logistics excellence. Apparently I *was* still active in their system. This new automatically-generated message—not the first seemingly composed by an alien robot with a third-grade education speaking English as a second language—awkwardly notified me that there was another opening for the same job I had applied for in a nearby area at a different hub. Somehow still optimistic, I went through the laborious yet inexplicably required re-application process and again submitted my candidacy. I then received another email with the final details about where and when to go for my second interview. This time I was instructed to show up two days later, over 2,000 miles away in California! I gave up on the shipping company, now fully convinced that their international logistical and business prowess did not extend to their human resources or hiring protocol.

I went back to selling shoes and sending out resumes for writing and editing jobs, but not long after wasting my time with the temp agency and the shipping company, I bungled an opportunity to move up in the *rapidly changing and constantly demanding world of retail* and ended up jobless again. An old heavy metal buddy named Sam who worked in insurance—and knew I was on the lookout for something that paid better than the shoe department—got in touch, letting me know that a co-worker had put in her notice. According to Sam, whose blunt honesty was much appreciated as I waded through one cesspool of corporate job application nonsense after another, there was an immediate need for an "office bitch."

Still eager for an alternative to retail, bereft of writing jobs as usual and thus intrigued, I flashed back to my two previous cubicular experiences and intermittent periods of unemployment. I figured I'd give it a shot. The thought of working in insurance held zero appeal, but the idea of a little more money and a stable work schedule that did not include weekends, nights, holidays or fetching shoes for irritated parents of screaming children during cleat season was worth considering.

Again I found myself ready for a change, but by now my expectations were lowered to the point of going for incremental improvements as I pinballed from one unsatisfying post to another. I never stopped trying all the while to find meaningful work tied to my education and interest in writing, but more practical concerns were at the forefront of my thoughts, as a "career" remained unattainable. Though I did get along well with my co-workers at the sporting goods store, my track record with jobs had convinced me that the idea of enjoying my work was an indulgence I should do my best to permanently annihilate from my expectations when starting a new position.

As far as I could tell from the stories Sam and Jake (my two musician friends who worked insurance jobs) told, it seemed that being an insurance claims adjuster was divided between two equally unappealing scenarios: either striving to save the corporation money by depriving injured or otherwise deserving people of appropriate compensation by attempting to appease them with undervalued gifts or payoffs in exchange for giving up their right to sue, or wrestling with liars who were trying to scam as much money as they could from the insurance corporation and suffering their unyielding verbal abuse.

Given this alternative—an administrative support position—I thought I could probably handle being the "office bitch," however humiliating it might sound. I interviewed with three women in a new glass and brick office park and was confident. I sat suited at the head of an enormous mahogany conference room desk in a comfortable leather chair and fielded questions from all three interviewers, answering their final question frankly that my "one most difficult struggle in life" had been that of finding meaningful, satisfying work. I received an offer via voicemail as I walked in the door to my apartment after the drive home.

What complicated things was that on the previous day at the sporting goods store, I had found out that the lead associate in footwear had been fired without warning, due to an apparent misuse of her company discount. Our new store manager, recently transferred from another state, had mentioned that she had me in mind as her first choice to fill the newly available lead position. I received no offer, however, as she made it clear that she was required to post the job as open and conduct interviews. I wanted to know how long this process would take, how much of a raise I might expect, how this would affect my schedule and responsibilities, etc., so I asked her if I could meet with her briefly at some point in the day when she had a few minutes. I knew she planned to be away on business for the next several days and realized I might need to make a decision immediately if my interview at the insurer went well. She said yes, that she would be happy to speak with me later that day about the details, but she either forgot or had no intention to do so and left the store after her shift without speaking to me.

A few days later, lacking adequate information to decide between the insurance job I had been offered and the footwear job I *expected* to be offered, the insurance people made it clear that they wanted me immediately, pointing out that there was a line of people behind me ready to accept the job for less money than they had offered me, which amounted to a salary of a little more than $10 an hour, a raise of $1.50 after taxes, but the regular schedule with weekends and holidays off was tempting. The shoe department manager—a great guy I really liked named Dan— who reported to the new store manager who had taken off, told me that he thought I could probably get an hourly wage of about $11 if I got the footwear lead position, and the insurance job would require a substantial commute through rush hour traffic.

The decision was tricky to make and decided under pressure without complete information because the offer of the insurance gig expired before the sporting goods manager returned. I opted for the insurance job and agreed not to give a two-week notice as I would prefer, but to jump right in, due to their urgent need to fill the position and demand that I decide immediately. I managed to cover my week's worth of scheduled shifts at the sporting goods store and apologized to my immediate manager Dan (who was both understanding and encouraging). The overall store manager returned on my last day in the footwear department, and I apologized to her for being unable to give adequate notice, thanking her for her confidence in me as a good candidate for the new job and wishing her the best of luck, though I was still frustrated at having been forced to make a decision without a firm offer or any information from her about my supposed promotion. She nodded but didn't say anything.

Thus began my brief foray into the insurance office. I lasted the better part of five days. I got up early and drove an hour through the morning traffic rush. I trained with the soft-spoken young woman I was replacing who had recently become engaged to a police officer in training. She was very nice and as helpful as she could be, though she had only worked there six months or so. It was apparent that she thought the job was stupid and boring, and she never wanted to work in insurance again.

I was handed various training manuals—file folders, worker's compensation claim forms, doctor and lawyer bills—and tried to be a sponge, expecting to be a bit overwhelmed as is often the case with new jobs. I toured the massive maze of cubicles and was introduced to 40 or 50 people assigned to various companies directly or tangentially related to the business of handling insurance claims by workers injured on the job. I was shown the handful of databases I'd be using to plug in little bits of relevant information like names, dates and numbers, under this or that tab, in one drop-down menu or checked box or fill-in window or another. My one chance to actually write anything during the day was when I typed a brief sentence like

"Allegedly, employee was opening a package of turkey when she slipped and lacerated her left index finger,"

or

"Allegedly, employee strained his back when lifting a patient from his bed."

While I was feeling a bit pressured to learn everything very fast, I wasn't worried about my ability to do so. I knew there would of course be a period of getting to know the work and the business and my responsibilities, but the more I learned about both, the less I wanted to have anything to do with either. I could tell pretty quickly that the job, once I got used to it, would be another mind-numbing, mundane, enthusiasm-for-life sucking vortex. I realized that there would be no moving up in insurance. Who was I kidding? I hated insurance. If I moved up, I'd probably have to be a claims adjuster, and that option didn't look appealing at all. They'd already told me there wouldn't be any raises in my future, and as I sat in the cubicle and crunched a few numbers, I could see that I wasn't doing any better than I could have, had I dragged my feet and landed the lead job in footwear at the sporting goods store, especially when I factored in the commute and wear and tear on my car.

My little cubicle started to shrink. I felt a steadily building pressure as the walls squeezed me in. Looking ahead a few months into my inevitable misery, I began to feel trapped, realizing I'd made the wrong call. I texted Dan and asked if anyone had been hired for the lead position yet. He said no.

"How's the new job?" he asked.

"I picked the wrong one," I said.

I asked if I might still have a shot at the footwear lead position; though certainly not my dream job, it was looking pretty good from where I was sitting. He said that he'd love to have me back, but that the new store manager over him had a "bad taste in her mouth" about my leaving without giving a two-week notice, even though I'd explained the situation to her in person, covered my shifts with Dan and requested a meeting with her that she had agreed to and ditched.

I went home to see family for the holidays, wrestling with the situation in my head and avoiding questions from everyone about my new job. I dreaded going back to the insurance office already and harbored a sinking feeling that I wouldn't hear back from Dan—that I had somehow managed to fumble the one chance I had at the job I should have had in the first place.

On Monday when I returned after New Year's for my first day back at the insurance company, the pressure returned, and I couldn't shake a tunnel-vision image of my future, chained to the bland beige box running Windows 2000, booting up databases and punching in codes, checking boxes, highlighting tabs, printing and emailing and filing an infinite barrage of nothing, generating limitless, inane data. I could not seem to find any positive angles. There was nothing to look forward to and no argument that I could discover to convince myself to stay, other than to soldier on for my wife, which wasn't enough. I knew that if she felt about her job like I did about this one, I'd have been happy for her to quit, and we'd discussed this very scenario in much detail. I remembered how she had told me long ago that she'd rather live in a broken down shack and eat beans than be forced to sit in a soul-sucking office job that had nothing to do with her interests or the creativity that defines her. I emailed my superiors and my friend Sam, with as sincere an apology as I could author. I wasn't cut out to be the office bitch. I stood up and walked out of the building. I knew I would never be able to get used to this field of work or the desperate, sinking feelings it engendered.

As I exited the office park, I called my wife. She was still home for her holiday break and was stunned by my news. She knew how hard it had been for me to even find the retail job, and we had both looked at the insurance job as something of an opportunity, as a way to ease the pressure she was feeling as the sole breadwinner. Words failed me, and any explanation I came up with seemed inadequate and probably was. What kind of person walks away from a decent job when so many people are unable to find work, when your own wife is struggling and stressed out because of money? All I could say was that I was sorry. That I just couldn't face it. The last thing I ever wanted to do was to make things more difficult for the woman I love, but I knew she would understand, and I would find something else. I simply had to…and besides, I knew that we both really liked beans and rice.

Temp Agency Trials, Insurance Office Bile and the International Lunatics of Logistics

Passengers, Hot Tips and The Barn As Art

You know, I'm sick of following my dreams, man. I'm just gonna ask where they're goin' and hook up with them later.[1]

—Mitch Hedberg

Sometimes when I was lucky, I'd have a passenger ride with me to share the trials and tribulations of barn hauling, but this was extremely rare, so it really was a treat to have someone along to visit and catch up with all day instead of becoming lost in my own thoughts or blocking it all out with audio books or music. Also, when I had someone to share the insanity with, it was easier to laugh at things that might otherwise have had me screaming with rage in the truck and punching the steering wheel. I've already written about how I royally screwed up a repo when my wife was riding with me. Whether things go smoothly or not, she is a calming force in a storm of barntacular insanity. She rode with me probably four or five times, and it was always a better day when she was along. Not only did she pack a great lunch, but she usually charmed the hell out of whatever crazy person I was dealing with, distracting them so I could get my job done and get us both out of there.

  Once there was an extremely old man at the house we were delivering to, and he was immediately enthralled with my wife. Somewhat suspiciously, he lured her into a dark shed in the corner of the property while I was working on delivering the barn. I kept a lookout from the corner of my eye, but I figured she could probably take the old man down if he tried anything weird. She works out. Anyway, a few moments later she emerged from the shed with the old guy and an armful of treasures from

---

1 Hedberg, Mitch. "Movie Plot." *Mitch All Together*. New York: Comedy Central, 2003.

decades of old. Apparently the old man collected all kinds of records and magazines from as long ago as the 1930s, and he let her pick out a few of whatever looked interesting. She ended up bringing home a few ancient pre-vinyl shellac records and movie star magazines from the early '40s. As an artist, my wife enjoys discovering oddities in advertising and elsewhere for inspiration for her work, which often involves collage. One notable bit of extreme weirdness she found in one of these old magazines was an ad for Lysol disinfectant spray. If you didn't know about this before, look it up. You may be shocked to know what women were once encouraged to do with this chemical household cleaner.

Once, my father-in-law rode with me in the truck, and we had a fun time. He would get out of the passenger side at each delivery site and chat up the customer, and he was about as good at charming them as his daughter was. His opening line was:

"I'm this guy's father-in-law, and I'm here to make sure he actually goes to work!"

That usually warmed them up a little, and by the time I finished with the delivery and set up, he had most likely extracted a life story and done his best to resolve whatever domestic squabbles any given customers may have had. I remember one couple that started out screaming insults and yelling at each other to shut up, but by the time we left, thanks to my father-in-law's intervention, they were thoughtfully discussing how lucky they were to have each other. The guy really gets to people and is a natural peacemaker. I never would have dreamed of involving myself in people's well-established dysfunctional relationships, but I admired him for leaving a trail of happiness as we drove along.

My Dad rode with me a few times too, and I always looked forward to that. We too rarely have the opportunity to spend an entire day together, catching up face-to-face. Plus, he had a chance to see firsthand how I was using the three college degrees he helped pay for! On one of those occasions, I was delivering two barns to one home, and we were winding down the customer's treacherous, steep, dirt, trench-filled driveway into the woods, the tires sinking into ditches in the driveway, so deep that the truck listed over to one side and then the other, so violently that he and I were bouncing on the seats, knocking our heads into the roof of the truck. We descended into this pitiful excuse for a driveway, plummeting at such an angle that we were hanging from our seatbelts toward the slope, then flopping side-to-side against each other as we dropped in and out of the deep crevasses that crisscrossed the pile of dirt serving as a path toward the mobile home trailer hidden deep within the woods. Trying to maintain forward momentum in an attempt to avoid getting stuck, we plunged hard and fast down the hill and lurched heavily to one side again when rounding a sharp curve in the path. The left side of the truck and trailer sank deeply into a trench, and one of the barns on my trailer toppled over sideways into the brush, crashing into some trees. That was a great way to impress my Dad with my prowess as a barn-hauling professional, I thought. Not only can I find no use for the education he helped pay for, but I can also demonstrate my complete lack of skill at the job I am instead stuck with! Great.

Turns out I had forgotten to secure the barn with straps—so, it fell off. I had never lost a barn before. I had done all kinds of damage to barns and trucks, but a barn actually falling off of the trailer—this was a first (and luckily a last) for me. Usually I was delivering one barn at a time, and pulling the chains tight from back to front with the winch was plenty to keep the barn secured in place. This time, however, I was delivering two barns at once, and if I had been on at least semi-level ground, the force of the two barns pressing against each other would have easily held them in place. The steep grade of the poor excuse for a driveway was enough to tip the larger barn over, however, and it was my own fault for assuming I wouldn't need to strap down the sides. The next fun challenge was attempting to use straps, chains, a nearby tree and the winch cable to configure and implement an elaborate pulley system that would theoretically flip the damn thing back over, righting it back onto the trailer again without breaking anything or squishing me underneath. I wrapped cables around surrounding trees and tied extra straps across the barn runners, fired up the little gasoline engine

Passengers, Hot Tips and The Barn As Art

on the top of the trailer and tried to implement my homemade physics project, which eventually worked. I was able to jump out of the way as the barn lifted slowly from the broken tree limbs and smashed back down onto the trailer. Once we finally secured it, made our way down the rest of the driveway and delivered both barns, I was glad to discover that the customer called himself a carpenter and wouldn't mind fixing the broken parts on the roof of the fallen barn. He assured me that it was no problem; he would fix it up right away, no sweat. I liked the sound of that, but of course I was back in a few months to repossess both barns, and (surprise) the roof hadn't been fixed at all, so I had to repair it anyway.

It's funny how sometimes the worst things happened when I had a guest riding with me in the truck. Things would go smoothly for a while—for barn hauling, at least—and then blow up when I had someone along for a day's visit. Mark, one of my best old pals from high school, was visiting and rode with me for a couple days in the truck. He is a teacher and was fascinated with my random adventures in barn hauling. I guess he couldn't believe I actually did this for a living and wanted to witness it firsthand. Well, he got what he wanted.

Just before Mark arrived in town, I had attempted to deliver another 12X36 monster into the impossibly steep front yard of a customer whose house overlooked a country road. The man's driveway carved a path straight up and across the lawn, parallel to the street below. Driving up the hill with a building on a trailer—if one could manage the angle in the first place, with the front lawn looming over the passenger's side and a sheer drop-off threatening to derail the whole ludicrous exercise on the driver's side—I could barely see straight ahead through the windshield because of the slope. In this man's yard, a ridiculous spot, impractical for a building of that size, I was unsuccessful in my first attempt at delivery. Even if I'd had a construction crane attached to a helicopter piloted by Yoda, the front entrance to the barn would've been at least 12 feet off the ground. The man wanted the building to sit next to the house, perpendicular to the driveway and road below it.

The customer and his unruly mother, who scurried in and out of the house in a nightshirt to squawk unintelligible commands at her son, absolutely refused to acknowledge my pleas for a reasonable assessment of the situation. The man played good cop to his mean old mother's bad cop. She never left the encircling porches of her house; she just wandered around the perimeter in her slippers every 15 minutes or so, criticizing (or maybe colluding with) her son, who was old enough to be my Dad. He translated her rants for me disarmingly with an

"aw shucks, that's just how maw is."

The good ol' boy filter of her son's charming demeanor worked in tandem with her hateful stance as they used each other's personalities against me. Logic never entered the equation, as her demands for how and where to place the building were clearly in-fucking-sane, ignoring the plight of the working man tasked with the job, the serious slope of the land and the obvious size and weight of the objects in question. Was she even looking at the same piece of ground, the same truck, the same giant building that I was? She would need climbing gear and a considerably higher degree of fitness than she appeared to demonstrate in order to ascend the mountain of stairs required to access the building if I were miraculously able to install it where she insisted it be situated. I tried but could not make the combative pair comprehend the ridiculousness of their demands. I discovered quickly that I was up against a thinly disguised brick wall of relentless inflexibility coupled with an undeniable lack of ability or simple refusal to recognize the reality of the physics on the ground, but *bless my heart*, this inarguable fact was delivered with the syrupy sheen of southern gentility, a two-faced and disgusting strategy.

The house was on an incredibly steep slope above the main road, and even getting the huge building anywhere near the yard was going to be fit for an episode of *Extremely Stupid & Death Defying Challenges: Barnman versus Jimmy & Maw*, or something similar. I can't believe that nobody has produced a reality TV series about hauling barns. Maybe I should pitch it.

After many tries, I couldn't get the barn even close to where the customer wanted it, going up the driveway forward and backward, again and again, maneuvering every which way I could think of. Whenever I got somewhere in the general vicinity of where the customer wanted the barn, my truck almost fell off the edge of the driveway, essentially a sheer cliff overhanging the road below. I wasted a significant portion of my day like this before I returned to the sales lot and unloaded the barn again. I explained the situation to Mitch later that afternoon, and he asked me to go back the next day and record a video of the location so he could get a better idea of what we were up against. I returned, shot the video, complete with snarky commentary, and returned home to show the film to Mitch, who agreed that the situation looked pretty difficult. It would take at least two of us to make a stronger attempt at delivering the gigantic building in this incredibly stupid location.

Mark had picked a perfect time to visit and witness the true absurdity of barn hauling. He squeezed into the half-sized back seat of the truck, Mitch took shotgun, and the three of us went together to try and deliver this thing. This third trip to the residence—and second delivery attempt—ultimately proved semi-successful after approximately three hours of struggle against equipment and barn on the steep slope at Jimmy and Maw's house. Mitch and I took turns wrestling with the wheel while Mark and whichever one of us wasn't driving yelled directions at each other from the side of the truck and the far end of the trailer. We tried to stuff wooden blocks in front of and behind spinning or slipping tires on the truck and trailer while attempting to force the barn into place without hurling the truck over the edge of the driveway. Though we didn't get the building placed where the customer had wanted—this proved impossible—we got it into the yard, perpendicular to the requested location, and that was simply as good as it would get. Jimmy said he was satisfied, and we left, convinced or perhaps merely reminded that a significant portion of barn customers have no brains.

What followed was a months-long saga of complaints, unfounded demands and manipulations by Team Jimmy and Maw. Though he had shaken our hands and said he was satisfied, thanking us for our hard work, he and Maw kept calling the sales lot, insisting that we move the barn again, face it a different direction, re-level it, add more concrete blocks, etc. Jimmy and Maw, like other opportunistic customers I encountered over years of many public service jobs, relished and exploited the role of the customer scorned to the fullest extent of vendor cooperation that they could possibly provoke. Preying on a barn seller, manufacturer and delivery driver's general sense of goodwill and desire to please customers, their bet was that they were always right—no matter what—so they tried to milk it for all it was worth and then some, demanding whatever they could get. This particular sort of customer was indeed *always an asshole.* The situation reminded me of another barn customer who had bragged to me as I leveled his barn about how he and his wife had gone to a grocery store, squirted dish detergent on the floor, slipped in it on purpose, faked an injury, threatened to sue the store, then retired in their 40s to a trailer park with the monetary settlement they were able to squeeze out of the grocery with the help of their lawyer.

Jimmy and Maw were no different. If you lack a sense of common decency and have no qualms about ignoring the plight of the workers who had already labored over three delivery trips and many extra hours at no additional charge to try and accommodate your outrageous demands, why not campaign even harder against the barn company itself and squeeze out every penny you can get? The lies about things we had supposedly said or done were grandiose and multitudinous, the accusations baseless. No, we had never "cussed them out." Not once had we "promised to do whatever it takes to make them happy no matter what." Yes, we had indeed refused to level the barn on the slope of their yard, which would have require more than 12 feet of stairs to access on level ground. What could have been quickly resolved as a sensible build-on-site situation, had the man and his mother behaved the slightest bit rationally from the beginning, devolved into an epic struggle of even more return trips to the property by me and Mitch, a barrage of nasty letters to Mitch and the barn company, and several ugly and threatening visits to the sales lot by Jimmy and Maw, leaving the little old ladies who worked there at their wits' ends. Where did these horrible people come from, and how the hell did I end up in their yard again? I wondered, as yet another shuddering wave of existential ennui washed over me.

The point is that the delivery process was nuts, and so were the customers, but we got it done, and usually, nobody got hurt. The point is also that if you are in need of a barn on the side of a steep-ass mountain, hire a contractor with helicopters, climbing harnesses, cranes and bulldozers to build it onsite. Just because someone sells portable storage sheds with free delivery and set-up, do not expect someone to drive it to the edge of the mountain on a truck and drop it off, like the guy who told me that I'd be placing his 30-foot barn on blocks on a "level" spot on the side of an actual mountain when I actually needed five feet of stacked blocks on one end of the thing in order to level it out. Come to think of it, if you live in any kind of non-level area composed of radically uneven topography seemingly established by Mother Nature on crack, don't order a portable barn! Again, have that barn built onsite. Don't leave instructions with small children while avoiding the barn hauler yourself and expect the barn to be delivered on the side of a hill, requiring $200 worth of cinder blocks to make it level enough to walk into and then stiff me for the bill, not answering your phone and forcing these small children to lie about your whereabouts, as that scumbag I mentioned a few chapters earlier did.

While we're at it, here are a few more **hot tips** for those interested in purchasing or renting-to-own a pre-built portable storage barn:

1. Figure out which way the driver should load the barn on the truck and tell him before he loads the building and drives out to your property. It's really not that hard. It can only be loaded two ways. Should the doors face the driver's side or the passenger's side, the front or rear of the truck? Look at the picture of the truck and trailer on the sales brochure. Now think hard and create a mental picture of your delivery site. Visualize

your barn on the trailer behind the delivery truck. Or better yet, draw yourself a picture. Now think about where you want that barn to be set up in your yard. Which way is it facing? Are you concentrating? Is it facing your house? Is it next to a tree? Is that trash fire in the way? Should you cut some limbs? Should you move those broken-down cars? Should you wait until the big pile of mud you call a backyard has a chance to dry out? Which way should the driver load the building in order to be able to place it where you want it and still have room to drive out from underneath it with his truck and trailer? He really doesn't want to load and unload it three times because you told him to face it the wrong way.

2. The driver doesn't want to take apart your fence, move your trampoline, bush-hog the wild field you call a lawn or dismantle your stupid above-ground pool. Are your stinking dog kennels in his way? What about farm animals? Out-houses? If you live 150 miles away from the sales lot, it's a safe bet that you can get a better deal closer to home. If you are going to expect a driver to bring a 12-foot-wide building that distance through downtown rush-hour traffic in a busy city, you are going to have to pay for it.

3. Inventory takes a while, and a driver isn't just hauling your barn; he's also hauling inventory for the sales lot. That's part of the reason he can't tell you an exact time for your delivery. Sometimes a driver has to wait in line to get his barns for inventory at the manufacturer's lot because there are other drivers ahead of him. He might need to load his truck with concrete and wooden blocks. He might have to cut the wooden blocks if they are not readily available. He might have to drive to a hardware store to buy concrete blocks. Give him some leeway. You don't call the UPS man and ask what time he'll be at your door, do you? Really, do you? The cable guy gets a four-hour window. I'm hauling an *entire building*. Be flexible. As one observant and sympathetic friend once observed, "It's a goddamn barn! Not a pizza!"

4. Don't invite your neighbors to come over and enjoy the spectacle of your barn delivery. Neighbors just get in the way. They love to putter over

with their four-wheelers and make suggestions that increase the workload for the driver and complicate the easy decisions of the actual customer:

"Doncha' thank he ought'a turn it more thattaway? Ya'll don't want it tah sit on this here flat spot. Don't yall want it up 'ere on 'at hillside outta yer way? He kin do that. I seen 'em with 'em jacks. Kin ya scoot it more over thissaway? Y'all should really think about puttin' it up on two or three layers of 'em concrete block. Aw, he should be able ta' do that. I usta' drive a truck, an' blah blah blah."

While there are plenty of crazy barn customers who could use these tips, I doubt many of those folks will be reading this, and believe it or not, friendly, reasonable barn customers exist too. But who wouldn't remember the crazies? A few of the kind and friendly ones tended to get creative with their barns. Maybe some of these folks had unexpressed artistic streaks that lay dormant until the barns arrived and piqued their creative juices, or maybe they already were budding interior/exterior designers, but barns for some were a blank canvas of possibilities.

Maybe it was easier for me to get along with the creative types. People expressed all kinds of rural individualism with their barns. Storage is only the most obvious option. Some folks think outside the barn—some live in them; some keep dogs or horses or cats in them; some turn them into garages, game rooms, greenhouses, restaurants, weight rooms, snack bars, poker joints, ceramics factories, crystal-meth labs, artist studios, campground cabins, writing retreats (in one rare professor's case), or hunting lodges. Some purchase multiple barns, drag them together and cut holes in them, creating a peculiar, modular community of barns disguised as mobile housing units, painted different colors, balanced on concrete blocks stacked precariously at heights according to the slope of the ground, rarely lining up or sealing correctly, with ramps connecting the holes in the buildings like gangplanks on a boat dock, kind of like *Waterworld*.

Some install hardwood flooring, carpeting, refrigerators, wild game freezers, microwaves, televisions, stereo systems, showers, sinks or pink toilets. One guy said he was going to turn his barn into a dance club, but the overwhelming majority of barn customers would just buy one barn and fill it with a bunch of dirty, useless, disorganized junk. However, some people do go above and beyond, redefining the role of a portable storage barn and unleashing their creative impulses on their neighbors and passersby, proudly broadcasting the irrefutable uniqueness of their customized barns. The Tiki Bar[n] was definitely one of those barns.

The Tiki Bar[n] was the next of four storage buildings already on the customer's property when I arrived to deliver this fifth barn. Other drivers had preceded me, as I did not recognize any of the four barns lined across the yard. I had delivered two barns on one piece of property before and hauled three at a time to sales lots, but these people were true collectors. They had so much stuff that they kept buying more buildings to house it all. Why not get a bigger house? Or better yet, get rid of some of your damn stuff? Whatever works for you.

"Honey, it's time fer another buildin.' We don' have 'nuff room fer the stuff in the uther four buildin's we got, an' the trailer's full, an hell, we got more yard sales on Saturdee!"

The couple who had ordered their fifth barn were nice folks, and they were so eager to show me The Tiki Bar[n]—that's what the oval sign read in Flintstones font above the door. I added the [n]. The friendly husband and wife invited me in and showed me around after I had finished setting up their newest addition. I felt like I was in Jimmy Buffett's seven-year-old daughter's playroom, or at some kind of tropically themed motel. I'm not sure why they put a bathtub out front and filled it with conch shells and various moon and star trinkets. This style of barn came with a porch, and every conceivable inch of space was taken advantage of.

Blue plastic flamingos stood at attention among the tiki torches, beaded curtains and rocking chairs. Wooden wind chimes lined the ceiling above the coconut porch light. A plywood cutout of a cartoon toucan with a spiked mane of neon green hair, a purple Hawaiian shirt and a margarita with a little umbrella in it beckoned to visitors with a drunken grin amid pointed arrow signs directing non-existent tourists to imaginary venues nearby, such as the Coconut Path, the Volcano Trail, the Hot Tub, the Beach and the Villa.

I stepped inside through the added screen door to discover a little wood stove for those cold tropical nights, plus an exercise bike and treadmill. A color television set, DVD player, air conditioner and lighted ceiling fan. An antique wooden end table with a reading lamp covered with flowery Hawaiian leis. A full-sized bed with island-themed pillowcases and comforter. Beach mats mounted on the walls with carpet and bamboo mats on the floor. A full chest of drawers with a blue-glass ashtray and a purple lava lamp. Toucan toys and plastic coconuts. Collectible T-shirts—some tie dyed, some beach themed—and shell chimes with colored glass buoys hanging aloft from ropes.

The whole thing reminded me of the southern beach-junk chain store called Wings, a franchised retail monument to plastic tourist garbage. Maybe you stopped by one on a family vacation somewhere for a souvenir Big Johnson T-shirt, some salt water taffy and a fun noodle. Maybe you needed a beach ball, an airbrushed license plate, and a corn-cob pipe? Wings is likely second only to Wal-Mart in its contribution to US landfills, at least in southeastern coastal states.

Passengers, Hot Tips and The Barn As Art

Liberal Arts and Other Effective Ways To Waste Your Life

A liberal arts education, the pride of the American undergraduate system, increasingly looks like a road to financial distress.[1]
—*TIME* magazine, October 2011

At this point maybe it's obvious, but in my mind, graduate school was more of a means of continuing my education, learning for the love of it and exploring my options than a predetermined path toward a particular career. As far as careers were concerned, I still lacked a plan. All I knew was that I loved reading and writing, had a certain facility with it and wanted to do more of it. Before barns came along, I was intrigued by the possibility of pursuing the life of a perpetual student. Liberal arts and the humanities seemed like a perfect path to continue my education in graduate school. What could be better than simply studying interesting things? The Human Condition? Great Works of Art and Literature? History and Music? I could worry about this "career" concept later. As long as I could read and write about *interesting* things and learn stuff, I thought I'd be happy and somehow figure out how to earn a living along the way. And besides, with a master's degree, someone would have to hire me to do something, *wouldn't they*?

I wasn't kidding anyone. I was no brainiac over-achiever. I went to a state school that nobody's ever heard of. I just wanted to be a relatively well-educated, well-rounded person and, in the words of Wendell Berry, submit to the "old duty" and earn my own "cultural and intellectual

---

[1] Dell, Kristina. "I Owe U: Student Debt Is On Track To Top $1 Trillion This Year. What Happens When Diplomas Stop Opening Doors?" *TIME Magazine*, Monday, Oct. 31, 2011.

inheritance"[2] rather than focusing the course of my studies unilaterally on my future means of earning money. It sounded good, anyway. I'm still working on that. Surely the rest of my life would eventually work itself out without career counseling or a burning desire to commit to Job X for the rest of my working life. Wasn't that era over anyway? The days of retiring from a single company after decades of service and receiving a pension and a gold watch afterward were long gone by the time I entered the workforce as one of the last of the Gen-Xers.

    I had thought for the three years following undergrad that I was just starting to get into the good stuff when I had finished that bachelor's degree in English. I found that I still had a real passion for reading and writing, and what better place to pursue both than in graduate school? I didn't know what else to do but felt like I had more to explore in school. Willing to do what needed to be done to pay the bills, I figured I could always find a job working outside doing physical labor if grad school didn't get me anywhere, but I sure hoped that it would. I liked working with my hands and getting exercise, and a healthy bit of perspective was helpful. Most people in the world don't have the luxury of searching for meaningful work. They just have to take whatever work they can find. I recognized my privilege despite my job struggles. So what was I complaining about? I could always do construction, landscaping or warehouse work again, land a retail job, flip burgers or do something to make ends meet if I had to, but I couldn't help wanting more than that from my working life. I simply wasn't content to major in something I wasn't fascinated by just because it led to a certain job or a career. I wanted to study subjects that honed my skills and piqued my interest. No matter how useless my education might prove to be, I thought there would always be blue-collar or customer service work I could fall back on to scrape together a living. Little did I know how prescient that thought would prove to be.

---

2 Berry, Wendell. "Feminism, the Body, and the Machine." *The Art of the Commonplace: The Agrarian Essays of Wendell Berry*. Ed. Norman Wirzba. Washington, DC: Counterpoint, 2002.

HARDBARNED!
One Man's Quest for Meaningful Work in the American South

I decided to return to school in the fall of 2003, applied and was accepted on a graduate teaching assistantship to an MA program, studying English and film. I loved reading, writing and movies, and I assumed that whether or not I became a teacher sooner or later, surely somehow I could eke out an existence with some useful letters after my name and experience studying useful things like reading and writing. I moved out of the nice apartment I shared with my buddy Donnie and his girlfriend and moved into an old house directly across from campus with four or five other roommates, where rent was a lot cheaper, and I could walk to class. Write Club was born in this house's cavernous basement.

Write Club was a small group of close friends with whom I met regularly to work on shared and individual writing projects and exercises, to offer each other a venue for brutally honest feedback and writing-related discussion, and to eat potato chips, drink beer and make each other laugh. Sometimes it's easier to motivate yourself to write if you have buddies who want to read and respond over cold beer; this is akin to how it's easier to lift weights if a buddy is screaming "Come On! Bull Neck!" in your face, I guess.

We all tried to entertain each other with what we wrote on the spot, but we had our personal and more "serious" ongoing writing projects as well. Everyone worked on different things: songs, poems, short stories, novels, memoirs and whatever we each needed to get out. We shared what we had written on our own, brought copies and wrote comments and suggestions on each other's drafts and did on-the-spot writing too. We often used random prompts with background music from an iPod plugged into a decaying Voltron-like conglomeration of discarded stereo parts. One of us would point blindly to a single word in a book opened to a random page for a prompt, and we would all write whatever we were inspired to for the duration of the playlist. Then we'd take turns reading what we'd written aloud.

The house was an ancient monstrosity divided into four apartments. Creaky wooden steps led down from the dusty hallway into the dark and filthy basement. Legend had it that more than a century before, it had housed nuns, but if so, they were long gone. Hundreds of beer bottles of every brand imaginable decorated the steel I-beams that lined the basement ceiling. Posters of Bob Dylan, At The Drive In, and Beers Of The World shared wall space with Cracker Barrel employee training posters, and street and road signs of unknown origin. Though insects of undiscovered genus inhabited the dark corners of the basement under stacks of broken appliances, furniture, tools and discarded junk, gigantic four-inch camel crickets, known scientifically as the Rhaphidophoridae, which sound like horrible man-eating denizens of the Sarlacc Pit from *Return of The Jedi* but were actually harmless, albeit unpleasant creatures, would often leap unexpectedly onto the table or into one's lap during a Write Club session.

The Rhaphidophoridae also liked to escape the basement and invade the living quarters upstairs via the air-conditioning vents. A dank, earthy smell seeped upward on the way down the stairs and lingered throughout each visit to the Write Club basement. The web of exposed electrical wiring, rusty water pipes, phone lines, Internet, cable and television wires dangled from the ceiling in an intricately tangled mess of code violation. A round glass table covered with a fuzzy yellow blanket was illuminated by a single, low-hanging poker light, which gave the surrounding darkness and shadows a sinister yet welcoming vibe. The perpetual hum of the house's washer and dryer was punctuated by the periodic roar of the exposed gas furnace, its blue flames pulsing visibly from the partially dismantled machine of eras past. Asbestos-covered lead pipes leaked their powdery remains onto the floor in dusty piles from a variety of ancient wounds. It was always too hot or too cold in the Write Club basement, but some real writing happened down there. We laughed a lot, and we were nearly moved to tears on occasion. We were fearless in what we were willing to write about and share with each other. Write Club attempted a long-distance revival once or twice but ultimately trickled out. The members have since scattered far and wide, but I like to think we all benefitted from the time we spent together in that unique basement and that our writing skills improved because of it.

As part of my graduate teaching assistantship, which covered my tuition and provided a $700 check once a month (books, rent, beer, beans, rice), I was required to work in the University Writing Center (UWC) as a tutor and to teach my own classroom section of freshman writing. I had never been a teacher or a tutor before, but I had received math tutoring from grade school through college algebra, so I had some idea of how it was supposed to work. I liked working with one student at a time, focusing on individual projects and struggles. I felt like I could always find something useful to share that might help the student improve his or her writing. Sometimes it was merely about being able to listen effectively, giving the student a chance to explain the work, the assignment, and the challenges they faced with deadlines and guidelines. Tutoring was something entirely different from teaching my own class. Sessions lasted 30 minutes, and "tutees" made their own appointments. I just had to be available and ready to help when I was scheduled.

I really enjoyed working with students, one-on-one with their writing projects. I felt effective and helpful a lot of the time, and being useful felt good…like *meaningful work*. I still think tutoring can be a huge help, whether it's with writing or with math, or whatever it is. I felt like I could help out most of the students I worked with, making at least a small difference in their lives, and I wasn't dealing with behavior problems or attention deficits. It is hard *not* to be focused when you're reading your paper aloud to your tutor, huddling over the pages together.

While I found that being able to listen to a single student and making gentle suggestions was a great way to help, standing in front of an entire class of freshman writing students and generalizing about technique was tougher for me. I found that I ran out of helpful things to say in front of everyone after a half hour or so, but I could always manage to be helpful with one student at a time, so I often initiated group work in my classroom and roamed around the class, helping individuals here and there, incorporating my tutoring technique into my classroom approach. Running a classroom was at times vexing, entertaining, frustrating, satisfying and occasionally infuriating. I only spent one semester in front of my own class, and I was actually a bit disappointed when I learned that I'd be without one for the following semester due to an enrollment drop in the spring. I'd put a lot of work into revising my new syllabus and knew I'd be a better teacher in the second semester, but I never got the chance to prove it.

Kids from every stereotypical high-school clique were students in my collegiate freshman writing class: the Jock, the Overachiever, the Cheerleader, the Metalhead, the Clown, the Smartass, the Cheater, the Quiet Guy, but I expected more from them than these trivial categories would belie. I tried to recognize their individuality and worked hard to cultivate a free-thinking environment where ideas were analyzed and debated. I tried everything I could think of to keep them interested. I bought a boom box and let the students bring in a song to share with the class, using music as a writing prompt. I had them come up with topics for in-class essays that we wrote together. I encouraged them to voice their opinions and ideas, and I promoted collaborative working environments, often requiring them to interact with each other. Some strategies worked better than others, and sometimes I had trouble filling the whole 75 minutes with teaching ideas, so sometimes I let them go early.

I established rules about late work and attendance on the first day and stuck to my guns. I believed firmly that a freshman's first English class was important and required real effort. I didn't give them an excessive amount of work and stuck to the general guidelines, but I was sincere in showing them that their successes or failures depended, directly, on the effort that they contributed to the class and to improving their writing. I wanted them to learn how to construct an effective argument and to understand that they wouldn't pass the class just by showing up. I constantly stressed to them that I was available in my office or after class if they had questions about their assignments, and I reminded them to go to the UWC for writing assistance.

Despite my efforts to help, some of them cheated, didn't show up or ignored me in class, and some of them paid no attention to the assignments, but that's how it goes. Perhaps three of my students came to see me on their own time outside of class to get help with their writing. The most dedicated of these freshmen was on the absolute opposite end of the spectrum from me politically, and so I enjoyed helping him improve his writing while trying to keep my own views obscured. It was a fun exercise (for both of us), focusing on helping him articulate and solidify his written arguments, most of which I disagreed with. This kid was sharp, and he thanked me at the end of the semester for helping him so much with his writing. He wanted me to know that he knew that I didn't agree with a lot of what he wrote, but he had appreciated my fairness and felt that he had become a much better writer.

This interaction meant a lot to me. For the first time in a long line of meaningless jobs, I actually felt like I'd made a positive difference in someone's life. This proved to be a rare and solitary victory. One young woman was struggling with my assignments, not showing up, not turning in essays. I talked with her outside of class and could see she was in pain. I listened for a while and ended up encouraging her to leave school. She was having trouble with her personal life, and I told her that college would be there when she decided to come back—that she shouldn't be there unless she wanted to be there for herself, at a time when she could focus. She was failing the class, and I stressed that she should drop the class before the drop deadline in order to avoid the F and take an Incomplete. Inexplicably, she never dropped the class, and I never saw or heard from her again.

The Metalhead was really starting to improve. I had spoken with him about his writing and how he needed to apply himself more seriously. He then wrote the best paper he had written by far, vividly detailing his dream life on the stage with a guitar, playing in a heavy metal band, his hair blowing in the wind from onstage fans, the drummer lit up with pyrotechnic explosions. I was eager to speak with him about his huge improvement, but he never showed up again, missed all the rest of the assignments, earned an F for the semester and will never know how well he did on that essay. Another student turned in a paper on a film I had screened in class, plagiarizing entire paragraphs blatantly from a review of the film on a prominent website. He failed the class and had the audacity to call me after the semester to ask if I'd give him a passing grade. I didn't even have a policy that failed a student automatically after one instance of plagiarism, though many teachers did. He had cheated spectacularly on one essay and failed to turn in one of the others, and he still thought he deserved to pass my class, with grades of zero on two out of five essays. As incredulous as John McEnroe after a bad call from a linesman, I said,

"You can't be serious!" I told him he was stuck with the F.

Meanwhile, at the writing center, I was asked to work as the assistant director, a position I shared with another grad student, my friend Rozelle. Roz and I worked well together, on projects like revising the tutor training manual, putting together rock shows at local bars to benefit the writing center and get the word out about its services, and various daily operational tasks, like organizing schedules, managing the staff of other graduate students and representing the UWC during freshman orientation week. We collaborated on a paper we wrote about using "punk pedagogy" as writing instructors, a teaching strategy involving punk approaches to empowering the student—theories we borrowed and cobbled together from teaching scholars Paulo Friere, Seth Kahn-Egan, James Berlin and others—and we presented together at a writing center conference in South Carolina.

When the director of graduate studies told us that graduate teaching assistants would not be paid for one month out of the summer, offering us no explanation, several other grad students and I formed a coalition and wrote to the dean of liberal arts with our case. As a result, we received our checks within a week. The director of graduate studies then asked me never to "go over her head" again. Why wouldn't I? It worked, and she wasn't helping us. We got the money we were entitled to, despite the fact that she was too busy or not interested enough to take up our cause. I remain grateful to her, however, because she allowed and even encouraged me to research and write about film in her graduate research seminar, something not all tenured professors deemed worthy of scholarship at that time. Traditionalists labeled film studies and other popular culture topics a less than acceptable area of study for academics, though that stigma is evaporating. One friend and former classmate of mine has since earned her PhD with a dissertation on *The Simpsons*.

Despite my extended inability to generate a writing career for the five years following graduation, not to mention the decade-plus of student loan debt I accumulated, I'm glad I went to graduate school. I realize that it is partially my own fault that I couldn't find writing or editing jobs, having entered the MA program without a clearly defined career plan, but with a simple desire to learn more and to read and improve my writing on topics that interested me. I'm still baffled as to how aspiring writers break into any (most) industries where every job seems to require three to five years of experience in a specialized field or a history of published work to become published or to land a job. The few academic essays I published while in grad school didn't open many doors for a long time. I did consider that by studying liberal arts while being unsure (at best) about the possibility of ever becoming a teacher was setting myself up for a certain degree of post-graduate employment challenges, but this is part of who I am and what has therefore determined my path into quite a few deeply unsatisfying employment situations.

Until I stepped into the ring with barns, I'd always been willing to do whatever it took to make ends meet while considering employment nothing more than a means to an end. This approach was not what I would have preferred but inevitable because I had yet to find the right job that made me feel like I was contributing something worthwhile for an objective of which I could be proud to be a part. Being paid to study what you find interesting is a special position to find yourself in, even if you don't really want to be a teacher, you're paid peanuts, your students cheat and you have little hope of earning a decent living as a tutor, but working through these kinds of situations and writing about them was a cathartic learning experience, and career challenges aside, grad school helped make me a better reader, writer and thinker.

I finished my MA in May 2005, halfheartedly applied for two doctoral programs (only one of which I really wanted to attend) and was rejected by both. Failing to extend my academic goal lines, I wasn't sure exactly what to do next. I soon found myself in pretty much the same situation I had been in five years before, this time with another English degree under my belt, but with no clear opportunities for professional employment as a writer or editor. I kept reading articles about the dwindling relevance of the humanities[3] and unemployed PhDs[4] and wasn't sure I'd be in better shape with a few more letters after my name anyway, so I didn't apply elsewhere. Evidence in the news[5] and in the experiences of friends choosing to remain in stagnant higher-education careers as underappreciated, undercompensated, benefit-free, perpetual adjuncts convinced me that my career outlook may not have been much sunnier

---

3 "Although people in humanities have always lamented the state of the field, they have never felt quite as much of a panic that their field is becoming irrelevant,' said Randall Delbanco, Director of American studies at Columbia University." Cohen, Patricia. "In Tough Times, the Humanities Must Justify Their Worth." *The New York Times*: February 24, 2009.
4 "The reality is that less than half of all doctorate holders—after nearly a decade of preparation, on average—will ever find tenure-track positions." Benton, Thomas H. "Graduate School in the Humanities: Just Don't Go." *The Chronicle of Higher Education*: January 30, 2009.
5 "Public colleges and universities that educate more than 70 percent of this country's students were burdened by rising costs and dwindling state revenues long before the recession. They reacted by raising tuition, slashing course offerings and, sometimes, by cutting enrollment. They also cut labor costs by replacing full-time professors who retired with part-time instructors, who typically have no health or pension benefits and are often abysmally paid, earning in the vicinity of $3,000 per course. The part-timers are often considered 'invisible faculty,' because they rarely participate in academic life and typically bolt from campus the moment class ends. That researchers still know little about them—or how well they do their jobs—is especially startling given that a little more than half of all college faculty members are now part-timers, and they far outnumber full-time faculty members on most community college campuses." The Editorial Board. "The College Faculty Crisis." *The New York Times*: April 13, 2014.

had I gone on to become even more debt-saddled[6] by earning that elusive and perhaps ill-advised PhD.[7] I could have even ended up on food stamps.[8] Still, I can't help thinking that if I had been accepted into one of those programs, this would probably be quite a different book.

---

[6] Between 2002 and 2012, the average cost of a four-year college degree rose 33 percent, student debt increased from $56.5 billion to $117.9 billion, and student loan defaults rose from 5.4% to 10%. The average student loan is nearly $30,000. And yet, a degree remains "more vital than ever," increasing annual full-time earnings for 25 to 32-year-olds by $17,500 over peers with only a high-school diploma. Sweetland Edwards, Haley. "Should U.S. Colleges be Graded by the Government?" *TIME* Magazine, April 28, 2014.

[7] "I now realize graduate school was a terrible idea because the full-time, tenure-track literature professorship is extinct. After four years of trying, I've finally gotten it through my thick head that I will not get a job—and if you go to graduate school, neither will you." Schuman, Rebecca. "Thesis Hatement: Getting a Literature Ph.D. Will Turn You Into An Emotional Trainwreck, Not A Professor." *Slate*: April 5, 2013.

[8] Patton, Stacey. "The Ph.D. Now Comes With Food Stamps." *The Chronicle of Higher Education*. May 6, 2012.

Hanging Up The Barn Boots for Reflections and Ramifications

Your chances of success are directly proportional to the degree of pleasure you derive from what you do. If you are in a job you hate, face the fact squarely and get out.[1]
—Michael Korda

Sure, Michael. Then go look for another job with greater potential for pleasure derivation, and when you've looked long enough but can't find something pleasurable that pays the grocery bill, and necessity and desperation get the better of you, go do something else until you realize you hate that job too, face that fact squarely and then get out again. Then do it all over again.
—The author

Toward the end of three years in barn hauling, I was loading a couple of barns on my truck at one of the builder's lots when I encountered another driver I had met once or twice before. Somehow I remembered his name, though he had forgotten mine.

"You look a lot older than you did last year!" he said, smiling.

"You really should get another job soon!"

I couldn't have agreed more.

"I'm working on it."

He was right. There were probably reasons why I was starting to look older. I definitely felt older and had noticed more wrinkles on my face and gray hairs on my head and in my beard. I got used to my perpetual collection of cuts and bruises and grew accustomed to the endless parade of eccentric characters that, at this point, actually made the job more interesting. My rage had downshifted toward a more simple kind of resignation, but it was still wearing me down, and I didn't want resignation to my fate to evolve into depression. I felt that a change was imminent, but I couldn't figure out what it was or how to escape.

---

[1] Korda, Michael. *Success! How Every Man and Woman Can Achieve It*. New York, Random House, 1977.

HARDBARNED!
One Man's Quest for Meaningful Work in the American South

Hauling barns late in year two, I still longed for the day when I would somehow get a writing job and make my exit from Barn Land, the bizarre and foreign world in which I could never quite feel at home. The barn life was beating me down, and as the three-year mark loomed, I realized I had to get out, despite the utter lack of prospects I continued to face. For so long, I had felt unable to quit, worried about where my next paycheck might come from, unwilling to violate the conventional wisdom of not quitting a job when you don't have another one to replace it, but I was starting to hate my life.

I had put up with barns so much longer than I had ever intended to, and at a certain point, the money didn't matter anymore. Of course I was dogged by a fear of being useless and failing to contribute to the world in any kind of meaningful way. I felt like I had squandered my abilities and wasted my costly education; I was afraid of becoming a husband who couldn't provide for his wife, of disappointing the people who loved me. But more powerful than any of those fears, the booming voice of doom that echoed through my flesh and into my bones and back—every day—was the fear of being trapped in a life that wasn't right for me, failing to make good on the potential I knew I had. It was a selfish fear, but it was honest. I had to exit this barn train. My wife had even started asking me to quit. She didn't like what the work was doing to me mentally or emotionally, and she worried about my physical safety.

I was worn down. I was laughing at my misery instead of surrendering to it, but that didn't always work. The looming three-year mark seemed like an appropriate time for me to call it quits. There wasn't a clearly defined breaking point. I thought I had reached several of those points a long time before, but I had stuck with the job because I was paying off debt and supporting my wife while she too sought to make use of her graduate degree and faced similar difficulties in finding appropriate jobs in line with her education that paid a living wage. I felt a sense of duty to provide and still worried about my chances of finding another job, but even if I had to go back to washing dishes, so be it. I was done.

My wife was relieved when in late November of 2008, I told her that I thought I was finally ready to pull the plug and give Mitch a month's notice. She had witnessed firsthand how the job was affecting my personal relationships and general attitude about everything. I couldn't face the crushing defeat I knew I'd feel if I had to begin year four in the truck. I didn't care that the world economy was tanking and unemployment was hitting a 70-year high. Barns took three years away from my life. I wasn't willing to give them any more of my remaining years. I realized that life came down to time, and I resented barns for burgling all of mine up, despite my sincere gratitude to Mitch for giving me a chance to work for him. She completely agreed.

This book is the natural result of my desire to make productive use of those three years, and a catalyst to help me strive harder toward spending my life and my energy on things I'm passionate about, like writing and music. For those of us who are able to find reliable employment, it is far too easy to fall prey to the seductive allure of steady income and job security when those rewards are finally in our grasp, which all too often forces us to abandon the things in life that mean the most to us, like our creative expressions, whatever shape they may take. When it comes down to the choice between money and time, I'm going to have to take less money and more time because I can't face the prospect of spending any more of my life trapped in a job I have no passion for. That is, at least until I get another job offer that I can't refuse, one that offers me yet another chance to take yet another sizeable chunk out of my indefatigable student loans, forcing me into yet another game of How Long Can He Take It Until He Is Driven Insane By Meaningless Work?

Well, here's to finding the courage to walk away from the things in our lives that make us miserable. Yeah, I mean it, but is courage really the right word? Maybe I mean audacity or stubbornness or irresponsibility. I guess that all depends on your perspective. Walking away from a job that pays well still makes me feel like a horrible, guilty, privileged and spoiled American who has the luxury to complain about his jobs and switch them at will (more or less). Millions of people all over the world struggle every day at crap jobs that pay next-to-nothing because it is the only option they have. That really sucks, and I have empathy for them, but I'm not sure how to reconcile this guilt with the very real taste of misery that consumed me in Barn Land. Does forcing myself to stay in a job that I hate for year after year make me some sort of hero? No. Does it alleviate the suffering of any of the millions who are toiling for decades in jobs that are much worse? No. Does writing an entire book full of complaints about most of the jobs I've had over my whole middle-class life in America make me a privileged asshole? Probably.

Still, anyone is lucky to have a good job while unemployment remains high, and millions have been out of work for months or even years. Millions more are overeducated and underemployed like I was, able to offer much more to the world than the demands of the crap job that they are forced to take when alternatives are just not possible. You have to do what you have to do, even if it really sucks sometimes. Again, it all depends on your perspective. I didn't have to walk eight miles from the local well with 100 pounds of water on my back every day to feed children and livestock, but some people on this planet do. I didn't have to crawl at gunpoint through a muddy hole in the ground and dig for diamonds with my hands all day, but some people do. I don't have to slaughter and eviscerate animals all day in a bloody meatpacking factory, but some folks do because they lack alternatives. So why should I complain, you ask? Because I can, I guess. That's the answer. I'm a spoiled American with first-world problems who has the luxury of choices. I'm full of empathy for people who suffer and animosity for those who create their suffering, but I'm a walking contradiction. I can complain about a crappy job and be thankful that I had it. I don't pretend to have this all figured out, but unless Shirley MacLaine has it right, we only get one shot at this, and I'm just trying to make the best of it without wasting time. Life and jobs are complicated, and I'm not sure I'll never master either one.

Of course, barn hauling provided a few positive benefits; otherwise,

I never would have made it through three years of it. Other than paying off considerable student loan debt and working for a great friend, I was unwittingly enrolled in a three-year course in anger management, and I like to think I passed. I learned how to convert rage into humor and laugh at my own misery. I can't pinpoint the actual moment when it happened, but I was able to stop screaming obscenities in the truck. I stopped beating the shit out of the steering wheel and tensing up my muscles until my head felt like it would pop like Michael Ironside's did in David Cronenberg's sci-fi mind-control film *Scanners*. It probably took two years to get to this headspace with barns, but for the last year or so that I worked the job, I laughed more. I was still feeling just as angry, sad and awful, but I managed to flip an internal switch and laughed at it instead of trying to punch an adversary that didn't exist. I watched more comedy and less documentary and heavy drama. It helped a little and appealed to me more than Prozac.

After all, I couldn't escape. I was still unhappy, but my unhappiness had lost its enthusiasm. I could punch or kick the barn, and I did, more than once, but that wasn't hurting anyone but me, of course. I learned to expect the worst and laugh in its face when I encountered it. The worst shitstorm of barntacular insanity would no longer cause me physical pain and dangerous levels of high blood pressure because I expected to greet it every day when I jumped into that truck.

Thinking back now, it makes perfect sense. I've always liked dark humor. Most kinds of art or music or film or painting that resonate with me are still dark. Life is pain, right? Well, I'm not depressed, but there are a lot of things to be depressed about. I'd rather laugh at them than wallow in them, however. If it's possible to be a negative person with a positive outlook, he is I, and I am he. Barns tried to break me down. They tried to kill me. They squandered my days on countless occasions. They cancelled my band practice and ruined my dinner dates. They made me an angry man. Eventually that changed, and I just laughed. Most people have it a lot worse, and it's all about perspective. I mean, when you think about it, it really was funny as hell.

After leaving barns, I was a much happier man. I was a lot poorer—that's for sure—but I didn't dread the coming day every morning when I woke up, and I didn't hate the world quite as viciously when I went to sleep. I smiled more often and laughed more easily, and I had fewer cuts and bruises. My car had no trailer, and it fit between the lines on the road. I had more time for music and writing and enjoying the company of my wife and friends. I relished simple pleasures like cooking and exercising that I didn't have time for or interest in when barns were effectively consuming my life and all of my energy. Surely this couldn't last.

Epilogue

Both as workers and as consumers, we feel we move in channels that have been projected from afar by vast impersonal forces. We worry that we are becoming stupider, and begin to wonder if getting an adequate grasp on the world, intellectually, depends on getting a handle on it in some literal and active sense.[1]

—Matthew B. Crawford

Crawford, who left his high-salary, high-stress, low-satisfaction, doctorate-level office job to become a motorcycle mechanic, sings the praises of physical labor. His book is fascinating, and his story is compelling, but I'm still searching for my employment nirvana. Maybe I should get another bike and break out the wrenches. I have been guilty of the greener-grass syndrome at times: sitting in an office-plex, gazing out at the sunshine, craving the fresh air and exercise of outdoor work. And yet, while digging ditches for peanuts, or when pinned under a barn in the mud and the shit, with customers yammering gibberish at me, I missed the clean shirt and the air conditioning.

    I am unemployed as I write this, but there will likely be more jobs in my future that have nothing to do with my perception of my own identity or my inherent need to make use of what I went to school for, what I'm good at, what I enjoy doing, what I'm interested in or what I care about. Until I find a job worth holding on to, one that contains at least a small portion of those key aspects of *me* within it, one that gives me a reason to be excited about the work that I perform in that cubicle or wherever I happen to be anchored, it's likely that I'm going to have to work more unsatisfying jobs simply to make money, albeit remaining burdened with

---

[1] Crawford, Matthew B. *Shop Class as Soulcraft: An Inquiry Into the Value of Work.* New York: The Penguin Press, 2009.

an unyielding desire to derive meaning and satisfaction from my working life. I could never erase my inherent need to pursue meaningful work, so it is pointless to try, but does my condition doom me to a lifetime of unsatisfying jobs? I hope not.

What I discovered on my journey through a few decades of random labor is not something easily resolved at the end of this book. It's not an inspiring anecdote that you can take with you on your journey toward more meaningful work. I don't have anything resolved, and there is no grand revelation or tidy, into-the sunset resolution. I'm still striving to find a way to make a living while engaging my interests, skill set and values. For most of us, the perfect job will remain elusive and out of reach, but deciding whether to settle and stop striving for it is something everyone must decide alone.

Any job has ups and downs, pros and cons, positives and negatives. Everyone must realize this at some level, but some of us have a much harder time accepting it. Until I convince someone to pay me a living wage to write about something I care about, am inspired by and feel passionately engaged with, I just have to figure out what I'm willing to put up with on a daily basis for rent and groceries. And so do you. Every new job offers additional lessons, and I intend to always be learning. I have to find a way to balance my need for income with my unwillingness to be perpetually uninspired, and then I'll have a job I can tolerate…but I think I'll be okay.

I'm not hauling barns. Yeah, that's right. I think I need to type that again, if you'll indulge me. I AM NOT HAULING BARNS. That feels pretty damn good. On the other side of three years in Barn Land, every other job I've had really does seem easy…but is it *meaningful work*? That's the question. Hmmm. In the meantime, if you'll excuse me, I need to fill out a few more job applications…

HARD END!

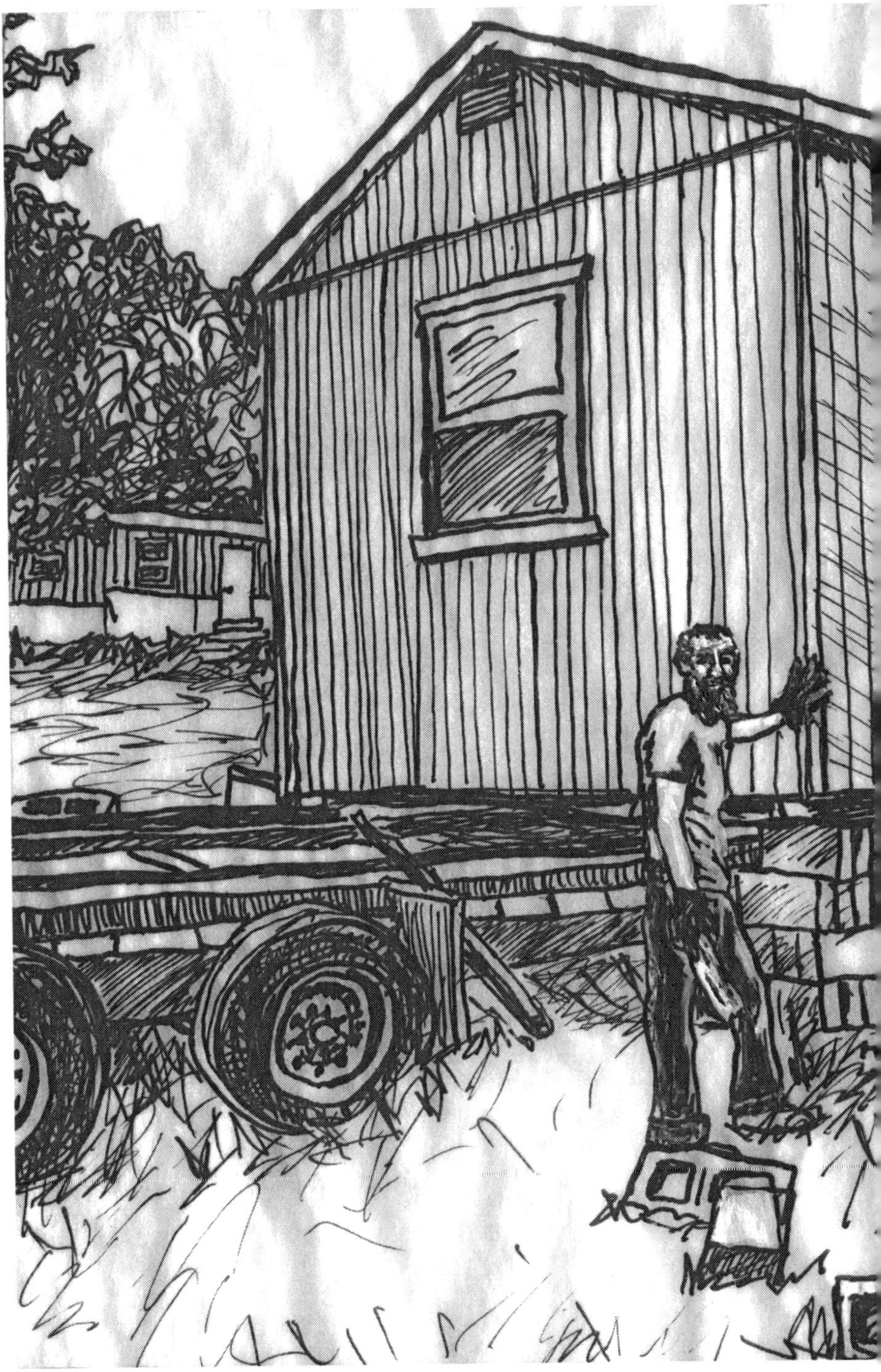

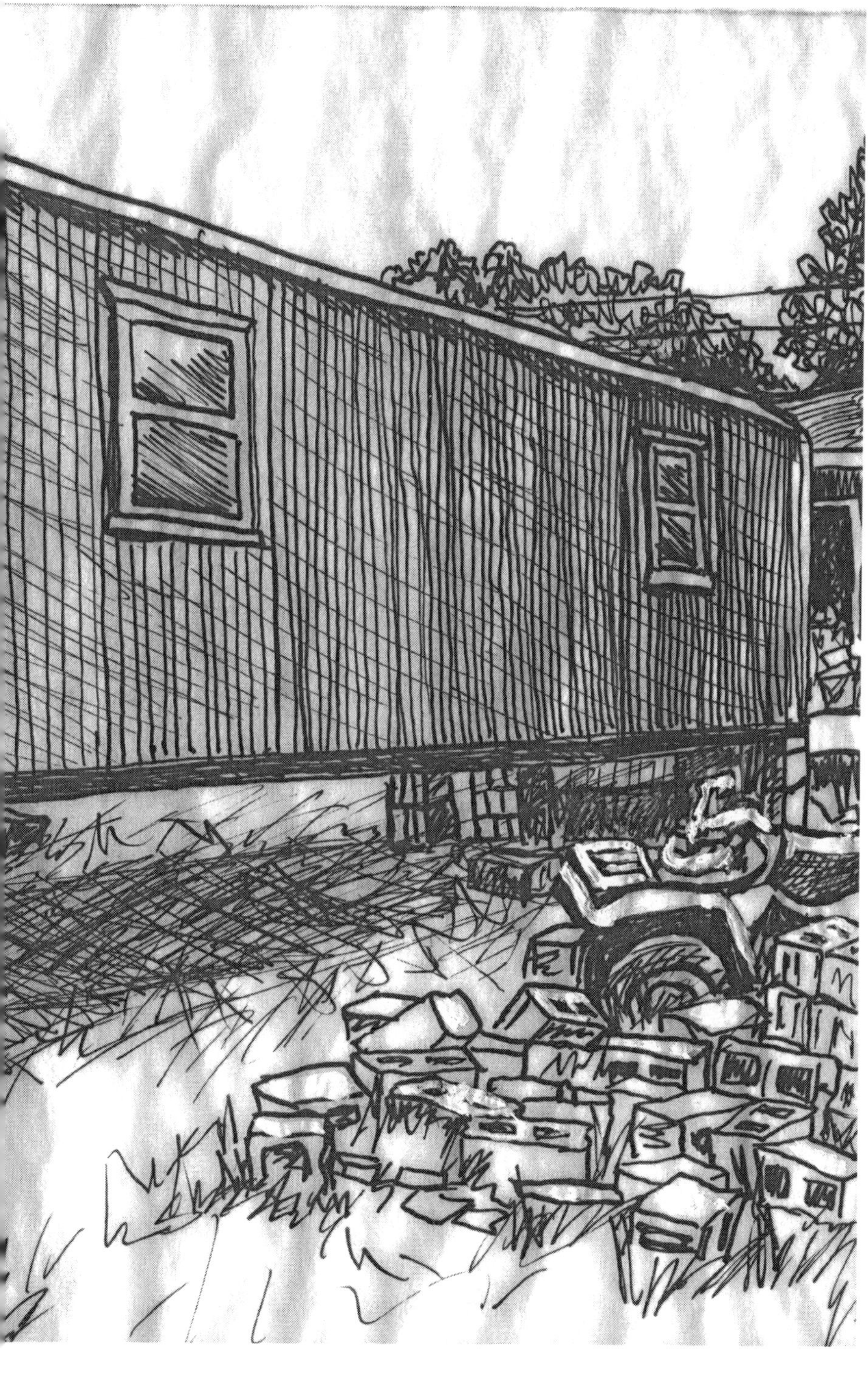

Every day I do the same thing.
I concentrate and waste time on stuff that means nothing.
Faces change but the story—it's the same.
I don't wanna go to school and be a doctor.
I don't wanna go to school and be a lawyer.
I don't wanna end up in a room behind a desk.

I hate my job.

My specific duties are endless and boring.
Might rather be in high school economics and snoring.
'Least then I'd have someone to talk to and some time for lunch.
Sure feels like I'm headed for nowhere.
If I had gas money I might not even care.
But I've still gotta eat and pay car insurance.

I hate my job.

Hating your job sure seems like a cliché.
But I don't care, I'll do it anyway.
'Least I've got some time to kill and a few words to say.
I don't wanna go school and be a doctor.
I don't wanna to go to school and be a lawyer.
I don't wanna end up in room behind a desk.

I hate my job.[1]

—The author, age 18

---

[1] Free Dirt. "Zest Everyday." *Jason's Basement*. No Label, 1995. http://freedirtoakridge.bandcamp.com/.

There are memoirs, and then there are refrigerator doors.[2]

—Lev Grossman

---

[2] Grossman, Lev. "Rough Magic: Joan Didion Faces Her Daughter's Death, And Her Own" *TIME Magazine*. Nov. 7, 2011.

HARDBARNED!
One Man's Quest for Meaningful Work in the American South

HARDTHANKS!

Thank you, Kelly Agee and Todd Anderson, my editorial Dream Team, for your superior editing skills, insights and vital feedback on multiple drafts. Any poor editorial decisions or errors that remain are all on me. Check out Todd's great writing, music, podcasts, short films and photos at www.heytodda.com.

Thank you, Will Ingram, Dallas Thomas and Greg Love, for your critical input, camaraderie and support—RIP WRITECLUB!

Thank you, LAGDM, TND, Jason Taylor, Mark Jackson, Grady Eades and Tracy Cabanis for your thoughtful responses to early drafts.

Thank you, Mom and Dad, for instilling a true love of reading, writing, learning, language and communication that cannot be satiated, for prioritizing education and for remaining proud of me when I had nothing to show for it but student loan debt.

Thank you TND, love of my life, for your fantastic illustrations, your steady encouragement, and your indefatigable beauty and grace. You're my best friend, and you make everything so much better.

About the Author and Illustrator

Author Christopher J. Driver lives in the scenic hills of East Tennessee with his lovely wife Tarri. In 2010, five long years after grad school, he finally found a full-time job with the word "writer" in it and has since tempered his rage against the employment machine…at least a little. Chris wrote his master's thesis on the science fiction films *Blade Runner* and *Solaris*. *HARDBARNED!* is his first book but hopefully not his last. Follow his continuing adventures and random observations at www.hardbarned.com.

Multi-talented illustrator and visual artist Tarri N. Driver majored in fine arts, with an emphasis on painting and a minor in psychology. She then earned a master's degree in education with a focus on expressive therapies. For a decade she worked as a board-certified, registered art therapist, licensed professional counselor and mental health services provider in inner-city schools and a children's hospital before leaving the mental health field to focus on her art. In addition to painting and drawing, she enjoys profiling inspiring women on her blog and working in collage. She is currently writing and illustrating the first in her brilliant, forthcoming *Lunar Mooner Lula* series of colorful and educational adventure books for children, which she expects to publish in 2016. Visit Lula at www.lunarmoonerlula.com.

CPSIA information can be obtained
at www.ICGtesting.com
Printed in the USA
FFOW02n0058290716
26160FF